Doing What You Really Want

Doing What You Really Want

An Introduction to the Philosophy of Mengzi

FRANKLIN PERKINS

OXFORD
UNIVERSITY PRESS

OXFORD
UNIVERSITY PRESS

Oxford University Press is a department of the University of Oxford. It furthers
the University's objective of excellence in research, scholarship, and education
by publishing worldwide. Oxford is a registered trade mark of Oxford University
Press in the UK and certain other countries.

Published in the United States of America by Oxford University Press
198 Madison Avenue, New York, NY 10016, United States of America.

© Oxford University Press 2022

Library of Congress Cataloging-in-Publication Data
Names: Perkins, Franklin, author.
Title: Doing what you really want : an introduction to the philosophy of
Mengzi / Franklin Perkins.
Description: New York, NY : Oxford University Press, [2022] |
Includes bibliographical references and index.
Identifiers: LCCN 2021031237 (print) | LCCN 2021031238 (ebook) |
ISBN 9780197574911 (hardback) | ISBN 9780197574928 (paperback) |
ISBN 9780197574935 (updf) | ISBN 9780197574959 (oso) |
ISBN 9780197574942 (epub)
Subjects: LCSH: Mencius. | Philosophy, Chinese—To 221 B.C. |
Philosophy, Confucian—China.
Classification: LCC B128.M324 P47 2021 (print) | LCC B128.M324 (ebook) |
DDC 181/.112—dc23
LC record available at https://lccn.loc.gov/2021031237
LC ebook record available at https://lccn.loc.gov/2021031238

DOI: 10.1093/oso/9780197574911.001.0001

1 3 5 7 9 8 6 4 2

Paperback printed by Marquis, Canada
Hardback printed by Bridgeport National Bindery, Inc., United States of America

Contents

Acknowledgments

This manuscript has existed in one form or another for almost my whole academic career. It would be impossible for me to grasp, let alone list, all of the influences on it. The initial draft was written in Berlin with the support of a Faculty Research Grant from DePaul University. Parts of it have been written while I worked at DePaul University (in Chicago), Nanyang Technological University (in Singapore), and now at the University of Hawaiʻi at Mānoa. All of those places have left marks on this book, and I am grateful to the supportive and stimulating colleagues I have had along the way.

My interpretation of Mengzi's philosophy builds on the work of many other scholars. As someone who came into the field from the outside, I am deeply indebted to the many people who took time to help me in developing my understanding of Mengzi and Chinese philosophy. A few people have given detailed and valuable feedback on the whole manuscript: Brook Ziporyn, Stephen C. Angle, Jing Liu, and my wife, Rachel Adams. This book is much better than it would have been without their help. I am also grateful to the anonymous reviewers of the manuscript, who saw its focus more clearly than I did. Some of the core ideas presented here have appeared in different forms in other papers, and I am thankful for comments I received early on from Bryan Van Norden, Philip J. Ivanhoe, and On-cho Ng. I have often thought of Henry Rosemont Jr. while writing this book, and I wish I had finished it in time for him to read it.

What I say here came as much from teaching as from discussions with other scholars and I am grateful to the many students, at DePaul, NTU, and UHM, who helped me to refine it, particularly to the small group of graduate students at DePaul who were daring enough to enroll in my first graduate course in Chinese philosophy. I first tried out my interpretation of Mengzi with them. Robin R. Wang read an early draft of the manuscript and tested it with her students at Loyola Marymount University, and am thankful for their feedback. Students in my Chinese Philosophy courses at UHM have also read chapters and given me helpful suggestions.

I would like to thank Peter Ohlin, my editor at OUP, for his thoughtful guidance on how to focus this book. I am also grateful to Haripriya Ravichandran, Madeleine Freeman, and the rest of the editorial team at OUP for their careful work in preparing the manuscript for publication.

My greatest debt in writing this book is to my wife, Rachel Adams. She has read and commented on multiple versions, helping with everything from reorganizing the chapters to finding the right word for the right place. She has also been quick to point out when I fall into needlessly academic jargon. Without her encouragement and support, this book may never have come to completion. Since I first read them in college, I've been drawn more to Mengzi when my life is going well and more toward Zhuangzi when it isn't. Rachel has kept my life in a Mengzi phase for a long time. I am also grateful to Kestrel and Granite, who have helped keep me grounded while revising this.

My imaginary audience while writing this book has often been my parents and my sister. My mother was the most interested in philosophy and I think she would have liked this book. I wish she could have read it. My family always encouraged me to try for things that I'm not sure any of us actually thought were possible. I owe everything to that.

It is difficult to know what my life would have become were it not for generous financial support for my undergraduate education. I would like once again to express my gratitude for a Dean's Select scholarship from Vanderbilt University and scholarships from the Citizens Foundation and Richardson Foundation.

Abbreviated References

TX Daxue (Greatest Learning)

Passages are cited by the numbering in Ian Johnston and Wang Ping, *Daxue & Zhongyong* (Hong Kong: Chinese University Press, 2012). That edition includes the Chinese text, as well as various commentaries.

LY Lunyu (Analects)

Passages are cited by passage number. For the Chinese text, I rely on Liu Baonan 劉寶楠, *Lunyu zhengyi* 論語正義 (Beijing: Zhonghua Shuju, 1990). For an English translation, I recommend Edward Slingerland, *Confucius Analects, with Selections from Traditional Commentaries* (Indianapolis: Hackett, 2003). For an alternate translation, see Roger T. Ames and Henry Rosemont Jr., trans, *The Analects of Confucius: A Philosophical Translation* (New York: Ballantine Books, 1999).

M Mengzi

Passages are cited by passage number. For the Chinese text, I rely on Jiao Xun 焦循, *Mengzi zhengyi* 孟子正義, 2 vols. (Beijing: Zhonghua Shuju, 1987). For an English translation, I recommend Bryan Van Norden, *Mengzi, with Selections from Traditional Commentaries* (Indianapolis: Hackett, 2008).

ZY Zhongyong (Centering in the Ordinary)

Passages are cited by the numbering in Johnston and Wang, *Daxue & Zhongyong*. That edition includes the Chinese text, as well as commentaries. For an alternate translation, see Roger T. Ames and David L. Hall, trans, *Focusing the Familiar: A Translation and Philosophical Interpretation of the* Zhongyong (Honolulu: University of Hawaii Press, 2001).

Introduction

Why Confucianism?

From the sixth to third century BCE, China was the setting for one of the world's richest outbursts of philosophical activity. It was also among the bloodiest times. The unifying political power of the Zhou dynasty, founded in the 11th century BCE, took a decisive blow when the capital was sacked in 771 BCE and the new emperor was forced to move the capital to the east. Small states and independent cities began to compete openly for power, the more successful conquering and incorporating their neighbors. For centuries, hardly a single year passed without at least one war, usually more. This period of struggle—divided into the "Spring and Autumn" and then "Warring States" periods—lasted until the Qin state overcame the last of its rivals in 221 BCE, unifying China. The Qin dynasty lasted just 15 years, but it set the foundation for the Han dynasty, which held China more or less together for four centuries.

The suffering brought by centuries of constant warfare is almost impossible to imagine. Mozi, one of the most important philosophers of that time, describes how the victors acted:

They enter the borders, mow down their grains, chop down their trees, and topple their city walls to fill in the moats and ponds. They burn down their ancestral temples and kill their sacrificial animals. Those of the people who resist are executed; those who do not resist are bound and brought back, the men used to care

Doing What You Really Want. Franklin Perkins, Oxford University Press. © Oxford University Press 2022. DOI: 10.1093/oso/9780197574911.003.0001

for livestock or serve in chains, the women used to pound grain and pour drinks.[1]

Those not killed on the battlefield are enslaved, their livelihood destroyed. Occupied with entering or fleeing battles, few were left to plant or harvest, adding famines to the suffering. Mengzi, the Confucian philosopher at the center of this book, describes one state he visited:

> The current system for the people's livelihood is such that above there is not enough to serve their parents and below there is not enough to raise a wife and children. In good years, the people live their whole lives in hardship and, in bad years, they cannot avoid death and destruction. They strive only to avoid death and yet fear they won't succeed. How can they spare time to cultivate propriety and rightness! (M 1A7)

Even in relatively good years, people can think of nothing but bare survival, and desperate circumstances lead to desperate actions. As Mengzi goes on to say, few people have a steady heart if they do not have a steady livelihood.

The political and economic turmoil of the declining centuries of the Zhou dynasty upset the whole complex of Zhou culture—customs, rituals, ethics, family relations, political authority, religion. The founders of the dynasty, King Wen and King Wu, claimed that their success demonstrated divine support, and that this support came because of their superior virtue (*dé* 德) and care for the people. They had the "mandate of heaven" (*tiānmìng* 天命). That world made sense. Centuries of suffering without effective political leadership made it hard to believe. The traditions were not working; no divine being came to the rescue. This crisis led to an explosion of philosophical and religious views, with each thinker offering advice for how to live in and make sense of this seemingly chaotic and cruel world.

While the authority of the past broke down, pressures to innovate increased. The lack of central power elevated competition among states, families, and individuals. Social order was destabilized. A person who was particularly clever, ruthless, or lucky could rise to power. A class of educated, skilled advisers emerged, known as *shì* 士. The *shi* lacked high-level hereditary positions but had access to power as consultants, administrators, critics, and teachers. The term is sometimes translated as "officials," and a verbal form of the character (*shì* 仕) specifically means to hold office, but one could be a *shi* without an official position. One could even refuse to take office and still be a *shi*, a "*shi* in hiding" (*yǐnshì* 隱士). The power of the *shi* came through their education and cultural capital, so another common translation is "scholar." That is misleading, as even when engaged in what we would call scholarly activities, the main concern of the *shi* was political engagement. In his study of early Chinese political thought, Yuri Pines argues against translating the term at all, but suggests that "intellectual" is often appropriate.[2] Kurtis Hagen and Steve Coutinho generally translate *shi* as "aspirant," which nicely implies both aspiring to a position of power and aspiring toward an ethical idea.[3] Another possible translation of *shi* would be "leaders," if we allow that someone could be a leader without holding an official position. Modern society does not have the same social group, but our equivalent would be those who lack immense inherited wealth but whose education gives them influence and potential access to power. If you are reading this book, the *shi* would likely include you.

This classical period is called the time of "one hundred schools" to represent its diversity. Some promoted ways of reforming the world in order to bring peace; some advanced strategies for accumulating power and personal benefits; some advocated withdrawing from the world of politics and struggle, preferring the safety and contentment of a life of simplicity. All of these views appear in a context of immense turmoil and suffering for regular people and the breakdown of traditional forms of authority. Most of those we now

call philosophers were *shi*: leaders/intellectuals/aspirants. They
tried to solve conceptual problems and determine the truth, but
that was not their primary aim or activity. If we limit our standards
to contemporary academia, we might doubt that these *shi* were
philosophers (even if they undeniably did some philosophy).
Contemporary academic philosophy, though, is a recent and pe-
culiar invention.[4] Through most of European history, the purpose
of philosophy was to live philosophically. This conception of philosophy, which we might follow Pierre Hadot in calling "philosophy as a way of life," has been a common endeavor across cultures,
appearing in India, China, and the classical Mediterranean.[5] Both
within and across these traditions one finds common ideals and
techniques but also disagreements and disputes. Differences in
material conditions lead to distinctive approaches. Chinese philosophy arose not just from speculation or wonder and not just from
the pursuit of personal excellence or enlightenment but also in response to widespread hardship and misery. Chinese philosophers
were also unusually this-worldly in their orientation, attaching no
significance to a life after death or release from this world. These
factors make early Chinese philosophy inherently political. Even
those who refused to engage in political life did so through a critique of politics. We can say that the central question at the origin
of Chinese philosophy was—how can we fix the problems of the
world? The goal of the philosopher was not just to determine the
right answer to that question but to actually fix the problems. More
precisely, the goal was to become the kind of person who could fix
those problems. There have been plenty of philosophers in Europe
whom Kongzi and Mengzi would recognize as fellow *shi*—Seneca,
Marcus Aurelius, Wilhelm Gottfried Leibniz, and John Locke come
to mind—but that is no longer the paradigm of philosophical life.

So how do we fix the world? There were many responses in China,
including those who said that trying to fix it will only make it worse.
This book systematically presents a way that became the dominant Chinese tradition for those seeking to fix the world, known in

English as "Confucianism" and in Chinese as Rú 儒. Kongzi 孔子, better known by the Latinized name Confucius, was one of the many *shi* who traveled from state to state, offering advice and explaining why his way was better than others. His ideas are known through short quotations and dialogues that were handed down and eventually collected into books. The most influential of these collections is the *Lunyu* 論語, known in English as the *Analects*. Kongzi had little immediate political influence. His impact was through his followers and later generations of philosophers who developed his ideas, often in quite different forms. The core of this book comes from one of those philosophers, Mengzi 孟子 (Mencius). Mengzi was born around 385 BCE in a small state called Zou in what is now Shandong province. He considered himself an interpreter, defender, and follower of Kongzi. At some point, Mengzi set out to save the world by engaging in politics, traveling from state to state, giving advice to rulers and seeking a position from which to enact his ideals. Although he succeeded in meeting (and insulting) some of the most powerful rulers of his time, he never convinced one to practice his Confucian way. Like Kongzi, Mengzi's main influence was on later generations. For more than two thousand years, his writings have been a source of guidance and inspiration for those set on doing something about the state of the world.

Worrying about peace of mind

This book is an introduction to the philosophy of Mengzi, but I didn't write it as a history lesson. I wrote it because Mengzi's philosophy has much to offer in making sense of how a meaningful life involves attempting to change the world. The core of the manuscript was written in a 6-week frenzy almost 20 years ago, in the summer of 2002. It was politically a tense time, the summer between the US invasion of Afghanistan and the second invasion of Iraq. It was also a time of personal crisis for me. The previous summer I had moved to a new city and started my first job as a professor. I was having serious doubts about the value of academic philosophy. My application to move into a communal house for people dedicated to social justice was rejected, and even I wasn't fully convinced by my arguments for the value of philosophy. I had started doing a little work at a center for assisting refugees and became involved with organizing to prevent the Iraq war. In that time, I was profoundly impressed by several people I met who were truly dedicated to living ethically and who focused their life on working to make the world a better place. Many of them were deeply religious. I began teaching at a Catholic university that took seriously the mission of St. Vincent DePaul. I also found myself in discussions with people interested in Asian philosophies, but almost always either Buddhism or Daoism (usually in some Americanized form). In these various contexts, I could not resist advocating Mengzi's form of Confucianism, but when people asked me what they should read, I was at a loss. The original texts compile fragments that are difficult to make sense of, let alone appreciate. Books about Confucianism are usually too introductory or too academic. In that summer of 2002, facing two months alone in Berlin with a grant to do research I had already finished, I tried to write the book I could give those people to read.

What attracted me to Mengzi's philosophy? Historically, religion has been an inspiration for changing the world but also an obstacle. Religions inspire activism and quietism. Consider the claim that the world was created by a God who is perfectly good. If God is good, then we should be good, and if being good involves making the world a better place, then God wants us to work for change. There is a problem, though. If this God is also omnipotent and made this world, isn't the world already the way that it should be? As Leibniz pointed out, if God is good and all powerful, this must be the best of all possible worlds. So shouldn't we accept the world as expressing God's will? When that is difficult, we can say things like "God works in mysterious ways." Throw in the comfort of an afterlife where everyone gets what they deserve, and you can see why Karl Marx called Christianity the "opiate of the masses." A Christian can reply that we must work for change because that is what God wants us to do, but the effort still seems superfluous. If God wanted there to be a better world, it would already exist. Our struggles have no more significance than a training ground or tryout for the afterlife. Beliefs based on karma avoid the awkwardness of having a god command us to do things that need no doing, but they have a similar outcome. If everything happens according to karma, then it all works out fairly no matter what we do. The problem exists for any religion that believes the ultimate ground of the universe is good or fair. The Confucians do not make such claims, nor do they believe it all gets worked out after death.[6] If the world is to be better, it is up to human beings to make it so.

The basic problem applies even to vaguer forms of spirituality. To commit to changing the world is to reject the way things are. That contradicts spiritual positions based on embracing, accepting, or affirming the world. Activism is inherently oppositional, while religion relies on an impulse toward reconciliation and acceptance, whether directed toward a transcendent god or the world itself. These two attitudes are not easily reconciled. It is hard to embrace the world at the same time that one fights to change it. Mengzi's philosophy is dedicated to changing the world and yet it maintains an element of reconciliation. That is why I wanted people to read it. On one side, Mengzi argues that a life dedicated to making the world a better place is more fulfilling, more in keeping with our natural desires, than a life of contemplation or a life accumulating wealth and power. On the other side, he roots the struggle for change in a continuity and harmony with nature and the divine, in his terms, with *tiān* 天 (heaven). How this reconciliation works out will be a central theme of this book.

The tension between opposition and reconciliation has an emotional dimension. Across time and traditions, many of those who take philosophy as a way of life do so to promote peace of mind.

That goes along with accepting the world as it is. This concern is particularly common in popular spirituality that draws on Asian traditions, such as Buddhism, Daoism, or yoga. Such views have great attraction and great power, as a trip to any bookstore confirms. It is easy to see why. If the problem we face is unfulfilled desire, solving it can go in two ways. One way is to increase our power so that we can fulfill our desires, getting the things we want. The other way is to reduce our desires so as to be more easily fulfilled. Nearly every wisdom tradition recognizes the futility of the former, yet we live in a culture that relentlessly teaches us the opposite. Our entire economic order depends on making us want more and more. Consumer culture uses desires that have been recognized as dangerous for thousands of years— the desire for sex, the craving for prestige, and the thrill of violence. It does not take a sage to see that such a culture leads to dissatisfaction and unrest. In this context, realizing that happiness lies down a different path is a relief, even a little subversive. That is good.

The problem with seeking contentment is that we live in a world where terrible things happen, often. Every one of us is implicated in the global systems that enable those things. In such a world, it seems we should fight injustice rather than cultivate peace of mind. Imagine what the world would be like if all the hours spent on "self-help" activities, including practices such as meditation and yoga, were instead spent helping other people. Confucians recognize the need for contentment and happiness, but they are suspicious of them. The 20th-century Confucian philosopher Xu Fuguan 徐復觀 advocated a "sense of concern and worry," *yōuhuàn yìshí* 憂患意識 and a feeling of awe or reverence (*jìng* 敬) at the responsibility borne by each of us.[7] This complex sense of responsibility, anxiety, and awe, is fundamental to Confucianism as a way of life. As the Song dynasty Confucian Fan Zhongyan 范仲淹 famously put it: "Go ahead in worrying about the world's worries; go behind in enjoying the world's joys."[8]

I find Fan's words inspiring, but part of me finds them ridiculous. Promising extra worry and less enjoyment won't get you far as a self-help guru. Even Mengzi thinks it isn't always the best advice. Yet Mengzi's philosophy justifies and makes sense of this orientation, not as a sacrifice that we should make out of duty but rather as an expression of what we really want. Understanding the coherence of that way of life requires a broad account of Mengzi's philosophy. I begin with his views of the world and the place of human beings in nature (chapter 1). The next two chapters explain natural human tendencies (chapter 2) and the value and nature of emotions (chapter 3). These three chapters set up the account of reality that justifies the way of life Mengzi promotes. They are followed by three chapters on the ways in which we can deliberately change and cultivate ourselves: by managing emotions and desires (chapter 4), through study and learning (chapter 5), and in rituals and embodied practices (chapter 6). That completes Mengzi's account of the good life for human beings, but Mengzi was most concerned about getting things done, so the final two chapters turn to issues that arise in practice. Chapter 7 gathers advice from Mengzi and other Confucians on how to address six things that tempt us away from improving the world. Chapter 8 turns to a Confucian analysis of power and how to have an impact.

I have tried to bring out the coherence of Mengzi's way, ranging from his philosophy of nature to human psychology to practical advice, and to let him speak for himself, sometimes with long quotations. My goal is to explain his philosophy in a plausible way, and that involves showing how his advice is grounded in a coherent vision of human beings and the world. At the same time, learning from Mengzi does not require accepting the whole system. In some cases, he might be wrong in the details but right at a more general level. In other cases, key positions in his philosophy can be replaced with different claims that do the same work. Because of their practical focus, many of his claims and advice can be taken from his context and placed into others. The history of Confucianism reveals just this kind of process of adaptation, revision, and renewal. What you read here unavoidably is a result of my own processing of the text, but I have tried to leave as much space as possible for the reader to do that work as well.

Mengzi in context

It should be clear by now that I am approaching ancient Chinese texts with my own concerns. If we want to learn from other cultures rather than just describe them, we must bring them into our own terms and make them living options. At the same time, we must try to understand the other culture in its own terms, to recreate what Mengzi himself thought and how he saw the world, and to see the coherence in the various things he says. Without that effort, we just project our own thoughts into words that sound more exotic and profound. That deprives us of any new insights, which is the point of turning to another culture in the first place. Europeans have a long history of appropriating Chinese thought for their own purposes, from the Jesuit missionaries who first translated and named "Confucius" and "Mencius" in Latin to the contemporary "translators" of the *Daodejing* who do not read Chinese. Popular writings on Asian thought usually err in the direction of appropriation. That was the case with the original draft of this book, written before I could read much of the original Chinese. Academic writings err in the opposite direction, sacrificing relevance for precision. I have tried to strike the right balance in this book, which should be seen as coauthored by me and a less academic version of me from a long time ago. It could not have been written by either of us alone.

In his own context, Mengzi was most concerned with fighting greed and the glorification of power, war, and luxury. That is still where his philosophy is most relevant. Among other *shi* philosophers, he said that his two main rivals were Yang Zhu and

Mozi (M 7A26). We know little about Yang Zhu.[9] Mengzi says that he advocated being concerned only for his own self or body, and that if he could benefit the world by pulling out one hair from his body, he still wouldn't do it. Yang's point probably was that we should take care of our own health and our own life and let other things follow their own course. We know much more about the thought of Mozi.[10] He was a fascinating figure with a philosophy based on concern for the lower classes and opposition to offensive wars. His best-known position is inclusive or impartial care, *jiān ài* 兼愛, which claimed that the benefit of all people should be considered in decisions, not just that of our family, friends, or compatriots. Mengzi absorbed aspects of this doctrine but also argued that it contradicted natural human feelings and undermined the importance of the family. The Mohists vehemently criticized the extravagance of the ruling classes, specifically arguing for reducing elaborate funeral ceremonies and for eliminating musical performances. As ritual specialists, the Ru responded by justifying the value of ritual and music on humanistic grounds. The Mohist system was supported by a belief in *tiān* 天 (heaven) as a vaguely anthropomorphic deity that rewarded those who cared inclusively and punished those who were selfish and biased. That provided an easy answer to the question: Why should I be good? If you aren't, heaven will punish you. The Mohists accused the Ru of denying a providential deity, and at least in the case of Mengzi and Xunzi, their charge is correct. In the Warring States period, the Confucians and the Mohists were the two dominant philosophical movements directed toward making the world better through political action. That made them fierce competitors, but they had much in common, so much so that the phrase "Ru-Mo" became a general term for people dedicated to using an ethical vision to reform the world.

Although Mengzi presents Mozi and Yang Zhu as his main rivals, I want to set him against one other perspective, that best exemplified in parts of the *Zhuangzi* 莊子.[11] Zhuangzi lived a little later than Mengzi. He is considered one of the two originators of

Daoist philosophy, along with Laozi 老子, the supposed author of the *Daodejing* 道德經. The book known as the *Zhuangzi* contains many different viewpoints, and we do not know which parts reflect the ideas of Zhuangzi himself. I use "Zhuangzi" to label one of those viewpoints, the view dominant in the first seven chapters of the text (known as the "Inner Chapters"). The philosophy of these chapters is sophisticated but slippery, presented in anecdotes and short dialogues that career from one perspective to another. While there are debates on the place of ethics in this philosophy, no one will deny that these chapters of the *Zhuangzi* are profoundly antiactivist. This stance arises from a skeptical attack on human categories, judgments, and labels, which follows a radical rejection of anthropocentrism. Nature does not center on us. Our values, concepts, and concerns have no priority; they are merely ours, lacking an objective foundation in nature itself. Once we give up our labels and judgments, we can appreciate the moment, find joy in whatever the world brings, and skillfully respond to immediate circumstances. We can call this outcome "peace of mind." Zhuangzi calls it *xiāo yáo yóu* 逍遙遊, which Burton Watson translates as "free and easy wandering" and Brook Ziporyn as "wandering far and unfettered."[12] To equate Zhuangzi with popular spirituality concentrated on peace of mind misses the radicalness and the complexity of Zhuangzi's philosophy. Nonetheless, the ways in which the philosophy of Mengzi resists the position of Zhuangzi are also the ways in which Mengzi is most relevant now.

Authors and texts

This book discusses a time nearly 2,500 years ago. As much as I strive to give an accurate account, speaking of Mengzi or Zhuangzi, Confucianism or Daoism, involves retrospective construction. As in Greece and India, Chinese philosophy began in oral discussions and debates. At some point before Mengzi's birth, people began to write philosophical ideas on strips of bamboo, which were then tied into bundles that could be rolled out and read, rolled up and put away. Copied by hand and disseminated from person to person and state to state, the wording could shift and phrases might be added or cut. The same lines or stories could end up in different texts making different points or spoken by different people. During the Han dynasty, these earlier materials were gathered, compared, edited, and combined. Books like the *Mengzi*, *Zhuangzi*, and *Lunyu* are products of that effort.

Archeologists in China have recently found many texts from before the Han dynasty, including several collections that were probably buried in Mengzi's youth.[13] Those bamboo texts give us direct evidence about early Chinese philosophy, but they also reveal how heavily revised and edited the transmitted texts must be. To make matters worse, the authoritative weight of the past led later thinkers to attribute their own ideas to earlier philosophers. The text taken as the most authoritative source on the thought of Kongzi, the *Lunyu* or *Analects*, contains numerous sayings attributed to Kongzi, yet we have no way of knowing if Kongzi really said them, and even if he did, we do not know how much the wording shifted over time. The *Mengzi* is taken as more consistently representing the viewpoint of one person, but surely some of the lines attributed to Mengzi were really said by his disciples, his teachers, or later interpreters. No one knows how much these sayings changed over the thousands of years they took to reach us.

Regardless of authorship, the *Mengzi* is consistent in expressing a vision of human life that derives goodness from our natural ways of responding to the world. That philosophy is the core of this book, and for convenience I refer to its author as Mengzi. There are many different and conflicting Confucian philosophies but they largely agree in practice, so on many issues I draw freely from texts other than the *Mengzi*, most of all from the *Lunyu* but also from the *Liji* 禮記, the *Record of Rituals*, particularly the *Zhongyong* 中庸, best known in English as the *Doctrine of the Mean*, and the *Daxue* 大學,

the *Greatest Learning*. My approach follows a long-standing Confucian tradition of reading the "Four Books" (*sìshū* 四書) together. I also draw materials from recently excavated texts, and even from Xunzi, a self-proclaimed opponent of Mengzi who argued that our natural dispositions lead us astray. In spite of their theoretical differences, these Confucians can be seen as sharing a common way of life dedicated to social change. In that sense, this book itself is a Confucian project, but my goal is not to promote "Confucianism" as a movement, religion, or tradition. That would require much more attention to the bad aspects of Confucianism, most of all its long and deep tradition of patriarchy. Here, I just draw out a core philosophy that I find relevant, interesting, and plausible.

Anyone who claims to have the true meaning of a classical Chinese text is fooling you or fooling themselves. The texts are inherently ambiguous. They make different philosophies when read from different perspectives. I have given my own interpretation in this book without much justification or alternate readings.[14] Those who want that kind of argument can consult my book, *Heaven and Earth Are Not Humane: The Problem of Evil in Classical Chinese Philosophy* (2014), which includes a chapter on Mengzi as well chapters on Zhuangzi and Mozi. I have cited works by other people only when I borrow specific ideas from them or when I think they might be of interest to a general reader seeking more information on a specific topic.

1

Harmony with Nature

On December 26, 2004, a massive earthquake occurred off the coast of Sumatra in Indonesia. In hours, waves as high as thirty meters hit Banda Ache, destroying everything within several kilometers of the coast. The displacement of water spread throughout the Indian Ocean, reaching as far as South Africa. In a short time 230,000 people lost their lives and another 1.7 million lost their homes. The tsunami killed without regard for nationality, class, age, or moral character. The cause was the movement of the continental plates, something essential to the structure of our planet. What would it mean to take harmony with *that* as an ideal, or to seek accord with a divine being that causes such events?

A similar catastrophe had a decisive impact on the philosophy of the European Enlightenment. On November 1, 1755, an earthquake struck off the coast of Portugal. The city of Lisbon was almost completely destroyed by the quake and the tsunamis and fires that followed. The death toll in Portugal, Spain, and Morocco is thought to have been nearly 50,000 people. In reaction, the French philosopher Voltaire (1694–1778) wrote "A Poem on the Lisbon Disaster." It begins:

> Unhappy mortals! Dark and mourning earth!
> Affrighted gathering of human kind!
> Eternal lingering of useless pain!
> Come, ye philosophers, who cry, "All's well,"
> And contemplate this ruin of a world.
> Behold these shreds and cinders of your race,
> This child and mother heaped in common wreck,

Doing What You Really Want. Franklin Perkins, Oxford University Press. © Oxford University Press 2022.
DOI: 10.1093/oso/9780197574911.003.0002

> These scattered limbs beneath the marble shafts—
> A hundred thousand whom the earth devours,
> Who, torn and bloody, palpitating yet,
> Entombed beneath their hospitable roofs,
> In racking torment end their stricken lives.[1]

Against the philosophers and theologians, Voltaire shouts: All is not well! We should not embrace or affirm this world. The problem goes back to God:

> But how conceive a God supremely good,
> Who heaps his favors on the sons he loves,
> Yet scatters evil with as large a hand?
> What eye can pierce the depth of his designs?
> From that all-perfect Being came not ill:
> And came it from no other, for he's lord:
> Yet it exists. O stern and numbing truth!
> O wondrous mingling of diversities!
> A God came down to lift our stricken race:
> He visited the earth, and changed it not![2]

Imagine someone who decided to act according to the principles by which nature appears to have been designed. That person would be monstrous by human standards. If a divine force is behind the order of nature, who could understand or affirm the choices it makes?

The problem is not eliminated by abandoning God. It applies to any ideal of following or harmonizing with nature. Nature has no sense of justice, as cancer strikes the good and the bad indifferently. Whenever anyone idealizes nature, I think of our old house cat when he happened to get hold of a mouse or a small rabbit. More than once it was we humans who would interrupt his play to put some unfortunate creature out of its misery. A fundamental divide separates the cold steady laws of nature and the things that most of us care about. Albert Camus (1913–1960) takes this condition as defining the absurd: "The absurd is born of this confrontation between human need and the unreasonable silence of the world."[3]

Anthropomorphism and a transcendent God

The challenges of thinking through the meaning of harmony with nature were fundamental to the formation of Chinese philosophy, and they shape any discussion of how to address the problems of the world. Before looking at the models that arose from those discussions, we must step back to consider how they viewed nature, the divine, and the place of human beings in the world, and before doing that, we should attend to aspects of European thought that we might take for granted. What appear to be commonalities between "Asian Philosophies" often just express the absence of certain European peculiarities. Buddhism, Hinduism, and Daoism end up looking the same only in the way that oranges, apples, and grapes are similar in not being yellow and long, that is, not being bananas. That approach tells us nothing about what Chinese philosophy *is*, only what it is *not*.

The clearest starting point for the peculiarities of European philosophy is the belief in a God who creates the world ex nihilo, from nothing. Belief in divine beings is common across cultures, but these are usually either within the world (Zeus, Thor, Indra, Shangdi) or an aspect of the world itself (Dao, Brahman, Buddha-nature). Either way, the divine is interwoven with nature. In contrast, God is the cause of the universe but exists outside of it. That makes the source of value, sacredness, and meaning external to the natural world. Nature might still be respected, but the respect is derivative. To worship the creation instead of the creator defines the sin of idolatry. That attitude easily slides into seeing the value of nature only in its usefulness for those beings who are made in God's image, that is, for us. The rise of science, technology, and the manipulation of nature are grounded in this view, for better and for worse.

Calling God a "Creator" implies an analogy to what we do in acts of creation. It implies that God has a mind like ours, and it is commonly thought that God shares our values, that God is good in some way that applies to us. The analogy between God and human beings makes the ultimate ground of the universe anthropomorphic. All things are made by God, but only human beings are *imago dei*, in the image of God. Human values are more than human. They are *objectively* valuable, held by the God who designed the universe. In the same way, if God thinks in the same categories as human beings, then our reasoning has an absolute foundation. All of this makes us very special, totally unlike deer or fish. From this we get the radical separation between human beings and the rest of nature, leading to a simple division between what is natural and what is artificial.

From a rational and scientific perspective, this worldview is implausible and few philosophers now accept it, but it has left many problems in its wake. If belief in God placed all meaning outside the world, what happens when faith in God is lost? The common result is crass materialism or existential angst. If confidence in human reason derived from its basis in God, what happens without that basis? It looks like we are just another animal with our own particular needs and perspectives. The extreme confidence in human science, reason, and moral concepts that one sees in many of the so-called New Atheists is ironically a legacy of Christianity itself. It continues the arrogant view of human beings as made in the image of God while denying the existence of that God. It is the *imago dei* but without the *dei*. Friedrich Nietzsche called this loss the "Death of God." That has little in common with what we might call the "absence of God" in classical Chinese philosophy.

The creation of the entire universe by a deliberate god is foreign to the early Chinese worldview, as are most of the problems that follow from it. In early China, nothing exists in isolation from nature. The meaning of the world lies within the world, and if anything is sacred or divine, it is within nature. Belief in gods or spirits within the world has been common throughout Chinese history, as has a sense of the divine as an aspect of nature itself. In the texts of the Warring States period, the most important terms for a divine force within the world are *tiān* 天, "heaven," and *dào* 道, the "way."

Tian became the most important divinity with the change from the Shang to the Zhou dynasty in the 11th century BCE. Originally, "heaven" was seen as a conscious god that enforced a certain ethics on rulers, supporting those who were good to the people and causing those who harmed the people to be overthrown. As one of the "Five Classics," the *Documents* (Shu 書) famously says: "Heaven sees from where my people see; heaven hears from where my people hear" (M 5A5).[4] Heaven aligns itself with the good of the people. The actions of heaven in promoting or thwarting rulers were called its command, *ming* 命, leading to the phrase *tiānmìng* 天命, conventionally translated as the "Mandate of Heaven." The sign that an emperor had lost the mandate was that his people rebelled. Even in this early context, heaven was still embedded in the order of nature. The same term, *tian*, also means sky, and the word for the world or realm in Classical Chinese is literally *tiānxià* 天下, what is "below the sky" or "under heaven." The association with both the divine and the sky explains the choice to translate *tian* as "heaven" or "the heavens," but the translation is misleading. *Tian* is not a place where good people go when they die.

This belief in heaven as a conscious force guiding the universe and looking out for the people broke down as centuries went by without peace. If heaven sees and hears as the people see and hear, why doesn't it help them? Some of the poems in the *Classic of Songs* (*Shijing* 詩經), another of the "Five Classics," likely date back to this time period. "Rain without Regularity" begins:

Great heaven, awesome and mighty, does not extend its virtue,
Sending down bereavement and starvation, spreading destruc-
tion throughout the states.
Expansive heaven, brutal and cruel, does not consider, does not
plan,
Leaving aside those with offences, fully concealing their crimes.
But as for these without offence, all are immersed in suffering.[5]

"Gazing Upward" starts with a similar message:

I gaze up toward great heaven, but it shows us no kindness.
Very long has there been no peace, these great disasters de-
scending down.
In the state, nothing is stable, leaders [shi] and the people are
diseased.
Insects stealing grain and causing sickness: there is no limit.
Those who offend are not caught in the net: there is no cure.[6]

These poems express grief, dismay, even outrage. They could have
been written by Voltaire after Lisbon, and they deal with the same
kind of evidence that European philosophers used to argue against
the existence of God, but the question here is different. Since
heaven or *tian* is an aspect of the world itself, it made no sense to
deny its *existence*. The question was whether or not *tian* supports
our values. In the *Documents*, heaven gave human life a reliable
foundation. With doubts about the justice of heaven, this foundation collapsed. What was right was what was in harmony with
heaven; if heaven no longer cares, why should we continue to do
what was right? The justification for political power was the mandate of heaven; if no mandate is given, who should hold power?
These questions demanded either new justifications for traditional
ethics and politics or new ethical codes and political visions better
suited to the real world. In philosophical texts that we have from
the Warring States period, only Mozi and his followers defend the

idea of heaven as a conscious force that consistently rewards the good and punishes the bad. In other texts, heaven is less a conscious force and more a reverent way of talking about the order of nature.

The other prominent word for the divine element in the world is *dào* 道, which literally means a path or way. As a verb, it meant to form a path or to guide along a path. A *dao* could refer to someone's teachings or the way that they advocate, as one could speak about the *dao* of the Mohists or the Confucian *dao*. In texts like the *Laozi*, *dao* was the term chosen to label the ultimate generative aspect of the natural world. Chapter 25 explains:

> There is a thing that took form in the undifferentiated, generated before heaven and earth.
>
> So silent! So still! Standing alone and unaltering, it can be considered the mother of heaven and earth.
>
> Its name is unknown, but its title is "*dao*"; if forced to make a name for it, we say "great."[7]

The ultimate ground of the world cannot be named, because it is not a thing or an object. If forced to refer to it, the best we can do is call it the "way" or "guide." Originally, the term *dao* was introduced to displace the dominance of *tian* (heaven), which retained connotations of an anthropomorphic force linked to political authority. As these connotations weakened, the distinction between heaven and the way diminished. The *Zhuangzi* uses both *tian* and *dao*.

Spontaneity versus creation

If early Chinese philosophers did not see the world as arising by conscious design, how did they explain it? Cosmogony (the genesis of the cosmos) became an important concern by the middle of the fourth century BCE.[8] To give one example, *Great Oneness Generates Water* begins:

> Great oneness generates water; water returns to assist great oneness, and by this heaven forms. Heaven returns to assist great oneness and by this earth forms.

Further generation occurs through the interaction of opposite pairs: heaven and earth assist each other to form spirit and luminosity (*shénmíng* 神明) and those interact to form *yīn* 陰 and *yáng* 陽. Yin and yang interact to form the four seasons, which then generate recurring patterns of cold and hot and wet and dry. These form a year or, literally, the harvest (*suì* 歲). This repeating cycle ends the progression. The passage concludes:

> Thus, the great oneness is contained in water, acts through the seasons, circulating and [beginning] again, . . . the mother of the myriad things. It waxes and wanes in alternation, acting as the thread that weaves together the myriad things. This is what heaven cannot kill, what earth cannot bury over, what yin and yang cannot bring to final completion.[9]

From an original unity, differentiation emerges on its own. As those differentiated forces interact, they produce further differentiation. Patterns emerge, culminating in the cyclical production of harvests.

In early Chinese cosmogonies, the universe is a multiplicity of interwoven forces, changing according to various tendencies and patterns. These forces came to be conceptualized as modalities and configurations of vital energies, *qì* 氣, a term which may be familiar from its role in martial arts or Chinese medicine (sometimes written as *ch'i*, or, from Japanese, *ki*). *Qi* originally meant air or breath. It is dynamic and material, described as flowing like a liquid. *Qi* animates the universe, forming heaven and earth, nourishing the plants that grow, filling the human body, and constituting our emotions. While *qi* is one kind of stuff, it took on different modalities, the most famous being a division into yin and yang. The character for yin originally referred to the shaded side of a mountain or a valley, but in this context, it labels movement that is soft and yielding, sometimes characterized as feminine. Yang referred to the sunny side and labels more active and forceful movements, characterized as masculine. Yin and yang are relational labels, not essential characteristics. The same thing might be yang in one relationship but yin in another, in the same way that we can consider any thing simultaneously as a cause (in one relationship) and an effect (in another). In this early Chinese view, any event can be analyzed into aspects that are yielding and receptive (yin) and those that are more forceful and active (yang).[10]

The world is in constant flux, but there are patterns within these changes. To survive and flourish, we must recognize these patterns and work with them. Since human life arises in the same way as anything else, these patterns encompass human psychology, social relations, family dynamics, and so on. The regularity of the patterns allows human beings to develop things like an art or *dao* of farming, and to gain some understanding of what makes human communities flourish. The patterns of change are cyclical, modeled on the consistent movements of the sun and moon and the regularity of the seasons. Cyclical repetition explains why nature can go on endlessly, without beginning or end. On a political level, this cyclical perspective tends against utopianism or unlimited progress. As much as Mengzi struggles to bring about peace in his own time, he did not believe peace could last forever (M 2B13). History follows cycles of order and disorder, so that there can be no perpetual peace (but also no perpetual disorder). Applied to the individual, a cyclical view means we cannot plan only for a life of happiness but must also cultivate ways of living with difficulties. No one avoids suffering, but suffering also passes.

Although scientific claims about the origins of the universe remain unsettled, they are closer to the Chinese account in which complexity emerges naturally and spontaneously from simplicity. Nonetheless, the claim that order emerges spontaneously may seem implausible to people familiar with arguments for intelligent design. A full response to this problem would go beyond the scope of this book, but there are good reasons to prefer something like the Chinese view. The assumption that every thing or event must have a cause leads to a paradox. Every cause will itself need a cause, which then needs a cause, and that needs a cause, and so on. Perhaps we could allow that chain of causes to go on to infinity, but we would still be left with the question—why does this particular infinite chain of causes exist? There is no way to avoid the conclusion that if anything exists, something must exist without a further cause, just existing by its own nature. That is the way that God is usually described, as "self-caused" (*causa sui*). But if we allow that something must be self-caused, why not the world itself? That is the Chinese view. Rather than use the language of a thing "causing" itself, they refer to zìrán 自然, which literally means to be so (*rán* 然) from itself (*zì* 自). The patterned differentiation of things arises spontaneously, of itself.

To just pronounce that spontaneous diversification is the nature of being may seem to beg the question. That feeling reveals an odd bias. We assume that order and existence require explanations or causes. If nothing existed, we would not need a reason for that. If the world were a chaotic mess, that would not need a cause. Nonexistence and chaos are the default conditions—anything else needs an explanation. But why would we assume that? After all, things exist and there is order. If anything, those are more likely to be the default condition. Maybe nonexistence and disorder are what need to be explained. That will appear strange, but it is just what theists say about God—God by its very nature is orderly and creative. Chinese philosophers just shift this claim to the world itself. Order and dynamic change are fundamental to the way the world is, and levels of patterns emerge naturally from the interplay of forces. We might say that for Chinese philosophers, the simplest form of being already has the characteristics of life, *shēng* 生. Being involves growth, organization, and complexity.

Nature as growth, nature as cycles

In this conception of the world, nature (or *tian* or *dao*) is the source of values and of the sacred. Human beings take their bearings from the world around them. Fitting in with nature becomes the main goal of life, just as obeying God is the main goal for monotheists. Philosophical discourse in China is closely interwoven with nature, as key philosophical points are made through metaphors and anecdotes drawn from the natural world: the flowing of water, the growth of plants, the timing of the seasons.[11] These metaphoric connections go to the heart of the Chinese language, as many concepts derive from images of natural phenomena. For example, the characters for beginning or foundation and end or result literally mean "root" and "branches." Both are based on the character for tree, which is an image: 木 *mù*. Root is 本 *běn* and branch is 末 *mò*. The character for being bright or for seeing clearly (and by extension for insight or understanding) unites an image of the sun 日 *rì* and an image of the moon 月 *yuè*, to form 明, *míng*.

It is hard to judge how much influence the images and the etymology of these characters had. We call the place where airplanes arrive and depart a "port" for the "air," but does this shape how we think of airports? Maybe not, but Chinese characters sometimes do retain connotations of their origins. The concept of *ben* as foundation or beginning frequently includes aspects of a root, including a sense of giving vitality and a natural direction of growth. While the beginning is not necessarily more important than the end, the *ben* (root) is always more important than the *mo* (branches). The image of the sun and moon in the term *ming* suggests impartiality, as the sun and moon illuminate all things alike.

Given that the divine is within nature and the ultimate goal for Chinese philosophers is harmony with nature, what does it mean to live in harmony with nature? The tendency in Daoist texts is to note patterns such as the cyclical nature of change, the instability of extremes, and the inevitable dissolution of particular things, and then to advocate following along with these patterns. In general, values and institutions that are peculiarly human, such as ritual, ethical ideals, and language, are seen as dangerous and in tension with *dao*. The problem with this position is that human beings are part of nature too. The separation between the artificial and the natural is itself artificial. If something is natural for us, then it is natural. Mengzi uses this point to argue that the human struggle to change the world is itself an expression of nature.

These different views of nature can be distinguished by their dominant metaphors. Chinese philosophers agreed that nature is cyclical. Life can be viewed in terms of these cycles, but that misses much of what it means to be a living thing. Plants make a natural progression from a beginning as seed, through growth, flourishing, reproduction, and, eventually, death and decay. They can be described as more or less healthy, and aspects of their environment can be described as more or less supportive. Mengzi relies on such metaphors of growth. In contrast, cycles have no natural beginning or end. They may include times of health and times of illness, but the cycle indifferently embraces both. Laozi and Zhuangzi highlight these cyclical metaphors.

Consider the significance of death. From the perspective of growth, death looms as an end. Living things are configurations of forces designed to keep death away. The process of growing and staying alive is spontaneous, but for human beings it is also conscious and affective. We make plans to eat and to avoid danger; we fear and mourn death. From a cyclical perspective, this all looks foolish. Winter comes, sooner or later. Death is the other side of birth, and no one would choose to live in a world that had no death. Later in the Warring States period, this cyclical view was even used to justify the naturalness of violence. In an explanation of frugality or conservation (*jiǎn* 儉) in chapter 67 of the *Laozi*, the *Hanfeizi* says:

> If heaven and earth cannot be always extravagant or always expending, how much less can human beings? Therefore, the myriad things must have prosperity and decline, the myriad affairs must have their rise and fall, a state must have the civil [*wén* 文] and the martial [*wǔ* 武], and government must have rewards and punishments.[12]

Just as there must be spring and autumn, a ruler must use kindness and violence, rewards and punishments, peace and war. In the Han dynasty, correlating human actions with natural patterns in this way became the dominant means of harmonizing with nature.

This correlative approach was not the only way that cycles were used. Earlier Daoist materials instead attend to the inevitability of change and the need to accept loss as natural and unavoidable. Zhuangzi uses natural cycles in a famous passage about the death of his wife. Soon after his wife dies, his friend and fellow philosopher, Huizi, visits. Finding Zhuangzi singing and banging on a tub, he scolds him for not mourning. Zhuangzi responds:

> It is not so! When she first died, how could I alone have no distress? But I looked to her beginning and that originally she was without life. Not only was she without life, originally she had no form. Not only did she have no form, originally she had no vital energies. Intermingling in the indefinite and vague, change happened and there was vital energy; vital energy changed and there was form; form changed and there was life; now there has been another change and she is dead. This is like the progression of the four seasons—spring, fall, winter, summer. There

she sleeps, reclining peacefully in a large chamber. If I wept and wailed, following her tearfully, I myself considered that it would have been not aligning with fate [*ming* 命]. So I stopped.[13]

Zhuangzi's initial reaction is what one would expect: grief at the loss of someone central to his life. Zhuangzi begins as one human being confronting the death of another, but he deliberately shifts his perspective. He turns to the cyclical transformations of nature through life and death, summer and winter. In that context, his wife was just a configuration of vital energies that gained momentary stability within a flux that requires both life and death. Mourning her would exhibit a failure to grasp processes that are inevitable and necessary.

These cyclical metaphors reflect nature on a grand scale. They are appealing, particularly in times of loss. Troubles that seem intense and world shattering to us can be placed in a vast horizon that makes our problems seem trivial, common, and unavoidable. Yet growth metaphors express a genuine aspect of nature too. While nature as a whole does not care who or what dies, each living thing does care. A mayfly will struggle to get away from a spider, though we might laugh and say—Why bother! You're going to die of natural causes in a day or two anyway! Nature unfolds a contradiction. Each part naturally treats its life and growth and relationships as if they were the most important things in the world. But nature itself cares not at all. Mourning death is natural and a rejection of nature. What does it mean then to follow or be in harmony with nature? For Zhuangzi, remaining bound to one provincial viewpoint is limiting, foolish, and sad. For Mengzi, we should maintain and cultivate the perspective and orientation natural to us.

The strangest thing about human beings is that we are able to entertain both perspectives—involved in our own pursuits and seeing their triviality in the big picture. That is why Camus says that human life is absurd. No wonder so many religions cling to the anthropomorphic view that our values lie in the foundations of reality! Mengzi does not use the divine to evade the fact that we are just one of the myriad things, nor does he engage in bad faith by ignoring our insignificance in nature. Yet he does not see life as absurd. His whole philosophy depends on maintaining the significance of human life while acknowledging the indifference of nature's cycles. That is its greatest strength in a contemporary context, particularly as a vision for a life dedicated to making the world more humane.

Roots and sprouts

Mengzi's portrayal of nature is constructed by the metaphors he chooses. One of the most common metaphors is the root. Youzi, one of Kongzi's disciples, said:

> The noble work on the roots. With the roots established, the way is born and grows. Filial piety and fraternal respect—aren't these the roots of benevolence? (LY 1.2)

The term translated here as "the noble" is *jūnzi* 君子, the most common word for the exemplary Confucian person. The word originally referred to a member of the ruling class or nobility, literally the son (*zǐ* 子) of a ruler (*jūn* 君). Confucians redeployed the word to refer to superiority or nobility in ethics and self-cultivation. Root, *běn* 本, here retains some of its natural connotations, not only as having priority over what follows after it but also as having a generative power that lets the way (*dao*) live and grow (*shēng* 生). If one works on the roots, benevolence follows naturally.

The metaphor of the sprout appears in one of the most important passages of the *Mengzi*:

> The heart of compassion and pain is the sprout of benevolence. The heart of shame and aversion is the sprout of rightness. The

heart of declining and yielding is the sprout of ritual propriety. The heart of affirming and negating is the sprout of wisdom. (M 2A6)

These lines will be the topic of chapter 2. The word translated as "sprout" is *duān* 端, which means a starting point or the tip of something. The character has two parts. The left, *lì* 立, means to stand or establish, and appears as an independent character in the previous passage (with the roots *established*). The graph on the right is the image of a sprout, *duān* 耑, with part above the ground and part below the ground. One of the recently discovered texts from Guodian uses this character to say, "Mourning is the sprout of benevolence."[14]

Metaphors of plant growth apply in many ways. They explain the influence of virtue:

Does your Majesty know about sprouts [*miáo* 苗]? In the dry times of the seventh and eight months, the sprouts wither. Clouds profusely rise in the heavens [*tian*], gushing rains descend, and then the sprouts spring up in vigor. When it is like this, who can stop it! Now among those of the world who shepherd other people, there are none who have no taste for killing other people. If there were someone with no taste for killing others, then the peoples of the world would crane their necks and gaze toward him. If it were genuinely like this, the people would come home to him, just as water goes to what is low. Gushing forth—who could stop it! (M 1A6)

Times are bad and people are desperate. If a good leader appears, they will follow him with the vigor of dry grass responding to rain. The metaphor points to a cyclical context, the seasonal patterns of rain, but the focus is not on the cycle but on the stimulation and growth of individual plants. A similar metaphor is used to explain the limited progress of a king Mengzi had been counseling. Mengzi compares the influence of his teachings to the warmth of the sun but notes that even plants that grow easily cannot thrive if they receive one day of warmth and ten days of cold (6A9). The sprouts of goodness respond to warmth, but they require consistent support. In another passage, the failure to become good is compared to a deforested mountain. Even when people came to cut down the trees for wood, its natural tendencies toward growth continued. It was only after sheep were repeatedly sent to graze that the mountain was unable to recover (M 6A8).

The tendency of plants to grow and spread usually illustrates good influences, but bad tendencies also proliferate. Mengzi says to one of his disciples:

> With the small tracks of mountains paths, if they are consistently used then they become roadways, but if they are unused for a time, wild grasses will fill in to block them. At this time, wild grasses fill in to block your heart. (M 7B21)

These metaphors come together in a famous story about a man from the state of Song:

> The man from Song was concerned that his sprouts [miao] were not growing, and so he tugged on them. He returned home looking worn out and said to his people, "I am exhausted today. I was helping the sprouts to grow." His son hurried off and went to look at them. The sprouts had withered.

Mengzi draws out the implications of the story:

> There are few in the world who do not help their sprouts to grow. Those who consider it of no benefit and abandon them are the ones who do not weed the sprouts. Those who help them grow are the ones who tug on the sprouts. Not only does that have no benefit, it harms them. (M 2A2)

Developing our own goodness is like cultivating plants. We must work on it and be attentive. We must check the spread of negative tendencies, which is the "weeding." As we weed, protect, and nourish, we must also be patient and let things develop naturally. Another passage says:

> The five domesticated grains are the finest of seeds, but if they do not ripen, they are not as good as barnyard millet or tare. So, benevolence also depends entirely on being ripened. (M 6A19)

Human effort is needed, but the growth itself must come about spontaneously through natural processes. The farmer from Song is foolish because he thinks we can willfully impose progress. As Mengzi recognizes, patience is particularly difficult for someone who really cares about the world.

Metaphors are not arguments, but they draw our attention to a certain way of construing the processes of nature, and thus what it would mean to follow or harmonize with them. It would be silly to say that nature (or heaven) wants plants to grow, or that it is more in harmony with heaven for a plant to grow than for it to wither in a drought or be eaten by sheep. Philosophers drawing on Aristotle like to talk about how an acorn has its natural end (a *telos*) in becoming a flourishing oak tree, but as Roger T. Ames points out, the vast majority of acorns become not trees but squirrels.[15] That is not unnatural or bad. Life and death both have a place in the cycles of nature. That is why looking at nature as a whole inclines us toward acceptance, harmony, and peace of mind, or in Zhuangzi's terms, free and easy wandering. Yet it would be wrong to conclude that it is unnatural for plants to strive to grow, for animals to fight to stay alive, or for human beings to work to make the world a better place. Nature (or *tian*) does not care, but it is still natural for us to struggle to live, to cultivate benevolence, and to end exploitation and violence. To relinquish these ideals because nature as a whole is indifferent to them would be like trees refusing to grow leaves because the leaves are just going to fall in a few months anyway.

Dispositions and tendencies

This understanding of nature explains the importance of *xing* 性, natural dispositions, in Mengzi's philosophy. As a concept, *xing* singles out the patterns and tendencies of particular organisms within the broader processes of nature as a whole. Since all processes are ultimately interconnected, what we pick out as an individual depends on context. The plant is inseparable from the field or the sun; the same goes for the plant's *xing*. There can be *xing* within *xing*, patterns within patterns, as we can speak of the *xing* of a person or of their mouth, the *xing* of a mountain ecosystem, of each tree in it, or of each leaf on the tree. *Xing* is often translated as "nature" in the sense of "human nature," but that misleadingly implies something fixed and essential. In a metaphysics based on change and mutual influence, *xing* is not a state but a way of reacting and responding. The *xing* of barley is how it responds to sunlight and soil; the *xing* of human beings includes hunger for food but also absorbing culture and tradition.

This conception of dispositions or tendencies disrupts the dichotomy of "nature versus nurture." The nature of any living thing is to be nurtured. It would be absurd to try to discover the true nature of an oak tree by isolating it in a dark room, freeing its nature from any trace of nurture. The nature of an oak can only be determined by its patterns of development, and that always involves an environment and locale. It is no less absurd to look to infants or feral children to understand the nature of human beings. At the same time, to have *xing* is not to just passively absorb influences. A plant does not just *change* or *react*, it *grows*. The language of *xing* defies the division between active and passive, just as it defies the split between nature and nurture.

Claims about human nature are dangerous because they are frequently used to "naturalize" socially constructed identities. Gender inequality and slavery have been rationalized as natural in just this way. Another danger is that the particularities of one powerful group become universalized as the standard for all human beings. Even now, when Anglo-American scholars list human universals, every item just happens to perfectly match an English word. They argue for a universal sense of justice, not a universal sense of *yì* 義. That puts Anglo-Americans at the center and other peoples at the periphery. Mengzi avoids these problems by rejecting a fixed human essence or nature and instead highlighting characteristic ways of responding to the world. Humanity is not defined by specific values, ideals, or concepts but by basic modes of socialization.

Mengzi usually argues for specific examples of common human dispositions and these will be considered in the next chapter. For now, we can examine a long argument that is more general. It begins with another plant metaphor:

> Now, consider barley. Spread the seeds and cover them over. If the soil is the same and the time of planting is also the same, it grows with vigor and when it comes to the time of summer solstice, it all is ripe. There might be differences, but that is due to the soil's being more fertile or barren, or the nourishing of the rain and dew or the human work not being even. Thus, all things of the same kind have similarities with each other—why doubt this in regard to human beings alone? We and the sages are of the same kind. (M 6A7)

Barley has characteristic ways of responding to stimuli, and under the same conditions, each plant will grow in roughly the same way. Without this consistency, farmers would never know what to do. If human beings are also natural beings, we would expect common tendencies among humans as well. The passage next applies the same argument to the parts of the body. If asked to make shoes, a shoemaker will not know the appropriate size but they will know the general shape of the shoe, because human feet are roughly the same.

So far, Mengzi's argument is on safe ground, but he then takes a more controversial step:

> In relating to flavors, all mouths savor the same tastes. Yi Ya first attained that which my mouth savors. If in relation to flavors the dispositions [xing] of his mouth differed from those other people, in the way that dogs and horses are not of the same kind as us, then how could the world's mouths all follow Yi Ya in what they savor? In taste, the world looks toward Yi Ya. That is the world's mouths being similar. Ears also are like this. In sound, the world looks toward Shi Kuang. That is the world's ears being similar. Eyes also are like this. When it comes to Zidu, no one in the world does not know his beauty. To not know Zidu's beauty would be to be without eyes.

Tastes in food and beauty are just the kinds of things people appeal to in arguing against universalism, but we shouldn't dismiss Mengzi's point too quickly. Our tastes have more in common than we might think, at least in contrast to dogs and horses. Just try eating a can of dog food. It is no coincidence that 2,500 years later, on the other side of the world, most people still enjoy "the meat of grass and grain-fed animals," while dogs still occasionally eat poop. Not everyone will agree on who is most beautiful, but we would probably all find Zidu more attractive than a fish or a deer, just as fish would consistently reject him. More important, dispositions are not fixed traits but characteristic ways of interacting with our environment. Under similar conditions people form similar preferences, because taste depends on common embodied structures. Without common ways of reacting and developing, taste would vary within cultures as much as it does across them. Mengzi's approach fits with the development of different kinds of taste: depending on education and experience, one might develop a taste for jazz or a taste for ska or a taste for Peking Opera. Mengzi says the people follow (*cóng* 從) Yi Ya or look to him in anticipation (*qī* 期). Yi Ya doesn't just give them what they already want; he guides their taste.

The final step applies these claims about the eyes and ears to another organ, the heart:

> Thus, I say, mouths in relation to flavor have the same tastes. Ears in relation to sounds have the same ways of listening. Eyes in relation to appearances have the same appreciation of beauty. Coming to the heart, is it alone without commonalities like this? What is it that hearts have in common? It is coherent patterns [*lǐ* 理] and rightness [*yì* 義]. Sagely people first attain what is common to my heart. Thus, my heart delighting in coherent patterns and rightness is like my mouth delighting in the meat of grass and grain-fed animals. (M 6A7)

The physical organ of the heart was taken as holding the functions we attribute to the brain and those we metaphorically attribute to "the heart." The heart is the basis for thinking and attending but also for emotions. If the human body has a common form and human taste works on common principles, the same should be true for our emotional and cognitive life.

Mengzi's argument follows from his vision of human beings as embodied creatures living within nature. That allows him to infer from barley, dogs, and horses to human beings, a move that would be denied by anyone who took human beings as radically different from other animals. In a similar way, Mengzi moves from feet to mouths to the heart because he does not accept any fundamental mind/body dualism. The character *xīn* 心 is an image of the physical heart and it has the same embodied status as the mouth or eyes or ears, whose characters also are images of those organs: mouth *kǒu* 口, ear *ěr* 耳, eye *mù* 目. Mengzi frequently speaks about the heart through analogies with other parts of the body, as in the following passage about priorities:

> Now, consider someone whose fourth finger is bent and will not straighten. This does not cause pain or hinder their work, and yet if there is someone who can straighten it, they will not consider the road to the distant states of Qin or Chu too far, because their finger is not like that of other people. If their finger is not like that of other people, they know to detest it, but if their heart is not like that of other people, they do not know to detest it. This is called not knowing how to sort things. (M 6A12)

People will go to great lengths seeking cosmetic surgery for some parts of the body, but show little concern for that part which is most important, the heart (or, as we would now say, the brain). Another passage argues that giving the eyes, ears, and mouth priority over the heart is as foolish as taking care of a finger while neglecting the shoulders and back (M 6A14). These passages contrast the heart with other body parts, but the heart has a priority among things of the same kind. We should take Mengzi literally when he says that my heart's desire for coherence and rightness is like my mouth's desire for good food.

For Mengzi, the process of "self" cultivation is a process of cultivating our embodied being. In fact, what we identify as the self just is the living body. That is the literal referent of character translated as "self" in "self-cultivation," *shēn* 身. Ultimately, a sage just realizes the full possibilities of the human body:

> The bodily form and appearance are from natural dispositions [*tiānxìng* 天性]. But only a sage can fully enact this form. (M 7A38)

This passage links nature as a whole (*tian*), our particular dispositions (*xing*), and our bodily form to a sage's attempt to change the world.

Naturalness and the struggle for change

Xing allows Mengzi to shift from the broader cycles of nature to the distinctive reactions and tendencies of particular things. The idea of transcending human desires and values because they are *merely* human is countered by the claim that *we* are merely human. We can see the distinctiveness of this view by contrast with a Zhuangzi passage that also compares human beings and other animals. In this dialogue, Gaptooth asks a sagely character named Wang Ni about right and wrong. Wang Ni responds:

> If people sleep in dampness, they wake up half dead and aching in the middle, but is this so for an eel? If they dwell in a tree, they tremble with terror, but is this so for a monkey? Of these three, which knows the correct dwelling? People eat the flesh of livestock, deer eat grass, centipedes savor snakes, and owls and crows relish mice. Of these four, which knows the correct taste? Monkeys take gibbons as partners, bucks exchange with does, loaches play with fish. Mao Qiang and Lady Li are what people consider beautiful, but if fish saw them they would enter the depths, if birds saw them they would fly high, and if deer saw them they would dash away. Of these four, which knows the world's correct allure? From where I see it, the sprouts of benevolence and rightness and the trails of right and wrong are all inextricably confused and chaotic. How could I know their distinctions?[16]

Different species have different needs and tastes, and it would be ridiculous for human beings to impose our standards on fish. Surely any Confucian would agree. Zhuangzi's conclusion, however, goes further—"the sprouts of benevolence and rightness and the trails of right and wrong are all inextricably confused and chaotic." The issue is not to avoid imposing human judgments onto fish but to avoid imposing them on ourselves. The intended effect is a reproach: you take your human values and concerns as if they were the most important things in the world, but they are not. The rest of nature pays them no attention. So why worry so much about them?

Both Mengzi and Zhuangzi rely on human beings having tastes that differ from those of fish or dogs, but they draw opposite conclusions. For Zhuangzi, the fact that these tastes are merely humans' means they lack an objective ground. If we cannot overcome them entirely, we should at least take them less seriously. For Mengzi, the fact that only humans have these tendencies does nothing to undermine their importance or their place in nature. All things under heaven have distinctive tendencies. We can admit that Lady Li is not objectively more beautiful than certain fish. That does not mean we should start lusting after fish.

Nature naturally differentiates into patterns and relationships. *Xing* marks this differentiation. Mengzi makes this point in a discussion with a philosopher named Gaozi:

Gaozi said: "Living is what is meant by dispositions."

Mengzi asked him, "Is saying 'living is what is meant by dispositions,' like saying 'white is what is meant by white'?"

He replied, "Yes."

Mengzi added, "Is the whiteness of a white feather like the whiteness of white snow? Is the whiteness of white snow like the whiteness of white jade?"

He replied, "Yes."

"But then are the dispositions of a dog like the dispositions of an ox? Are the dispositions of an ox like the dispositions of a human being?" (M 6A3)

Gaozi plays on the close connection between the terms for life and dispositions. *Shēng* means life, living, growth, and birth. The character originally represented a plant emerging from the soil: 生. *Xìng* differs only by adding the heart radical: 性 (or in the Guodian texts, by adding a radical representing the eye: 眚). Gaozi suggests that our natural dispositions are directed only toward living, consisting of the processes that drive us toward food, sex, and survival. Some philosophers at the time used this claim about our dispositions to argue that we should forget about virtues and culture and seek to preserve our lives undamaged. This was likely the position of Yang Zhu, but Gaozi expresses a Confucian account found in recently discovered bamboo texts. Virtues and culture are good, but they must be imposed on our nature through effort, study, and self-cultivation. At least initially, rightness is "external" to our natural feelings.

Mengzi disputes such views by saying that our dispositions include not just eating but also caring, learning, showing respect, and so on. Even in terms of basic life processes, the dispositions of human beings must be different from those of dogs and oxen— dogs, oxen, and humans all strive for food, but not the same foods. Every living thing has *xing*, but not in the way that all white things are white. This theory of *xing* allows Mengzi to distinguish different kinds of animals, different roles, and different reactions, while seeing all as equally part of nature and equally linked to heaven.

Mengzi uses *xing* to place human values and actions *within* nature. Ultimately, it allows him to theorize a struggle to change the world as a way of harmonizing with nature, because that struggle expresses the tendencies we human beings naturally have. This orientation contrasts both Zhuangzi and many European thinkers, who see deliberate effortful human action as interfering with rather than following nature.

A great expression of this Confucian spirit appears in a description of Yi Yin, who became a key minister to Tang, the founder of the Shang dynasty. Mengzi begins by describing the way Yi Yin was living:

Yi Yin tilled in the wilds of You Xin, delighting there in the way of Yao and Shun. If it opposed his rightness or opposed his way, even if offered the realm as payment, he would not consider it, nor would he look at having the horses for a thousand chariots. If it opposed his rightness or opposed his way, he would not give a blade of grass to another person, nor would he accept a blade of grass from another. (M 5A7)

Yao was the founder of the first Chinese dynasty, and Shun was his chosen successor. These two sage-kings were among the highest exemplars of virtue for the Confucians, and Mengzi mentions them often. The dynasty they founded, the Xia, had declined and Tang, another paradigm of virtue, was in the process of overthrowing the evil emperor Jie and founding a new dynasty. Tang hears of Yi Yin's virtue and sends messengers to recruit him. At first, Yi Yin refuses. He enjoys his simple life as a farmer, far from the troubles of the world, and he takes pride in the uncompromising integrity it allows. Tang persists and eventually Yi Yin changes his mind, saying:

Rather than residing in the midst of the fields and canals to delight in the way of Yao and Shun, would it not be better to make this sovereign become a sovereign like Yao or Shun, and make this people become like the people of a Yao or Shun? Isn't it better to see these for myself? Heaven gives birth to the people, making those first to know wake up those later to know, making those first to awaken wake up those later to awaken. I am among the first of heaven's people to awaken. I will use this way to wake up this people. If I do not wake them, who will?

Yi Yin risks not just his own life and pleasure but also his reputation. One cannot remain so pure when involved in the real work of creating a new political order. He justifies his decision by appeal to the patterns of heaven—it is natural (or divine) for those who awaken first to lead and awaken others. The driving force is Yi Yin's own feeling of responsibility. Mengzi explains:

> In thinking of the people of the world, if there was one man or one woman who did not receive the nurturing kindness of a Yao or Shun, it was like he himself shoved them into a ditch. That is the weight of taking the world as one's own responsibility. (M 5A7)

Yi Yin saw the suffering of other people as if it were something he himself caused. This attitude makes his initial stance untenable: it is impossible to remain virtuous and yet do nothing to help those in need. This feeling of responsibility is natural, and that is the crucial point. When we fail to treat other people well, or we live in and serve an exploitative system, or even when we just refuse to try to improve things, we thwart our own nature (*xing*) and defy our place in nature as whole (*tian*).

This passage stands in direct contrast to a story in which Zhuangzi is offered the chance to control the powerful southern state of Chu. Zhuangzi is fishing on the Pu River at the time. Without looking up, he replies:

> I have heard the state of Chu has a sacred tortoise, that has been dead already for three thousand years. The king wraps it and places it in a strong box, stored high in the ancestral temple. This tortoise, would it prefer to be dead and have the bones it left behind honored? Or would it prefer to live and drag its tails in the mud?

The messengers say the tortoise would rather be alive in the mud. Zhuangzi replies:

> Go away! I will drag my tail in the mud![17]

Zhuangzi's choice might seem selfish, but who could blame him? He wouldn't just have to give up his life of leisure. High minister of the state of Chu would be a miserable job, with constant struggles against other officials, frustrations with rulers who won't listen, and plenty of unpleasant compromises. Ministers often ended up dead. Zhuangzi is wise to claim that honor is not incentive enough. We can also see why Zhuangzi's choice might appear most natural. He chooses a life outside the constructs of the human world, remaining by a river and in the mud. He justifies that choice by imagining the preferences of a nonhuman animal, a tortoise. Finally, he chooses not to impose his human judgments on the world, letting things take their own course.

One could accept Zhuangzi's naturalness and then either reject politics (as he does) or reject naturalness as an ideal. Mengzi opposes this understanding of naturalness. We see this approach in his evaluation of a hermit who was praised for his extreme purity:

> Kuang Zhang said, "As for Chen Zhongzi, wasn't he truly a leader of incorruptible integrity? While living in Wuling, for three days he did not eat. His ears did not hear, his eyes did not see. Above a well there was a plum. Grubs had eaten its core more than halfway through. He crawled over and ate it. After three bites, his ears could hear and his eyes could see." Mengzi said, "Among the leaders [shi] of the state of Qi, I certainly consider Zhongzi as a thumb among fingers. Even so, how can Zhongzi be one of incorruptible integrity? To fulfill the actions of Zhongzi one must be an earthworm—only then can it be done. Now an earthworm eats withered soil above and drinks from the yellow spring below. Is the house where Zhongzi lives something that a Bo Yi built, or was it something that a Robber Zhi built? Is the grain he eats something grown by a Bo Yi or something grown by a Robber Zhi? We do not know. (M 3B10)

One might be compelled to live like Chen Zhongzi. In a corrupt world, a virtuous person will likely be excluded from the power structures and may have to live in poverty. Kongzi's favorite disciple Yan Hui was praised for his ability to remain happy while living in destitution. But this kind of life should not be an ideal. Mengzi's comparison of Chen Zhongzi to the earthworm indicates that what is natural for a worm (or a turtle) is not natural for a human being. A fully developed human being is essentially interconnected with other people. That was what Yi Yin realized: it is natural for those who understand to help those who do not. It was also what Yi Yin felt when he took responsibility for the suffering of others (M 5A7).

Even so, Chen Zhongzi's willingness to bear such hardship does at least prove his purity and integrity, doesn't it? Perhaps not. Mengzi believes the best way to overcome selfish desire is not asceticism but caring for other people. This is a crucial point. If the goal is to reduce selfishness, as almost all spiritual traditions advocate, many routes remain open. One is to live simply and to meditate or practice other spiritual disciplines. Another is to serve other people. Popular spirituality is strongly biased toward the first alternative, although its asceticism tends to be very weak. Confucians advocate the approach of helping others. One reason is that withdrawal and purity are not possible for human beings. The earthworm does not have to worry about the source of its house or its food, nor does the turtle. We do. We are bound to a world of human influence, entangled in ethical obligations. We cannot act naturally in the way a worm or a turtle does. Mengzi has in mind how Chen Zhongzi impacted his family, but we could easily apply the story to someone living in relative simplicity but without attention to the chemicals used to produce their food, the labor used to produce their clothes, or the global economic structures that allow for their leisure. Were these produced by a bandit like Robber Zhi, or a humanitarian like Bo Yi? We *naturally* should be concerned with these issues, because we *naturally* depend on extended social networks. An explanation of where Zhuangzi got his fishing pole, his house, and clothes, is conspicuously absent in the text. How did he support himself? We do not know.

Following nature

Mengzi theorizes a way of life dedicated to struggling to change the way the world is. Yet he goes out of his way to ground this way of life in continuity with nature or the divine. He explains:

> Those who exhaust their hearts know their natural dispositions. Knowing their dispositions, then they know heaven. Preserving their heart and nourishing their dispositions is that by which they serve heaven. Not thinking twice about long or short life and cultivating the self to await it is that by which one takes a firm stand toward what is outside our control. (M 7A1)

We do not serve heaven by following the will of an anthropomorphic god (as the Mohists argued) or by following the general patterns of nature (as in the *Daodejing* and parts of the *Zhuangzi*). We relate to what is natural through our dispositions. Human beings are not unique in this system. We are not the only ones with dispositions and all dispositions come from heaven. Growth is the way that barley "serves" heaven; eating grass is the proper way for sheep. Serving heaven certainly does not mean heaven will take care of us. It is natural for some times to be good and other times to be bad, to sometimes succeed and sometimes fail, for some to live long and others to die young, but these natural cycles should not directly guide our actions. They reflect no deeper meaning or point. That is just the way the world works. What keeps us consistent through good times and bad is our own spontaneous affective responses to events in the world. That is how one can take a firm stance (*lì* 立) toward events that are out of our control (*mìng* 命), not letting them draw us off course or erode our commitments.

If nature/heaven doesn't care what we do, why should we care about "serving" heaven? Why does harmony with nature matter at all? One reason is practical. We live within nature and nature has its patterns and intrinsic tendencies. Sustainable success can only be achieved through harmony with these patterns. Several passages emphasize this point in describing the way the sage-king Yu managed floods:

> Bai Gui said, "My managing of water surpasses that of Yu." Mengzi said, "You, sir, are wrong. Yu managed water by the way [dao] of water. Because of this, Yu used the four seas for drainage. Now you use neighboring states for drainage. Water going against its course is called overflowing water. Overflowing water is flooding water. That is what benevolent people detest. You are wrong!" (M 6B11)

Another passage broadens the criticism:

> What I detest in those who are wise is their chiseling through. If the wise resembled Yu in guiding water, then I would not detest this wisdom. Yu guided water by guiding it without anything requiring work. If the wise also guided without anything requiring work, that wisdom would indeed be great. (M 4B26)

Those so-called wise men know how to get things done, but not in a sustainable way. Their "chiseling through" means forcing things rather than following the dao of water or doing what requires no work (wúshì 無事).

The need to act in harmony with nature's patterns leads into rules for sustainability:

> If you do not violate the agricultural seasons, then the grain will be more than can be eaten. If fine meshed nets do not enter the ponds and pools, then fish and turtles will be more than can be

eaten. If axes and wedges enter the mountains and forests according to the season, then wood and lumber will be more than can be used up. When grain, fish, and turtles are more than can be eaten and wood is more than can be used up, the people can nourish the living and mourn the dead without regret. Nourishing the living and mourning the dead without regret—that is the beginning of the way of a true king. (M 1A3)

Working with nature allows us to succeed by doing what is easy. If we "chisel through," oblivious to the coherence of the world around us, the results will be violent and unsustainable, like trying to hold back a river rather than channeling its force.

This kind of ecological consciousness is not surprising given Mengzi's attention to relationships and his view of nature as interlocking forces that are self-organizing and self-regulating. With no ultimate beyond nature itself, we must form sustainable relationships that allow for human thriving. Mengzi himself shows little awareness of environmental crises, but if placed in our context, he surely would give a central role to actions mitigating climate change, reducing deforestation, and so on. At the same time, Mengzi is far from a preservationist stance aimed at separating nature from human beings. We see the complexity of his position in his story about the origins of Chinese civilization. Mengzi begins with a condition in which nonhuman animals seem to flourish but human beings lack room for a good life:

In the time of Yao, the world was still unsettled. Vast flooding waters flowed far and wide, inundating the world. Grass and trees spread and flourished, birds and beasts propagated and multiplied, the five types of grains did not ripen. Birds and beasts encroached on human beings and the paths [*dao*] of their tracks crossed the middle states. Yao alone was concerned about this, elevating Shun to bring order to it. Shun made Yi master of fire. Yi set fires in the mountains and swamps and burnt them clear.

The birds and beasts fled and hid. Yu channeled the nine rivers, opened up the Ji and Ta, leading them to the sea, dredged the Ru and Han, and directed the Huai and Si, leading them to the Yangtze. After that, the middle states could attain food to eat. At that time, Yu was out for eight years, passing his gate three times without entering. Even if he had wanted to spend time farming, how could he? Hou Ji taught the people sowing and harvesting and the cultivation of the five types of grain. When the five grains were ripe, the people were nurtured.

The passage seems to present a struggle between human beings and the rest of nature, but human beings are part of nature. Mengzi praises the ceaseless effort of Yu, saying eight years passed before had time to visit his home. The motives that led him to work so hard, like the initial motivations of Yao to bring stability, all express human dispositions. Human work in establishing agriculture is as natural as the effort birds put into building nests and ants put into caring for aphids. The final result is not a human world that opposes the world of nature but an integration of human animals with other living things. What made Yu successful was his ability to follow along with the tendencies of the water and the land. The naturalness of planting and growth is a common theme in the *Mengzi*.

The line between human beings and the rest of nature is further blurred as Mengzi's origin story continues:

With human beings, there is a way [*dao*]—if they eat their fill and wear warm clothes and relax at home but they do not have education, then they are almost like birds and beasts. The sage was concerned about this, and made Xie minister of instruction, teaching them through human relations: father and son have cherishing, sovereign and minister have rightness, husband and wife have differentiation, old and young have order, and friends have trust. (M 3A4)

This attitude toward human beings is exactly the same as toward any other part of nature. The five relationships are in some sense natural, but they do not take their particular forms without human guidance and effort. We must work with the tendencies we naturally have, encouraging and strengthening some while redirecting others. We cannot become better by forcing ourselves, tugging on the sprouts like the man from Song. If we want to have a life that is rich and worthwhile, we need to channel these tendencies rather than thwart them, harmonize them rather than let them tear us apart. Mengzi probably sees all of these tendencies and forces as configurations and trajectories of vital energies. The story of the man from Song who tugs on his plants to help them grow is given to illustrate the way of cultivating vital energies (M 2A2). When cared for and protected from "weeds," this vital energy will grow and flourish. It leads to a power that is manifested in health, a forceful sense of purpose, and a charismatic influence over other people. Mengzi claimed to have vital energy that was "flood-like" (M 2A2).

I have so far emphasized the pragmatic importance of following nature, but Mengzi's desire to ground human values in nature or the divine also has a religious or spiritual dimension. To see human beings as standing alone in defiance against the world of nature is plausible only in the wake of a view in which human beings are alien to nature and the source of meaning is a transcendent God. Without God, this conflictual stance hardly makes sense. If the ultimate is nature itself, on what else can we take our stand? What could justify such opposition? In any case, such a stance leaves most people with a feeling of alienation. Mengzi provides an alternative in which human beings maintain and extend their concerns while still being at home in the world:

> Now, benevolence is heaven's honored office and people's peaceful home. To not be benevolent when nothing prevents it—this is not wise. (M 2A7)

2

What People Really Want

On the morning of June 11, 1963, a Buddhist monk named Thích Quảng Đức arrived at a busy intersection in downtown Saigon with a small entourage. He sat in a meditative posture on a cushion placed on the road. One of his assistants poured a can of gasoline over him. Quảng Đức himself lit the match. He was consumed in flame and burned to death. His action was done to protest the treatment of Buddhists under the regime of Ngô Đình Diệm, the American-supported leader of South Vietnam. This event happened six years before I was born, but its impression on me derived from the impression it left on my father, solidifying his opposition to the Vietnam War, a war that lasted almost another decade and killed more than a million people.

People who attempt to bring about great social change put themselves in danger. They risk their jobs and social status, their health and safety. Some lose their lives. Western philosophy traces itself back to Socrates, who was condemned to die in ancient Athens by drinking hemlock. He was charged with corrupting the youth and promoting new gods. Socrates had several chances to avoid death, if he had just been more willing to compromise. In his trial, he explains his refusal to conform:

> To fear death, gentlemen, is no other than to think oneself wise when one is not, to think one knows what one does not know. No one knows whether death may not be the greatest of all blessings for a man, yet men fear it as if they knew that it is the greatest of evils. And surely it is the most blameworthy ignorance to believe that one knows what one does not know. [. . .] I know, however,

Doing What You Really Want. Franklin Perkins, Oxford University Press. © Oxford University Press 2022.
DOI: 10.1093/oso/9780197574911.003.0003

that it is wicked and shameful to do wrong, to disobey one's supe-
rior, be he god or man. I shall never fear or avoid things of which
I do not know whether they may be good rather than things that
I know to be bad.[1]

Socrates drank the hemlock and died.

We think of such people as exceptional, ones who in a Chinese
context might have been "sages" or at least "the noble." But the willingness to risk one's life for the sake of others is not as rare as we
might think. Frontline healthcare workers around the world put
themselves in danger. Thousands have died in the current pan-
demic. Every year hundreds of humanitarian aid workers are killed
and kidnapped. Journalists, firefighters, police, and protesters all
die doing what they believe is right. These people do not know they
are going to die, but they know they might. They take that risk.
Even when some unexpected event involves a random sampling of
people, regular people step up to risk their lives in order to save
others. On July 21, 2017 (as I revised this section), the French philosopher Anne Dufourmantelle died trying to save two children
from drowning.[2]

The fact that regular people willingly risk their lives for other
people is profoundly significant for understanding the natural
human dispositions mentioned in the last chapter. Mengzi gives it a
central place in his philosophy:

If in what people desire there was nothing deeper than life, then
if there were anything they could use to attain life, they would use
it. If in what people detest there were nothing deeper than death,
then if there were anything they could do to avoid death, they
would do it. Yet there are cases in which one could live but some
means are not used, or one could avoid death but some things
are not done. Thus, having what one desires more than life and
having what one detests more than death—it is not only worthies

that have this heart. All people have it. Worthies are just able to not lose it. (M 6A10)

Are there things you would refuse to do, even if you knew refusing meant death? Would you trample your mother in order to flee a burning building? Wrestle the last life jacket away from a child on a sinking ship? Under threat of death reveal secrets that would lead to the deaths of thousands of people? No one can say for sure what they would do in the moment, which is why such questions make good premises for movies. Yet most people seem to have limits on what they would do. Many would go further, actively risking their life in at least some circumstances, leaping in front of a car to pull a child out of the way or rushing into a burning building to save a sibling.

The illustration Mengzi gives with the his statement is less convincing:

> One basket of food, one cup of stew—if one attains them then they live but if they do not attain them they die. If someone sneers angrily and gives it, then a wanderer on the road will not receive it. If someone tramples on it and gives it, then a beggar will consider it unworthy. (M 6A10)

Perhaps only an exceptional person would choose to starve rather than be insulted, but imagine being forced to beg like a dog for that food. In any case, many people would turn down an obviously humiliating job even if they could make more money. Human beings have a sense of dignity that outweighs their desires for material benefits.

Mengzi gives a more powerful example in a dialogue about compromising rules. It begins with someone implicitly criticizing the Confucian insistence on propriety. He first gets Mengzi's disciple, Wuluzi, to state that propriety is more important than either food or sex. Then he offers a challenge:

What if by following propriety you will starve to death, but by not following propriety you can eat—do you have to follow propriety? What if you cannot attain a wife through the ritual of receiving her at her family's home, but if you do not receive her in this way, you can attain a wife—do you have to follow propriety? (M 6B1)

Wuluzi does not know how to reply. He has just said that propriety is most important, but it seems absurd to starve to death or stay celibate for some minor issue of etiquette. Wuluzi goes to Mengzi, who explains:

How is that difficult to answer? If you even out the tops without aligning the bottoms, then a square inch of wood can be made higher than a mountain peak. Gold is heavier than feathers, but how could this apply to a gold clasp and a cartload of feathers! If you take the weightiest of eating and the slightest of propriety and compare them, how is it just food that is weightier? If you take the weightiest of sex and the slightest of propriety and compare them, how is it just sex that is weightier? Go and respond to him by saying, "If you can attain food by twisting your older brother's arm and seizing his food, but cannot attain food if you do not twist his arm—will you twist it? If you can attain a wife by leaping over a family's eastern wall and dragging off their virgin daughter, but cannot attain a wife if you do not drag one off—will you drag one off?" (M 6B1)

Desires for food and sex (and reproduction) express our most basic biological drives, shared by all animals. As we saw in the last chapter, Gaozi argues that these desires are our *xing*, our natural dispositions. Mengzi agrees that they have value and sometimes justify ethical compromises, but they are not what we most deeply care about. What if the only way to avoid starvation were to fight your starving brother for his last food? If the only way to have sex were to kidnap your neighbor's daughter? Mengzi thinks that regular people would not do such things. If he is right, then our deepest desires are not for our own survival. Care for our family runs the deepest, but the case of kidnapping someone's daughter shows that some actions are abhorrent even when done to a stranger. That is what Mengzi calls having what one will not do and hating some actions more than death itself.

What we genuinely want goes far beyond our own comfort or pleasure. Just think about why we really do what we do throughout the day. We follow social conventions, not wanting to be rude or to stand out. We help the people we care about and fulfill the responsibilities we have taken on. We want people to like or admire or respect us. Some of these actions are backed up by material rewards and punishments, but that is rarely *why* we do them. This point alone proves the implausibility of the dominant ideology behind our economic system, consumer culture, and technological drive—that human beings are naturally self-interested and motivated most of all by material rewards and punishments. Mengzi makes an even stronger claim. It is not just that human beings naturally have other concerns but that these concerns are the deepest and the strongest. Death is the permanent end to all sensory pleasure and the elimination of the very possibility of self-interest, and yet there are actions that people will refuse to do even in order to survive. That is why Mengzi calls our natural dispositions good.

Does this mean that Mengzi promotes self-denial over self-interest? Is he saying that human beings are naturally unselfish? Not exactly. The dichotomy between self-interest and self-denial depends on a false conception of the self. The self is intertwined with the world. I identify as a teacher, which I cannot be without students. When a student of mine has a remarkable success, I feel like I have accomplished what *I* wanted, even if I get no credit for it. That success is as much a part of my interests as anything else, and it adds more to me than the pleasure of a good meal. The same goes for being a parent or a husband, a nurse or an artist, all of which incorporate the interests of others into our own interests. Are such actions selfish? Certainly not in the usual sense, but the question itself is flawed. To oppose altruism and self-interest already skews the debate by assuming an individualistic idea of self that contradicts our actual way of being in the world.

Mengzi introduces his claim that everyone has something they would die for through a comparison with taste:

> Fish is what I desire. Bear paw is also what I desire. If these two cannot be attained together, I give up the fish and take the bear paw. Life is what I desire. Rightness also is what I desire. If these two cannot be attained together, I give up life and take rightness. Life is what I desire, but what I desire has something deeper than life. Thus, I will not do just anything to attain life. Death is what I detest, but what I detest has something deeper than death. Thus, there are troubles I will not avoid. (M 6A10)

Mengzi likes to eat bear paw and he likes to eat fish. Ideally, he would eat both, but if he has to choose, he chooses bear paw, because that is what he wants more. In the same way, he loves life and he loves rightness. Both are good, and as we just saw, one might make some ethical compromises for the sake of staying alive (M 6B1). If forced into a hard choice between life and rightness, though, Mengzi goes with what he wants more. He loves some things more than life, just as he detests some more than death. It is not a matter of self-denial or self-sacrifice, of choosing what you *should* do over what you *want* to do, as the ideology of self-interest would like us to think. It is just a matter of going with what we most care about. If we think of morality as distinct from other kinds of norms, values, and desires, then Mengzi is not advocating morality at all. My aversion to the suffering of others is the same kind of thing as my aversion to bad music. In taking risks to help others, we are doing what we really want.

The basis for the distinction between desiring life and desiring rightness lies within the body. Mengzi explains in a dialogue with his disciple Gongduzi:

"People love all of their body/self [*shēn* 身] without discrimination; what they love without discrimination they nourish without discrimination. There is not a foot or inch of flesh they do not love in it, so there is not a foot or inch which they do not nourish. That by which one examines if a person is good or not—how can it be anything other than what they choose in relation to the body/self? The body [*tǐ* 體] has noble and lowly, lesser and greater. Do not use the lesser to harm the greater; do not use the lowly to harm the noble. One who nourishes the lesser becomes a lesser person. One who nourishes the greater becomes a greater person. Now, if there is a master gardener who abandons the valuable parasol and catalpa trees but nourishes the sour dates, then he becomes a lowly gardener. Someone who nourishes a single finger while unknowingly neglecting the shoulders and back is a person like a crazed wolf. Those who just eat and drink are seen by people as lowly, because they nourish the lesser and thereby lose the greater. (M 6A14)

Mengzi's distinction looks like a familiar division between higher and lower pleasures, the first being pleasures of the mind and the latter being pleasures of the body. But the great of our body is not the *mind*, it is the *heart*. Mengzi does not divide mind and body; he makes a division within the body (referred to first as *shēn* 身 and then as *tǐ* 體). It is a ranking among things of the same kind. The finger and the shoulder are all limbs, but the shoulder is more important. The mouth, the ears, and the heart are all sensing organs, but the heart is more important.

The centrality of embodiment is difficult to capture in translation. The first line says simultaneously that people love themselves and that people love their bodies. The term *shen* unites those two meanings. Rather than separating mind and body or dividing reason and feeling, Mengzi distinguishes different kinds of affective, embodied responses to our environment. Some draw us to food, some to music, some to our loved ones, and some to strangers. All are based in the responsiveness of bodily organs: heart, eyes, ears, and mouth. If most people have something they would die rather than do, that is because for most people the responses of the heart have priority. In the passage about the dignified beggar, Mengzi says that those who violate rightness for the sake of excessive wealth have lost their *běnxīn* 本心, the rooted heart (6A10). We have seen both characters. The first is the root, which has a sense of being most fundamental but also of being a natural source of growth. The second depicts the physical heart. These two terms situate our natural feelings in the body and in the natural world. To deny our feelings of concern or of aversion is like the root refusing to grow. It thwarts our natural desires, our bodies, and nature itself.

The distinction between the two kinds of motivation is commonly made not in the extreme terms of life and death but as the difference between pursuing benefit (*lì* 利) and pursuing rightness (*yi*) or goodness (*shàn* 善):

> One who rises when the roosters crow and works diligently for goodness is a follower of Shun. One who rises when the roosters crow and works diligently for benefit is a follower of Robber Zhi. If you desire to know the division between Shun and Zhi—it is nothing other than the space between benefit and goodness. (M 7A25)

Mengzi probably uses the term "benefit" with the Mohists in mind. For the Mohists, the highest good is to promote benefit inclusively for all people. They defined benefit in terms of the basic necessities needed for life: food for those who are hungry, clothing for those who are cold, and rest for those who are weary. Mengzi was not opposed to those benefits. He argues that promoting benevolence and rightness brings material benefits to the people, and that if people lack the basic necessities for life, they will be unable to become good. As with life and sensory pleasures, the question is of priorities. Giving priority to benefit encourages the desires of the lesser parts of the body, strengthening them while neglecting the social concerns of the heart. Ultimately, this weakens the real ground for social cohesion and cooperation, which lies in relationships of direct concern rather than calculated benefit. Even if the benefit is meant for the sake of all people, it encourages the parts of us that tend toward greed.

The sprouts of the virtues

The examples raised throughout this chapter already suggest some of the specific concerns that can outweigh the pursuit of benefit: attachment to family, an aversion to certain kinds of harmful actions, dedication to a cause, and a sense of dignity. In two passages, Mengzi divides the concerns of the heart into four basic ways of responding to the world, each tending toward one of the main virtues. The first passage explains what he means in saying that natural human dispositions are good:

> By their genuine feelings [qíng 情], they can become good. This is what good refers to. If people become not good, it is not the fault of their ability. Every person has a heart of compassion and pain. Every person has a heart of shame and aversion. Every person has a heart of respect and reverence. Every person has a heart of affirming and negating. The heart of compassion and pain is benevolence. The heart of shame and aversion is rightness. The heart of respect and reverence is propriety. The heart of affirming and negating is wisdom. Benevolence, rightness, propriety, and wisdom are not fused onto us from outside. We certainly have them, only we do not attend to them. Thus, it is said,

"If you seek it then you attain it; if you abandon it, then you lose it." (M 6A6)

The list appears with minor variations in the passage using the term "beginning" or "sprout":

> Looking at in this way, lacking a heart of compassion and pain is not human; lacking a heart of shame and aversion is not human; lacking a heart of declining and yielding is not human; lacking a heart of affirming and negating is not human. The heart of compassion and pain is the sprout of benevolence. The heart of shame and aversion is the sprout of rightness. The heart of declining and yielding is the sprout of propriety. The heart of affirming and negating is the sprout of wisdom. People have these four sprouts like they have four limbs. To have these four sprouts and say that you cannot do it is to rob yourself. To say that your sovereign cannot do it is to rob your sovereign. All have these four sprouts within themselves. Know how to broaden and fill them and they will be like a fire beginning to ignite or a spring beginning to flow. If you can fill them, they are enough to stabilize all within the four seas. If you cannot fill them, they are not enough to serve your father and mother. (M 2A6)

Mengzi does not believe all humans are virtuous, but we all have spontaneous ways of reacting to the world that naturally lead toward virtue, given the right circumstances. These feelings relate to the virtues as sprouts relate to healthy, grown plants. They extend under their own power, like spreading fire or a flowing spring. When developed, they lead toward concern for the whole world. Without development, even one's own family will be neglected.

The process of cultivating these sprouts will be discussed in later chapters. In this chapter, I will explain each one. First, we must look briefly at the four virtues. Benevolence, *rén* 仁, centers on care and compassion. It was associated with the natural feelings of care that emerge within the family and was taken as what defines us as human beings. That played on the connection between the *rén* 仁 meaning benevolence and the *rén* 人 meaning human being. Later Confucians connected benevolence with sensitivity to suffering in the world, comparing the way we feel pain in our body to the way we should feel the pain of others. A cultivated person takes the world as her body. The culmination of this extension is described by the Song dynasty neo-Confucian Zhang Zai 張載 (1020–1077) in his famous *Western Inscription* (Ximing 西銘):

> Heaven is father; earth is mother. Even a trifling thing like myself dwells immersed in their midst. Thus, what fills heaven and earth is embodied in me; what guides heaven and earth is natural disposition [*xing*] in me. The people are my siblings; living things are my companions.[3]

This interpretation was suggested because the phrase "not-*ren*" (the same character translated as benevolence) became a medical term for numbness or paralysis. To be not-*ren* is to be insensitive, unable to feel.

Rightness, *yì* 義, centers on performing the right actions in the right circumstances. It is traditionally explained with a character of similar sound, *yí* 宜, which means "appropriate." Benevolence and rightness highlight different sides of virtuous action, but for Mengzi, both require internal feeling and attunement to the external complexities of the world. The third virtue is propriety, *lǐ* 禮. The character itself contains parts picturing common objects from ceremonial sacrifices: an altar 示, food 豆, and a bowl 曲, but the meaning of *li* is much broader, including rituals, etiquette, and proper manners. It was often paired with music (*yuè* 樂). Music and propriety will be the topic of chapter 6. The fourth virtue, *zhì* 智, is wisdom. The Confucians emphasize wisdom as the ability to recognize those with virtue and talent and to adapt right behavior to different circumstances. It is as much a form of knowing-how as knowing-that.

The four virtues are interdependent and complementary. A virtuous person must express genuine care (*ren*) in appropriate actions (*yi*) with the correct manner (*li*) in recognition of changing circumstances (*zhi*). All exist as dynamic intersections of internal and external, feelings and knowledge. Putting all four on an equal footing as felt reactions to the world may be Mengzi's innovation. Before him, it was common to divide the virtues into the external and the internal. As one recently discovered text says: "Benevolence is internal; rightness is external; ritual and music are combined."[4] Another text says that some virtues come from the center and extend out, while others come from the outside and enter in. The first list includes benevolence, loyalty, and sincerity. The second list is missing, but would include rightness, and probably ritual and wisdom.[5] Mengzi rejects these distinctions, taking all of the virtues as coming through the interplay of our natural dispositions and our environment, the internal and external.

With this general account of the "sprouts" in place, we can turn to each of the four in more detail.

The heart of compassion and pain is the sprout of benevolence

The sprout of benevolence receives most attention, with two famous illustrations. The first is in a long dialogue between Mengzi and King Xuan of Qi, one of the most powerful rulers of the time:

> The king asked, "Is it possible for someone like me to protect and maintain the people?" Mengzi replied: "Yes."
> "How do you know?"
> Mengzi replied: "I heard your attendant Huhe say this: The king sat aloft in his hall when someone led an ox past the lower

part of it. The king saw it and said, 'Where is the ox going?' The man replied, 'It will be used to consecrate a bell.' The king said, 'Let it go! I cannot bear its terrified appearance, like an innocent going to the place of death.' The man responded, 'Then should we abandon the consecration of the bell?' The king said: 'How can it be abandoned? Use a sheep in its place.'" Mengzi added, "I do not know if this incident really happened."

The king replied "It did."

Mengzi said, "This heart suffices for being a real king. The people all took your Majesty as being stingy about the ox, but I know for sure that it was your Majesty's not being able to bear it."

The king said, "Yes, there really were people like that. But though Qi is a small and narrow state, how should I be stingy about one ox? Indeed, it was that I could not bear its terrified appearance, like an innocent going to the place of death, and so I had a sheep used in its place."

Mengzi pursued, "Your Majesty, do not consider it odd that the people thought you were stingy. You exchanged the larger for the smaller, how could they understand? If you felt pained at its being like an innocent going to the place of death, what difference is there in choosing between the ox and the sheep?"

The king laughed and said, "What really was my heart in the matter? I did not grudge its expense but exchanged it for a sheep. It is fitting that the people thought I was being stingy."

Mengzi replied, "There is no harm in it. This is the method of benevolence. You saw the ox but had not seen the sheep. The noble relate to birds and beasts such that seeing them alive they cannot bear to see them die; hearing their cries, they cannot bear to eat their flesh. Therefore, the noble stay far from the kitchen." (M 1A7)

This passage is one of the most important in the *Mengzi* and we will return to some of its odd aspects, such as the king's ignorance of his own motivations and the surprising line about avoiding the kitchen. For now, we can consider the story as illustrating the heart of compassion and pain, which is described in terms of finding the suffering of another unbearable (*bùrěn* 不忍). This feeling of concern appears in three relationships—in the king's feeling for the ox about to be sacrificed, in his thought of how he would feel seeing an innocent person going to the place of execution, and in the feeling of sympathy the noble have for an animal being slaughtered. All three feelings come as spontaneous reactions to the world. The king's limited compassion reflects his poorly developed character, but the point is that the king already cares about beings other than himself. If he can feel concern enough to save the ox, he can do the same for the people.

Mengzi gives his other example as an illustration of the sprout of benevolence, just before he introduces the four sprouts:

> For this reason, I say all people have a heart of not bearing in relation to other people: Now if people suddenly see a small child about to fall into a well, anyone will have a heart of alarm and compassion, not to get connections with the child's father and mother, not to seek praise among their neighbors and friends, and not for detesting the reputation of it. (M 2A6)

The power of this example to extend across two millennia of time and half a world of distance is itself a strong argument in support of Mengzi's claim for common human dispositions. Open wells are rare, but imagine the feeling of panic upon seeing an oblivious child chasing a ball toward a busy road. Mengzi draws our attention to the primitiveness of this reaction. It does not arise out of a judgment or calculation about benefit and consequences. It happens immediately. The situation seizes us. Mengzi again describes this feeling as a heart of "not bearing." In relation to other people, there are some things that we feel we just cannot accept or allow.

Excavated texts suggest that earlier Confucians saw benevolence as arising naturally from feelings within the family. One key virtue that Mengzi leaves off his list of four is *xiào* 孝, usually translated as filial piety. Filial piety may not make the list because it penetrates all of the virtues—without the right feelings for parents, one lacks benevolence; without acting appropriately toward family, one lacks rightness. The *feelings* for family are usually included within the description of benevolence. Mengzi says:

Of children carried in arms and just old enough to smile, none do not know loving their parents. When they grow, none do not know revering their older brothers. Cherishing parents is benevolence. Revering elders is rightness. There is nothing else but to extend them through the world. (M 7A15)

When people are young they adore their father and mother. When they become aware of alluring appearances, they adore youthful beauties. When they have a wife and children, they adore their wife and children. When they take office, they adore their sovereign—if they do not attain a sovereign then they burn inside. Great filial piety means to the end of one's life still adoring one's father and mother. (M 5A1)

Familial feelings are the clearest example of motivations that lead us to willingly sacrifice our individual material interests, but for Mengzi, our concern naturally extends beyond our own circle of family and friends. The child by the well is not related to us. The ox is not even of the same species. This explanation of benevolence as arising from feelings toward strangers as well as family is another of Mengzi's innovations, perhaps in response to Mohist criticisms of Confucian care as not inclusive enough.

The heart of shame and aversion is the sprout of rightness

People sacrifice their own benefit for the sake of what they consider right, and some will even give up their life. That is a fact, but the feeling behind such actions is more difficult to pinpoint. Mengzi derives rightness from feelings of shame and aversion. The term for shame, *xiū* 羞, appears in a dialogue between a wife and concubine. It begins with the wife expressing suspicions that their husband is not as great as he says he is:

> When our husband goes out, he always returns later full from wine and meat. When I ask with whom he eats and drinks, he names all of the wealthy and noble, and yet none of the illustrious ever come here. I will spy out where he goes.

She follows her husband to a burial ground outside the city and sees him asking for the leftovers from the funeral rituals. He goes from grave to grave eating in this way. The story concludes:

> His wife returned and said to his concubine, "Our husband is the one we must look toward for our whole lives, and he turns out to be like this!" She and the concubine vilified the husband and cried together in the middle of the courtyard. Unaware of this, the husband strolled in from outside, lording it over them. Looking at it from the point of view of the noble, there are very few whose means of seeking wealth and honor, benefit and success would not make their wife and concubine ashamed [*xiu*] and tearful. (M 4B33)

The story assumes that its readers will feel shame at the thought of begging for funeral leftovers, but that is just meant as an extreme example of the kinds of things people do in the pursuit of wealth. The emphasis is not on knowing what is right and wrong but rather on the feeling that holds one back from doing certain things. The wife and concubine have that feeling. Their husband does not.

The other emotion at the basis of rightness is *wù* 惡, to detest, have an aversion toward, or be disgusted by. As an adjective or noun (pronounced *è*), the same character means bad, ugly, or disgusting. The immediacy of this aversion is nicely expressed in a famous line from the "Greatest Learning" (*Daxue* 大學) chapter of the *Record of Rituals*:

> What is called making one's intention authentic and avoiding self-deception is like being disgusted by a disgusting smell or like loving those with an alluring appearance. This is called being sat-isfied in oneself. (TX3)

Just as the passage uses 惡 first as a verb (be disgusted by, detest) and then as an adjective (disgusting, detestable), it uses 好 as a verb (pronounced *hào*, meaning to love or want) and then as an adjective (pronounced *hǎo*, meaning good or attractive). "Appearance" is *sè* 色, a term often associated with erotic attraction and sex. Kongzi says elsewhere, "I have not seen one who loved virtue like they love those with alluring appearances" (LY 9.18). The point is that we should be attracted to good actions in the same visceral way we are spontaneously drawn to someone we find attractive, and we should react to bad deeds with the immediate and genuine repulsion we have toward a bad smell. Mengzi uses the same character when he says that he *detests* death, but there are things that he detests even more.

The clearest illustration of the heart of shame and aversion is given parallel to benevolence:

> People all have what they will not bear; extending that to what they will bear is benevolence. People all have what they will not do; extending that to what they will do is rightness. If people can fill out the heart that is without desires to harm other people,

then their benevolence cannot be used up. If people can fill out the heart that is without boring through and leaping over [walls], then their rightness cannot be used up. If people can fill out the core that will not accept being addressed with condescension, they will have rightness wherever they go. For leaders [shi] to speak when they should not speak is to manipulate with speech. For leaders to not speak when they should speak is to manipulate with silence. These are the same kind of thing as boring through or leaping over walls. (M 7B31)

By "boring through" and "leaping over," Mengzi means breaking into some place, perhaps to steal property or for an illicit meeting with a lover, actions he assumes most people would feel averse toward. Like the feelings of sympathy and familial concern, the feeling that some things cannot be done is considered common and natural. We must take the heart that cannot bear to hurt others and extend it to become benevolent. In the same way, we must take the heart that is averse to breaking through or jumping over walls and extend it to other wrong actions.

This need to extend natural feelings has already appeared in several passages, where something easily felt to be wrong is compared to a bad action that does not evoke the same aversion. King Xuan of Qi feels pity for an ox but not for his own people (M 1A7). People would feel shame about eating funeral leftovers, but they are undisturbed by the bad things they do in pursuit of wealth (4B33). After giving the example of the dignified beggar refusing to be humiliated, Mengzi contrasts that with what people will accept in pursuit of wealth, even though much less is at stake:

Yet ten thousand bushels of grain will be accepted without consideration of propriety or rightness. What can ten thousand bushels of grain add to me! For the beauty of palaces, the support of wives and concubines, so that people I know in adversity or need will consider me generous? (6A10)

That is what he calls losing the rooted heart (*benxin*). Part of the problem is the disjunction between what we *know* is wrong and what we *feel* as wrong. Mengzi recognizes that people react more strongly against simple and obvious wrongs like burglary than they do to so-called white-collar crimes, while knowing the latter often cause worse harms. It would take tens of thousands of burglars to do as much harm as was caused by the financial industry in the mortgage crisis of the mid-2000s, yet not a single person was punished like a burglar. These disjunctions appear on a personal level too. I feel a deep aversion to littering. I could hardly bear to throw trash out a car window. But eating meat does not bother me, even though I know that on almost any ethical theory, littering is a less significant harm.

In his examples of rightness, Mengzi contrasts the stifled feelings of more privileged people with the rooted feelings of someone more marginalized: wives and concubines in 4B33, a beggar in 6A10. The commonality of the four sprouts is not restricted by gender or social position. It also means that ambition, pride, and power obscure the directions of the heart. The beggar feels what the wealthy person does not. The contrast between those with power and those without also is a contrast between those with and without education, suggesting that education can erode our rooted heart. This point parallels criticisms of education found in the *Laozi*. The Confucians do not reject education but envision education as an art of stimulating the constructive tendencies of the heart. Confucian approaches to learning and education will be discussed in chapter 5.

John Locke (1632–1704) once argued against the existence of any innate moral principles by claiming that no moral rule exists in every culture.[6] Many anthropologists would agree. Yet even if no single rule is universal, all cultures have rules, from taboos to etiquette to divine commandments. That rules arise wherever human beings live together is a product of the kind of beings we are. Social rules would never take hold if there were no feelings supporting them. Why would we bother constraining ourselves with rules even when we had no chance of getting caught? How could mere knowledge of what is right consistently resist other desires and emotions, unless that knowledge were linked to some affective force of its own?

Mengzi is not claiming that human beings have innate knowledge of morality. The fact that we can *feel* an action as wrong presupposes some natural feeling, but that does not necessarily have a fixed content. Mengzi's philosophy is compatible with a claim that the rules we follow are socially constructed and must be learned. That means social norms can be bad. In a racist society, we might feel no shame at being racist; in a capitalist society, we might feel no shame at the poverty of others. Disgust may arise naturally and spontaneously in relation to things like rotting flesh, but its use to enforce social roles and mores is obviously learned. Regarding shame, a suspicious reader might even say that we do not care so much about *being good* but rather *being considered good*, particularly by our parents. When we feel shame while alone, that just means we have internalized that parental voice. I'm not sure Mengzi would disagree, but even if our direct concern is being respected by others, that feeling reveals our fundamental sociality. If we were purely rational beings looking out only for our own interests, why would we care so much how other people see us? There is something remarkably and strangely human about the fact that some people will die to preserve their honor or save face.

The heart of yielding to others is the sprout of propriety

None of us would think of putting ritual propriety in a list of our top four virtues, not even a top ten. It is difficult to imagine cases in which someone would die for the sake of propriety. At the same time, in daily life, propriety is one of the virtues we most often sacrifice our personal comfort and desires for. We do that whenever we politely open a door and let someone go before us, or when we wait to say what we want rather than interrupt. We do it when we put on clothes that are less comfortable than what we would lounge around the house in. Just think about what you wear if working at home. Teaching on Zoom, I haven't worn long pants or even shoes in eight months (it is Hawai'i). One excavated text that develops the philosophy of Mengzi gives a more extreme case—no matter how attractive a person was, if the only way to have sex with them was in front of your parents, would you do it?[7] The author thinks you would not.

If every culture has rituals, something about us human beings must drive us toward them. The variety of rituals across cultures does not alter the commonality of this drive. What common feeling leads to the development and importance of propriety? Mengzi himself may have been unsure of the answer. It is the only "sprout" formulated differently in the two versions of the list, and the examples he gives have little connection to either formulation. The core of the problem is that rituals fill many functions at the same, making them irreducible to any single feeling. The complex and multifaceted nature of ritual and music will be discussed in chapter 6. Here, I just briefly present Mengzi's explanation of their origins in human dispositions.

In 2A6, Mengzi says, "a heart of declining and yielding is the sprout of ritual propriety." The terms refer to declining (*cí* 辭) a position that is improper, such as resigning from a corrupt government, and to yielding (*ràng* 讓) what one desires to someone else, particular one's parents or older siblings. Mengzi gives no examples, but Xunzi, a Confucian who lived about a century later, associates the same phrase with ritual. For Xunzi, the opposite of yielding and declining is grasping things as we desire them. His example of yielding is at a family meal.[8] If we are hungry and follow our desires, we immediately grab the best dish and take a big serving. If we sit back and wait for our parents or guests to serve themselves first, that is because ritual restrains us. There is something truly bizarre about a group of hungry people sitting at a dinner table with food in front of them, not eating. Yet we do this regularly, when we wait for the last person to be served at a restaurant or for a slow family member to come to the table. Yielding to others is a common aspect of ritual or etiquette. For Xunzi, this proves that ritual involves a deliberate constraining of our natural desires. Mengzi says the yielding itself expresses a natural human feeling. Impatience at someone taking too long to come to the dinner table represents not a conflict between natural desire and self-discipline but between two natural desires—to eat and to show respect to the other person. Consider again the simple example of what clothes we wear. When I put on shoes and long pants to teach a class, am I forcing myself to do something I do not want? I don't think so. I could surely go to class in shorts and slippers, perhaps even barefoot, without getting in any trouble. I don't do that because it doesn't feel appropriate to me.

Mengzi's second version of the origins of propriety is a heart of respect (gōng 恭) and reverence (jìng 敬) (M 6A6). Confucians often named reverence and respect as the most important attitudes during rituals. This feeling of respect may be connected to what a recently discovered Confucian text describes as a heart oriented toward what is distant or other, literally toward what is external or foreign (wài 外). That text, known as the *Five Conducts* gives the following progression:

Using the heart that responds to otherness to interact with people is keeping a feeling of distance. Feeling distant and being dignified in it is reverence. Being reverent and not slacking off is seriousness. Being serious and in awe of it is respect. Being respectful and not arrogant is humility. Being humble and interacting widely is propriety.[9]

If this description is in the background of Mengzi's account, then respect is the opposite of a feeling of familiarity or casualness. Imagine the feeling of meeting your lover's parents for the first time, or having dinner with someone you have admired but have never met.

Feelings of respect and a desire to yield to others explain some aspects of propriety, but not all of it. Mengzi assumes a common Confucian belief that ritual derives not from one particular feeling but from the need to express any feeling. Just as feelings arise naturally through sensitivity to external circumstances, they naturally require some form of expression: "whatever is on the inside must take shape on the outside" (M 6B6). The main example that Mengzi gives is funerals. These express grief above all, and their emphasis on familial feelings connects them to the origins of benevolence. We can consider one example, a complex dialogue with a Mohist named Yizhi or Yizi (Master Yi). The Mohists advocated inclusive or impartial care. Yizi begins by quoting a Confucian saying: "The ancient people acted as if protecting a child."[10] He takes this to mean that one should care for all people without difference or rank, but that this care should first be implemented within the family. When Mengzi hears of this from his disciple, he replies:

Now does Yizi truly think people cherish their older brother's son just like they cherish their neighbor's son? What is taken from that saying is that if a crawling child is about go into a well, it is not the fault of the child. Moreover, in heaven's generating of things, it makes them have one root, but Yizi gives them two roots. Presumably, in the ancient past, some did not bury their parents. When their parents died, they lifted them up and discarded them into a ditch. On another day, they passed by and saw foxes eating them and insects swarming on them. Their foreheads sweat. They glanced but did not look. Now this sweating was not for the sake of other people. Their innermost heart reached through to their face and eyes. They went home and came back with baskets and shovels and covered them. If covering them thus was genuinely right, then the filial son and benevolent person, in burying their parents, must also have *dao*. (M 3A5)

The meaning of having one root will be discussed later in this chapter and this passage will come up again in the chapter on ritual. Here, we can just consider what it says about the origins of ritual and propriety. When the people see the corpses, feelings that are rooted in the heart immediately express themselves through the body, in the face and eyes, in the sweat on their foreheads. Ritual originates from these spontaneous expressions of emotions.

The heart of affirming and negating is the sprout of wisdom

Like the sprout that leads to ritual propriety, the sprout of affirming and negating gets little explanation from Mengzi. Literally, this origin is a heart that will *shì* 是 and *fēi* 非, key terms in argument and debate. To *shi* is to affirm something or agree that it is the case. To *fei* is to deny something or say that it is not the case. They involve motivation too: to *shi* something is to support it and to *fei* is to oppose it. We might think Mengzi is claiming human beings naturally know what is right and wrong, but that would break the parallel with the other three hearts that lead to the virtues. We are looking for a fundamental affective relationship to the world that naturally leads us to acquire knowledge and wisdom. Mengzi's point, I think, is that we are naturally drawn to sort and evaluate things. Human beings are born with a desire to learn, as we see in a child's unending curiosity. It is not just that this kind of curiosity is a prerequisite for wisdom—it leads toward wisdom by its own internal force. Children just need to be placed in the right conditions, so that their drive to learn can take them further and further. Placing the origin of wisdom in a feeling might seem strange, but it is comparable to seeing the origin of rightness in a feeling. Both virtues require extensive knowledge of the world, but this knowledge would not be possible without internal motivation. In the case of rightness, a felt need drives us to do the right things and to learn which actions are right. In achieving wisdom, a felt need drives us to makes sense of and judge things, leading to knowledge of the world. To quote an actual fortune cookie, "The root of wisdom is to desire it."

Mengzi never explains this sprout directly, but other Confucian texts associate wisdom with *hàoxué* 好學, the love of learning. The *Zhongyong* says simply: "Loving learning comes close to wisdom" (ZY15). Love of learning is the decisive trait of wise people. Kongzi is particularly associated with it:

> The master said, "In a village of ten families there is surely someone as dedicated and trustworthy as I am, but not one who loves learning like I do." (LY 5.28)

> Formerly Zigong asked Kongzi, "Master, are you a sage?" Kongzi responded, "Being a sage is something I cannot do. I learn without satiety and teach without tiring." Zigong said, "Learning without satiety is wisdom. Teaching without tiring is benevolence. Benevolent and wise, master you are a sage." (M 2A2)

The emphasis on love (using the same *hao* as in loving those with an alluring appearance) points to the basis of learning in responsiveness to the world around us:

> When Shun resided in the midst of deep mountains, dwelling with trees and stones and wandering with deer and hogs, that by which he differed from the wild people of the deep mountains was slight. But when he heard one good word or saw one good action, it was like releasing the Yangtze or Yellow River, gushing forth so that nothing could stop it. (M 7A16)

This passage echoes the description of Yi Yin working in the fields. When he heard of a benevolent government, he responded by rising up and entering its service. Shun exhibits a similar responsiveness, spontaneously flowing toward a good word or action. This drive toward learning has natural force like surging waters. If learning itself is natural, then so are its results, including a body of wisdom accumulated over time.

What it means to be human

What makes a human being distinctively human? One common answer is reason or rationality. Animals simply react to stimuli, while we humans deliberate and reason. Another possible answer is free will. Only the human will escape the chains of causality. Everything else follows the laws of nature. These attributes make sense in a Christian context, where human beings are super-natural and individuals must be entirely responsible for their actions. For Mengzi, human beings have no abilities that can be radically isolated from the world, whether that is an innate structure of rationality or a free will. Mengzi defines human beings according to the reactions of the heart. We could say he defines human beings by their emotions, but not just any kind of emotions. Mengzi's definition of human beings is not far from a definition given by Aristotle: human beings are social or political animals (*zoon politikon*). For Mengzi, dispositions naturally lead human beings to form bonds of compassion (*ren*), rules enforced by feelings of shame and aversion (*yi*), rituals and customs for expressing emotions (*li*), and some body of wisdom (*zhi*). Culture, social structures, and rules arise from the interplay of a concrete environment and the kinds of things human beings naturally care about. These same feelings, when developed, lead us to actively help others and strive to make the world a better place.

Defining human beings as social expresses the early Chinese view of being as life or growth. While many European philosophers saw the world as made up of distinct things called substances, Chinese philosophers thought that things dynamically become what they are through ways of mixing with their environment. The sprout takes in sun and soil and reworks them to grow into a tree. Rather than conceptualize this in terms of one thing and the influences of other things on it, it would be better to think of the growth of a sprout as a process involving a conjunction of factors, a node within a network of natural forces. Human beings also grow as a nexus of water, food, and shelter. We experience these interactions as desires and aversions. What makes us distinctive is that our existence as a center of relations and reactions is also experienced as emotions like love, fear, respect, and shame. It is not just that we are social but that our very identity incorporates our unique place in the world. Abstractly, we can say all human beings have a disposition to compassion, but that compassion arises in relation to particular events. I see that child near the edge of a well, I am saddened by the troubles of this friend, and I mourn the death of my mother. Walking around campus I notice a student and ask with concern about how he is doing. Another professor will pass him by but stop to ask one of her students. All people have something they would die for, but what it is that they would risk their lives for will depend on the circumstances, including cultural background. Different cultures will find different actions shameful or rude. A bird would have an entirely different perception.

The trouble is that while the particularities of our concerns make us who we are, we have the capacity to see that the two students are equally worthy of concern, that the death of my mother is no more tragic or deserving of sorrow than the death of any other person. Mohists like Yizi appealed to this kind of perspective to argue for inclusive care. From the perspective of heaven or nature, what would make one human life more valuable than another? I may have my preferences, but these are imposed on nature itself. In the passage on the origin of funerals, Mengzi accuses Yizi of giving human beings two roots instead of one. He doesn't say what those roots are, but we can now see an explanation—one root is our affective engagement with the world around us while the other root is the objective perspective of nature or heaven. Mengzi agrees that we should care for strangers and the whole world, but only as an extension of our concrete concerns in the world, which begins with our families. The danger of having two roots is that the objective perspective can erode our particularistic feelings of care, yet, for Mengzi, these feelings, based in the rooted heart, are the only possible basis for caring about anyone at all.

Another problem with the Mohist appeal to the inclusivity of heaven is that it goes too far. If heaven generates and covers all things, why single out human beings? Shouldn't all living things have equal value? The *Zhuangzi* frequently appeals to this point of view, as in a description of the sage Wang Tai:

> Viewing from differences, your liver and gall bladder are like the states of Chu and Yue. Viewing from sameness, the myriad things are all one. Someone like this does not even know what is suitable for his ears or eyes. He lets his heart wander playfully in the harmony of potency [*dé* 德]. As for things, he views what unifies them and does not view what is lost. He views the loss of his foot as dirt left behind.[11]

Distinctions are relative to some particular perspective. The states of Chu and Yue are far apart (from the perspective of walking between them) but the states of Chu and Yue are near to each other (from the perspective of England). This throws our distinctions into doubt. I see my foot as radically different from a clump of earth, but is it really so? They are all equally parts of nature, existing in various processes that change over time. The foot will become dirt someday.

If one can overcome distinctions in this way, then one can overcome attachment and loss, and that is probably a good way to deal with losing a foot. But should we see the loss of limbs due to the bombing of Iraq or Vietnam in the same way? What about the deaths of children? We *can* see them this way. They have entered back into the *dao*, as they once emerged from it. If we look in terms of what all things have in common, nothing is ever truly lost. What makes Mengzi's position so distinctive is that he accepts that from the perspective of nature or heaven, there is no greater value to my foot or my mother than there is to a clump of dirt. Our feet and our mothers are only different *to us*. Yet that difference matters. Although all things come from heaven and are in some sense natural, there are some things it is natural for human beings to resist, things like suffering and oppression. We should strive to change these, and this action harmonizes with heaven by expressing our natural dispositions. In times of trouble, we should respond like Yi Yin by rising out of the fields, not the wild mountain sage who rolls all things into one.

3

Emotions and Enjoying Life

The way of life that Mengzi promotes derives from and relies on natural human emotions. And yet, sages across the world warn us to beware of emotions. In the *Bhagavad-Gita*, when Arjuna is racked by feelings of concern for the friends and family members he is about to attack in battle, Lord Krishna counsels:

> When suffering does not disturb his mind,
> when his craving for pleasures has vanished,
> when attraction, fear, and anger are gone,
> he is called a sage whose thought is sure.
> When he shows no preference
> in fortune or misfortune
> and neither exults nor hates,
> his insight is sure.[1]

In the "Fire Sutra," the Buddha tells his disciples:

> The mind is burning, ideas are burning, mind-consciousness is burning, mind-contact is burning, also whatever is felt as pleasant or painful or neither-painful-nor-pleasant that arises with mind-contact for its indispensable condition, that too is burning. Burning with what? Burning with the fire of lust, with the fire of hate, with the fire of delusion. I say it is burning with birth, aging and death, with sorrows, with lamentations, with pains, with griefs, with despairs.[2]

Doing What You Really Want. Franklin Perkins, Oxford University Press. © Oxford University Press 2022. DOI: 10.1093/oso/9780197574911.003.0004

The Roman emperor and stoic philosopher Marcus Aurelius writes in his journal:

> Remember that your ruling centre becomes invincible when it withdraws into itself and rests content with itself [. . .]. By virtue of this, an intelligence free from passions is a mighty citadel; for man has no stronghold more secure to which he can retreat to remain unassailable from that time onward. One who has failed to see this is merely ignorant, but one who has seen it and fails to take refuge there is beyond the aid of fortune.[3]

The *Huainanzi*, a text compiled around 139 BCE based largely on Daoist views, says:

> Joy and anger are deviations from the way;
> Worry and grief are the loss of virtuosity [*de*];
> Loving and hating are the excesses of the heart;
> Cravings and desires are what burden our natural dispositions.
> For people, great anger breaks up the yin forces; great joy
>   topples the yang forces.
> Suppressing vital energy leads to muteness; fear and terror make
>   madness.
> When worry and grief accumulate with anger, sickness takes
>   form and gathers.
> When loving and hating pile up, one disaster will follow another.
> Thus, the heart not worrying or grieving is the utmost of
>   potency.
> Communing without change is the utmost of stillness.
> Not carrying along lusts and desires is the utmost of emptiness.
> Having nothing loved or hated is the utmost of peace.
> Not being distracted by things is the utmost of refined purity.[4]

Why do philosophers across traditions reach this same conclusion? What is wrong with emotions?

Surely at some point we have all come to regret actions driven by anger, fear, or jealousy. We recognize how emotions can cloud our judgment, and we have been around people making bad decisions under the sway of some strong emotion. There are reasons why the terms "fool" and "love" are associated, and why we say that emotions are blind. Emotions also make us lose control. It is no accident that emotions are called *passions*: they are that in which we are *passive*. The stoic philosopher Epictetus, who was literally a slave, explains:

> If someone turned your body over to just any person who happened to meet you, you would be angry. But are you not ashamed to turn over your own faculty of judgment to whoever happens along, so that if he abuses you it is upset and confused?[5]

You would be ashamed to let someone else take control of your body, but it is even worse to enslave your mind to others. That is what happens when you let someone else's actions "control" your emotions, for example, by allowing them to make you angry.

If the world is just a collection of independent substances, then either we control ourselves or we let things in the world control us. In that context, *dependence* on the world looks like *enslavement* to the world. Our goal is autonomy, literally giving law (*nomos*) to ourselves (*auto*). The alternative is having laws dictated to us by others, heteronomy. This idea of autonomy makes little sense if our being is essentially entangled with others. Even when Chinese philosophers criticize emotion and desire, the goal is not independence but shifting our dependence from particular things to what all things have in common. The *Zhuangzi* refers to this as "hiding the world in the world":

> You hide your boat in a ravine or your net in a swamp and call it secure. But in the middle of the night, one with strength lifts it on his shoulder and goes, and the ignorant know nothing about it. Hiding the small in the big is appropriate, but something still gets

away. If you hide the world in the world, there can be nothing that gets away.[6]

Freedom from the daily disruptions that come from attachment to particular things is achieved not through independence but by embracing what cannot be lost.

Neither action nor passion, both internal and external

If Mengzi's philosophy promotes a way of life built around emotions, he must have ways of dealing with these problems. That will be the theme of this chapter. I will begin with the question of agency and control. First of all, emotions are not simply blind or irrational. They have an embedded rationality involving distinctions, attention, and understanding. To feel concern for someone suffering requires discerning that they really are suffering, and that requires insight into their purposes and desires. For Mengzi, knowledge itself results from a felt need to make sense of things, the heart of affirming and negating. Even so, emotions do erode our self-control. Take love as an example. On the one hand, it is difficult if not impossible to control who one loves. They seize hold of us without explanation. So it happens that some people do not love the person they should or that they cannot help but love someone they shouldn't. On the other hand, when in love, we lose some control. If the person we love seems disinterested, we are anxious. If they hurt, we hurt. Their joy lifts our moods. To love means to no longer have full control—if your beloved could not make you upset, I would doubt you were really in love.

Loss of complete control does not mean we are enslaved or passive. The division between active and passive is embedded in our language and our thinking, but it does not fit our way of being in the world. I think—I am out walking and acting in the world. Some things I do; some things are done to me. But, if I walk down the street and a chirping bird draws my attention, who is active and who passive? The encounter would not happen if I did not have my own particular interests and an ability to attend to things, if I were too lost in thought or were listening to music. But the birdsong is what prompts me to pause and look. I respond to the call. We could try to divide the event into active and passive elements, but that would be an imposition on what is really a single process. Perhaps the bird began singing because it saw me. The encounter only happens because the bird and I both ended up in the park in the early morning, so perhaps the real agent is the sunrise? Or maybe it is the common air that transmits sound and makes both of our lives possible? The park only exists because of city planning, so perhaps the ultimate agent is Lee Kuan Yew (I write this part while living in Singapore)? The whole line of questioning is misdirected, revealing the absurdity of any strong idea of autonomy. What exists is a complex tangle of influences and relationships, patterns of stimulation and response.

Mengzi discusses the relational nature of emotions in two complex dialogues connected with Gaozi. The first begins with Gaozi staking out a philosophical claim: "Food and sex are natural dispositions. Benevolence is internal and not external. Rightness is external and not internal" (M 6A4). We have seen Gaozi's equation of natural dispositions (*xing*) with life (*sheng*) and so with dispositions toward food and sex. Here, his position shifts. He admits certain feelings of care arise in us spontaneously and naturally, so he says that benevolence is internal. In contrast, rules of conduct must be learned, so he says rightness is external. This position connects to another distinction, between benevolence as rooted in natural familial affection (thus internal to the home) and rightness as a public virtue of following and enforcing rules (outside the home).

When Mengzi asks him to justify his claim, the argument begins:

Gaozi said, "That person is an elder and I respect him as an elder. The elderliness is not within me. It is like that being white and me treating it as white. It follows its being white, which is external. Thus, I say it is external."

Mengzi said, "The white of a white horse is no different from the white of a white person, but I doubt that the elderliness of an old horse is no different from the elderliness of an old person. Moreover, is elderliness called rightness, or is respecting elderliness called rightness?"

The parallel between white (*bái* 白) and old age (*zhǎng* 長) in the argument is impossible to capture in English, because the passage uses each character as a noun, an adjective, and a verb. To "white" something as a verb is to treat it as white, and there is little difference in how we treat the whiteness of different things. In contrast, to "elder" a horse is to treat it as old, while to "elder" a person is to treat that person with respect. A basic ambiguity arises when Gaozi says, "That one is *zhang* (elderly) and I *zhang* (elder) him—*zhang* (elderliness/eldering) is not in me." As a noun, the elderliness is not within me, but as an action or attitude (eldering), it is from me. Even recognizing a person as an elder is not purely objective and external. In English, we say an elderly person but not an elderly horse.

Gaozi responds with a second example:

If it is my younger brother, then I love him. If it is the younger brother of a person from the state of Qin, then I do not love him. This shows that what is affirmed is from me and so I call it internal. I respect an elder of the people of the state of Chu as I respect my own elders. This shows that what is affirmed is from the age, so I call it external.

Love or care is internal because it is subjective—facing two people objectively the same, I love my brother more than a stranger. In contrast, respect is external because it follows what is objective—I respect anyone of the right age, no matter who they are. One can see some echo of the two roots discussed earlier in relation to the Mohists. For Gaozi, benevolence is rooted in the particularities of my own feelings. Rightness relies on an objective view of the world. Mengzi disputes this division with a counterexample:

> Desire for meat roasted by a person from the state of Qi is not different from desire for meat that I roast myself. It is like this with all things. Then is the desire for roast meat also external? (M 6A4)

The desire for good tasting food tracks objective qualities in the world, just as rightness tracks age as an objective quality. It even involves cultural factors, as what people recognize as good food varies across cultures. But to claim that desiring food has no basis in me would be absurd. It is *my* desire. In the same way, I respond to age no matter who the person is, but the respect I express must be mine. Mengzi does not deny the role of external factors but shifts from those factors to our relationships with them.

The second passage begins when Meng Jizi challenges Mengzi's disciple Gongduzi to justify the claim that rightness is internal:

> Meng Jizi asked Gongduzi, "Why do you say that rightness is internal?"
> Gongduzi said, "I enact my reverence, so I say it is internal." Jizi said, "If a villager is older than your older brother by one year, then who do you revere?" Gongduzi said, "I revere my older brother." Jizi said, "In pouring drinks, then who do you pour for first?" Gongduzi said, "I pour for the villager first." Jizi said, "You feel reverence toward this one but treat as an elder that one. As a result, it is external, not following the internal."

Meng Jizi leads Gongduzi into a split between his feelings of reverence (*jing*) and his actions demonstrating reverence toward an elder, again using *zhang* as a verb. His point is that feelings depend on us, which makes them internal, while showing respect is external.

Gongduzi does not know what to say, and goes to Mengzi, who replies:

> Say to him, "Do you revere your uncle? Or do you revere your younger brother?" He will say, "I revere my uncle." Then say, "If your younger brother is ritually in the place of the dead ancestor, then who do you revere?" He will say, "I revere my younger brother." Then you say, "What about the reverence you have for your uncle?" He will say, "It is because of position." You also say, "It is because of position. Normally I revere my older brother, but in that particular situation reverence is for the villager."

In this reply, Mengzi focuses on the feeling of reverence expressed both toward an older brother and a village elder. In both cases, the feeling is based in myself but tracks external factors in the world. It is not just that my *actions* depend on the context but my *feelings* do as well. When Jizi hears of this, he tries one more example:

> When I should revere my uncle then I revere him; when I should revere my younger brother then I revere him: ultimately it is external and not from the internal.

Reverence is external because it is determined by external factors. Gongduzi replies with another comparison to eating:

> In winter we drink hot soup but in summer we drink cool water. So then are drinking and eating also external? (M 6A5)

What food we desire changes radically by our external circumstances, but does that mean it has no basis in our own feelings? Of course not. In the same way, my feelings of respect change radically according to the circumstances, but they are still *my* feelings. It is worth remembering that Mengzi takes desires for food and desires to show respect as equally natural and part of our dispositions. It is no surprise that they work in similar ways.

Mengzi says benevolence and rightness are internal, but his arguments undermine the division between internal and external. Love for a sibling is bound up with evaluations of the external world; showing respect in a conventional ritual context engages feelings inside me. Emotions are not objective or subjective, external or internal. When I feel concern for someone suffering, something of myself, a heart of compassion, responds to something of the world, a child in danger. This concern expresses who I am as much as it expresses the world. Extending my felt connections to more and more of the world does not make me more and more passive but increases my sensitivity, extending my being further and further.

Sensitivity and suffering

Becoming more sensitive means becoming more vulnerable. That brings us to a harder problem. Emotions make us suffer, and who wants to suffer? Zhuangzi's embracing of all things follows from his views of nature but it has a practical goal—to find joy everywhere. Zhuangzi writes:

> The genuine human beings of the past did not know to approve of living or to detest dying. They came out without delight and they entered back without resistance. They were at ease in going and were at ease in coming, that's all. They did not forget what begins it and did not seek what ends it. Receiving they enjoyed it, losing they returned it. This is called not using the heart to harm *dao*, not using the human to aid heaven.[7]

In contrast, the Confucians say we should *not* find joy in or embrace all things. We have already seen examples in which we should not feel joy—a child in danger, the slaughter of an animal, an innocent person executed, the death of a parent, the suffering of the people.

Most Confucian examples involve family and friends. The *Lunyu* says:

> The master said, "The age of one's parents cannot be ignored. It is at once a cause for pleasure and a cause for worry." (LY 4.21)

We are pleased because they have lived this long, but worry that as they get older, death and illness become more likely. When one's parents die, the feeling of sorrow should be strong enough to disrupt our usual pleasures (LY 17.21). The same goes for the loss of a friend. Yan Yuan, better known as Yan Hui, was one of Kongzi's most promising students, but he lived in poverty and died young. Several passages describe Kongzi's response:

> When Yan Yuan died, the master cried for him and was carried away by grief. His disciples said, "Master, you are getting carried away." He replied: "Am I getting carried away? If I am not to be carried away by grief for this person, then for whom?" (LY 11.10)

The death of Kongzi evokes similar emotions in his followers:

> Formerly when Kongzi died and three years of mourning had passed, his disciples packed their things and were about to return home. They paid their respects to Zigong, looked at each other and cried so long that they lost their voices. Only then did they return home. Zigong turned back and built a house on the grounds, residing there alone for another three years. Only then did he return home. (M 3A4)

These passages advocate sorrow by describing the mourning of exemplary figures like Kongzi and his disciple Zigong.

A more complex account of proper unhappiness appears in a discussion of the legendary sage emperor Shun. The passage begins with Mengzi's disciple Wan Zhang asking about a legendary claim that Shun went out into the fields and cried out to heaven. Mengzi confirms the story, saying that Shun expressed a feeling of *yuànmù* 怨慕, a mix of frustration, resentment, and longing. Wan Zhang questions the appropriateness of that feeling. We should do our best to please our parents, but if we fail to attain results, we must accept that, not cry and complain. Mengzi quotes a similar response but then rejects it:

> Gongming Gao thought the heart of a filial son could not be so complacent as to think, "I exhaust myself working in the fields, just respectfully carrying out the role of a son. If my father and mother do not love me, what is it to me?"

There are cases in which we should resign ourselves and say we did our best, but sometimes the stakes are too high and we cannot but be upset. Mengzi explains:

> When Shun was still working in the fields and ditches, the emperor [Yao] had his nine sons and two daughters, the hundreds of officials, cattle and sheep, granaries and storehouses, all serve him. The world's scholars and leaders (*shi*) approached him in multitudes. The emperor took the whole world and transferred it to him. Yet because he did not have accord with his father and mother, he was like a destitute person with no home to return to. To be affirmed by the world's leaders is what people desire, but this was not enough to release his anxiety. Those with alluring appearances are what people desire and for wives he had daughters of the emperor but this was not enough to release his anxiety. Wealth is what people desire and for wealth he had the whole

world, but this was not enough to release his anxiety. Nobility is what people desire and for nobility he had the position of son of heaven, but this was not enough to release his anxiety. People delighting in him, those with alluring appearances, wealth and nobility—none of these were enough to release his anxiety. Only accord with his father and mother could release it. (M 5A1)

Shun had everything human beings desire and yet he cried out to heaven in misery, because he did not have the approval of his parents. To make matters worse, Shun's family was notoriously bad. They tried to kill him, once by locking him in a granary and then setting fire to it! When that failed, they asked him to repair a well and then filled it in while he was underground (M 5A2). Surely Zhuangzi would consider Shun's sorrow absurd, and even Mengzi's disciple questions it. Yet for Mengzi, Shun's story illustrates the primacy of human relationships, which outweigh desires for honor, beauty, wealth, and power. Since Mengzi thinks this is our natural orientation, it is just a matter of not losing the rooted heart.

The *Zhuangzi* mocks the Confucians for their worries and concerns. One passage compares Kongzi to a pitiful father searching for his lost son.[8] Isn't joy obviously good? Why not find joy in everything we can? Can the Confucian recommendation that we increase our sensitivity be justified? Mengzi might respond that our natural place in the world is to differentiate things and that taking all events as equally joyous puts us out of harmony with heaven by violating our natural dispositions. A stronger reason against finding joy in all things is that our common human dispositions make it unrealistic. We cannot help but become attached to people and things. Even if some people—through years of constant practice—are able to embrace all events equally, it is not a plausible life for most of us. Another possibility is that even if bad feelings are avoidable, they cannot be avoided if we fully engage human relationships. It is no coincidence that many peace of mind traditions advocate a monastic life without family. We cannot be pleased with the age of parents without a bit of the anxiety. We cannot enjoy true friends without being hurt by their loss, or their anger. We cannot celebrate the flourishing of others without suffering at their breakdown. Human relationships depend in both their good feelings and their bad feelings on particular connections. A parent or a true friend cannot be replaced. This uniqueness produces the joy and the anxiety.[9] Perhaps we can give up both, but we cannot keep only the joy. The overcoming of attachments would free us from suffering but would also destroy something valuable. That is Mengzi's view.

Another reason for cultivating sensitivity rather than peace of mind derives from the Confucian dedication to fixing the problems of the world. It seems dangerous to say that the oppressed should cultivate enjoyment of their oppression—what would motivate the drive for change? It seems outright vicious to say that those profiting from that oppression should find joy in affirming the same system. We need the feelings behind benevolence and rightness in order to avoid exploiting others. Several alternatives to this Confucian position are possible. One might say that we do not need *feelings* to motivate action. We can use reason to see what is right, and then use our will to choose it. Emotions would only confuse and cloud our judgment. Such a position appears in stoicism and its descendants. One might go further and say—Do right and rejoice! That is, find joy in all things while using reason and will to motivate the right actions. Such advice conflicts with the Confucian vision of the self as inseparable from a dynamic, interconnected world. For Mengzi, we always exist in emotive relationships that guide and move us. To free ourselves from emotions leaves us without motivation, because we have no pure, independent source of motivation within ourselves, no disconnected free will. Zhuangzi sees clearly that finding joy in all things removes our motivation to change the world, or as he puts it, our desire to use the human to aid heaven.

Enjoying life

The Confucian elevation of emotions like grief and compassion should not give the impression that their way of life is all gloom and doom. The ability to enjoy life is praised and good people cultivate it:

> The master said, "Those who know it are not equal to those who love it, and those who love it are not equal to those who enjoy it." (LY 6.20)

The "it" here might be the Confucian way, or study more specifically. We have seen the significance of aversion or disgust (*wù* 惡) as part of the sprout of rightness. The opposite motivation is necessary as well, to love or affirm, *hào* 好, the same term used in "love of learning" or "loving alluring appearances." Knowing you should do something is not as good as a deep desire to do it, and this desire or love is not as good as taking joy in the activity itself. The *Lunyu* opens with famous lines on enjoyment:

> The master said, "To learn and apply it in a timely way, is this not a pleasure? To have friends come from distant places, is this not a joy? To be unrecognized by others and yet not resentful, is this not a noble person?" (LY 1.1)

This passage brings together the main points of Confucianism: study and apply what you have learned, cherish personal relations, do not let failure upset you. The first two should bring joy; the last should not bring sorrow.

On a superficial level, advocating joy serves a practical purpose—who would want to be a Confucian if it meant being always unhappy? On a deeper level, Mengzi and other Confucians grapple with one of the most fundamental problems for anyone who cares deeply about other people and is concerned about suffering and injustice. There are just too many things to be sad, angry, and anxious about. Racism, misogyny, growing inequality, wars, climate change—how can a decent person enjoy life in such a world? It is tempting to turn away and ignore it, to remain fishing in the mud like Zhuangzi, but that isn't what we really want. Is the only alternative a life of continual anxiety, sorrow, and frustration? It is hard to see how anyone could live that way, let alone make the world any better.

As with many issues within philosophy as a way of life, there is no simple or definitive solution to this problem. Mengzi emphasizes balancing our various desires and emotions. When he says— "people love all of their body/self without discrimination" (M 6A14)—he does not mean this as a criticism but as a description. The problem is that sensory desires are so powerful. Few people detest bad actions like bad smells or love virtue with the same genuine spontaneity as they love sex. The proper response is not to deny our desires, sacrificing what we want for what we should do, but to cultivate the right balance. If the concerns of the heart can be maintained as the foundation, other sensory desires will take their proper place. Mengzi loved a tasty meal of bear paw and fish. He just loved rightness more.

Rather than offer a theoretical solution or principle, the Confucians present several strategies for achieving balance between the heart and the other sense organs. While desires cannot be eliminated, we can reduce and moderate them:

> Mengzi said, "To nourish the heart, there is nothing better than making the desires few. For people whose desires are few, although there may be cases in which they do not persevere, they will be few. For people whose desires are many, although there may be cases in which they persevere, they will be few." (M 7B35)

Different kinds of desires will be problems at different times. Kongzi gives advice for different stages of life:

Kongzi said, "There are three things which the noble guard against. In youth, when the blood and vital energies (*qi*) are not yet stable, they guard against erotic attraction. When they are adults and their blood and vital energies are firm, they guard against contentiousness. When they are old and their blood and vital energies have weakened, they guard against acquisitiveness." (LY 16.7)

Managing our desires depends on sensitivity to context and different people will have to watch out for different desires.

The most common Confucian strategy directs our desires into less problematic forms, like learning to enjoy simple things. Kongzi said:

Coarse grains to eat, water to drink, and my bended arm for a pillow—there is joy in these things. Wealth and honors acquired against rightness are to me like floating clouds. (LY 7.16)

The ability to enjoy plain rice and water is exactly what enables Kongzi to let ill-gotten wealth pass like clouds in the sky. If plain rice and clean water bring joy to the mouth, singing brings joy to the ears, and an arm for a pillow brings joy to the limbs, we rarely have to choose between the heart and the pleasures of the other organs. We can follow our duty wherever it leads while still enjoying life. That was the greatness of Yan Hui:

The master said, "What a worthy person was Hui! With a single dish of rice, a single gourd of drink, living in a narrow lane—others could not have endured the anxiety, but he did not allow it to alter his joy. What a worthy person was Hui!" (LY 6.11)

Another dialogue broadens the point:

Zigong said, "What about one who is poor but not obsequious, or rich but not arrogant?" The master replied, "They will do, but that is not as good as one who is poor yet joyful or rich but loves propriety." (LY 1.15)

We have already encountered Zigong in several passages. He was one of Kongzi's most important disciples, famous for his skill as a diplomat as well as his business acumen. Here he gives examples of correct behavior when in either a high or low position, but such behaviors are unstable if they run counter to our genuine feelings. It is not as good as finding joy when poor or loving correct behavior when rich.

There are many sources of joy. We should train ourselves to prefer those that support community.

Kongzi said, "There are three joys that are constructive and three joys that are destructive. To enjoy moderation through ritual and music, to enjoy guiding one's way by the goodness in other people, to enjoy having many worthy friends—these are constructive. To enjoy reckless abandon, to enjoy idle wandering, to enjoy feasting—these are destructive." (LY 16.5)

Mengzi said, "The noble have three joys and being king of the world is not one of them. Father and mother both alive and older and younger brothers having no strife: this is the first joy. Looking up without shame before heaven and looking down without shame before other people: this is the second joy. To attain the talented and able of the world and teach and nourish them: this is the third joy. The noble have three joys and being king of the world is not one of them." (M 7A20)

Even sensual pleasures can be constructive. Xunzi took that as a key function of ritual and music, which imbue social processes with sensory pleasure. Think of the effect of the beauty of a cathedral and choir in a mass.

Mengzi uses this strategy in several dialogues with rulers reluctant to give up their royal pleasures. King Xuan of Qi, the king who spared the ox, tells Mengzi that his weakness is his love of popular music. Mengzi replies with a question:

> Mengzi said, "To enjoy music alone or to enjoy music with other people, which is more enjoyable?" The king said, "It is better with other people." Mengzi said, "To enjoy music with a few or to enjoy music with many, which is more enjoyable?" The king said, "It is better with many."

The phrase "enjoying music" (樂樂) plays on the character 樂, which has two meanings and pronunciations: *yuè* meaning music and *lè* meaning pleasure or enjoyment. The meanings are closely connected, since music is a source of joy and an expression of joy. Another possible reading of Mengzi's question is: "Is it better to enjoy joys alone or to enjoy joys with other people?" The king agrees that it is better to enjoy music (or pleasures) with other people, and even better to enjoy it with many other people. Mengzi then describes the situation in his kingdom: the people are weary with labor and families are scattered apart. When they hear the king enjoying his music or going on a royal hunt, they are frustrated and resentful, not happy for him. Mengzi then illustrates what it would mean to have pleasure along with the people:

> In contrast, suppose the king is making music here, and the common people hear the sounds of the king's bells and drums and the tunes of his flutes and whistles. Together they are happy, and with a pleased appearance they say to each other, "Our king must be without sickness and pain! How else could he make music?" [. . .] This is nothing other than having enjoyment in common with the people. Now if the king has enjoyment together with the people, then he will be a true king. (M 1B1)

This dialogue makes several points. By describing the suffering of his people, Mengzi subtly shifts the king's attention from his ears to his heart. His heart makes him wish that the people would be pleased when he is happy rather than being resentful. At the same time, Mengzi tells the king that the pleasures of the ear are not in conflict with the heart. Mengzi is not just pandering. Even sensual pleasures have a social element. If I think of the times in which I've felt the greatest joy in hearing music, they all involve listening in a tightly packed crowd of moving people. When we hear a great song, we want to share it with others—thus the ancient art of the mixed tape. The desire for an excellent meal usually brings with it the desire to invite someone to dinner. Sharing photos can be narcissistic or bragging, but at its best we post a photo because we have seen something beautiful or interesting and we want others to see it too. The concerns of the heart ultimately blend in with the desires of the other senses. The Confucians just tell us to pay more attention to the social aspect.

Accepting limits

The Confucians advocate joy and find it in many sources—eating simple foods, listening to and playing music, participating in ceremonies, spending time with friends and family, seeing a student succeed or the world become more harmonious. In a perfect world, Confucians would be happy all of the time. That is not our world. The universe does not center on or particularly care about human beings. Things happen in spite of our natural desires and wishes. If we care about events in the world, we will sometimes be sad or angry. We will often be anxious.

To deal with uncertainty and failure, the Confucians use a strategy common among peace of mind traditions, appeals to fate. When Mengzi says that the way to know and serve heaven is not by direct obedience or imitation but through our natural dispositions, he immediately adds: "Not thinking twice about long or short life and cultivating the self to await it is that by which one takes a firm stand toward what is outside our control" (M 7A1). The Chinese term translated as "what is outside our control" is *ming* 命, the same word originally used for the mandate or command of heaven. By the time of Mengzi and Zhuangzi, *ming* rarely had any sense of intention or purpose, at least among philosophers. It can be translated as fate, but in the "shit happens" sense rather than "it was meant to be" or "it's my destiny." Fate (*ming*) labels all those things that are outside of our control. It can explain particular events like illness:

> Bo Niu was ill and the master asked for him. Holding his hand through the window, he said "Losing him is *ming*, alas! That such a man should have such an illness! That such a man should have such an illness!" (LY 6.10)

Another quotation makes a more general claim:

> Sima Niu anxiously said, "People all have their brothers, only I have none." Zixia said to him, "I have heard this: 'Death and life are *ming*; wealth and honors are heaven.'" (LY 12.5)

The distribution of life and death, wealth and honor, are not determined by one's own merit or actions. In this passage, heaven (*tian*) and fate (*ming*) are used interchangeably to refer to the whole conjunction of factors outside our control. Fate also can explain the conditions of the world:

> The master said, "If the way will be practiced, that is *ming*. If the way will be abandoned, that is *ming*. What can Gongbo Liao do about *ming*?" (LY 14.36)

Kongzi was blocked from meeting the leader of the Ji family by Gongbo Liao, and his disciple is upset about it. Kongzi points out that whether the world is peaceful and good or disorderly and violent is not something anyone can control.

Why make these appeals to fate? Understanding the limits of our control allows us to better direct our effort. Mengzi explains:

> If seeking attains it and abandoning loses it, then seeking has benefits for attaining. The seeking is within me. If seeking has the way but attaining involves fate, then seeking is of no benefit to attaining. This is seeking in the external. (M 7A3)

We can control our own virtue, but successful results exceed our control. That doesn't mean we can use fate as an excuse. Mengzi distinguishes between fate in general and fate that is proper or correct (zhèngmìng 正命):

> There is nothing that is not fated; compliantly accept what is correct in it. For this reason, one who knows fate does not stand below a collapsing wall. To die while fully implementing the way is correct fate. Dying in fetters and chains is not correct fate. (M 7A2)

We can insist on maintaining our virtue, on trying to do the right thing, no matter what external circumstances bring. We can be forced into difficult circumstances, perhaps even into a choice between death or committing some atrocity, but we still have a choice. To die would then be our correct fate; to commit the atrocity would not. That does not mean we should make no effort to stay alive or that we can use fate to excuse carelessness. Don't hang out in front of a wall that looks like it is about to collapse.

As the Stoics point out, seeing events as necessary or outside of our control makes them easier to accept. We recognize this in practice when we say, "there was nothing you could do about it," or, "it was meant to be." The distinction between what does and what does not fall under fate leads to the Confucian version of peace of mind:

Sima Niu asked about the noble. The master said, "The noble do not worry and do not fear." Niu said, "Having no worries and no fears—is this what it means to be noble?" The master said, "When internal examination reveals no faults, what is there to worry about? What is there to fear?" (LY 12.4)

The master said, "Having heard the way in the morning, one can accept dying in the evening." (LY 4.8)

Cultivated people are free from worries about the outcomes of their actions. Mengzi calls this an undisturbed heart, literally a heart that is not moved (búdòngxīn 不動心).

In the longest passage in the whole book, Mengzi contrasts three models for attaining an undisturbed heart, speaking of it in terms of bravery or resolve. One exemplar attained an unmoved heart through an inflexible rule and a strong sense of purpose. He did not think of risks or consequences. Another recognized that the outcome of an event was uncertain. He could only do his best. Mengzi then quotes Kongzi's disciple, Zengzi:

Do you love bravery? I once heard this about great bravery from the master: "If I examine myself and am not upright, facing a common person in coarse cloth, how can I not be afraid? If I examine myself and am upright, then facing thousands or tens of thousands of people, I will go forward." (M 2A2)

Zengzi worked on what he could control, his virtue, and did not worry about what he could not control. Doing what is right, he calmly faced any situation. That allows him to keep his commitments and follow the way, even in the face of poverty or death. Mengzi recommends this method as the best.

How to face danger calmly and resolutely was not an idle question. The Confucian mission was to persuade powerful people to reform. Mengzi is shockingly blunt in criticizing tyrants to their face. One of Kongzi's disciples, Zilu, was a minister in the state of Wei 衛 and died trying to protect the ruler during a rebellion. His corpse was displayed above the eastern gate of the city. Kongzi himself was frequently in danger. Many stories discuss one particular moment of difficulty, when Kongzi and his disciples were stranded without food between the states of Chen and Cai. My favorite of these ended up in the *Zhuangzi*. It begins with Zilu complaining that in spite of their goodness, they have ended up in failure and adversity (*qióng* 窮). He clings to the idea that good people will be rewarded with success. The conversation continues:

> Kongzi said, "What words are these! Succeeding in the way is what the noble call success. Failing in the way is what they call failing. Now, I embrace the way of benevolence and rightness to engage the troubles of a disordered age. How can that be called failure! So, examine the internal and do not fail in the way; in approaching difficulties, do not lose this virtue. When great cold is at the utmost and frost and snow fall, this is how we know the vigor of the pine and cypress. Being confined between Chen and Cai is lucky for us!" Kongzi calmly returned to his zither, strumming and singing. Zilu joyously grabbed a branch and danced. Zigong said, "I did not know the height of heaven or the depth of the earth!"[10]

Facing the threat of death and feeling weak from starvation, Confucius and his disciples jam.

The biggest challenge is keeping fear from determining our actions. Mengzi says:

> Resolute leaders do not forget the possibility of ending up in a ditch; brave leaders do not forget the chance of losing their head. (M 5B7)

The term "resolute" describes the intention or the direction of the heart, *zhì* 志. To be a determined leader, a resolute *shi*, is to have a stable or fixed *zhi*, a purpose or commitment that allows one to act deliberately in the world rather than being pushed and pulled by whatever appears. Truly determined *shi* keep to their purpose even in the face of death. The ability to stay committed through both success and failure appears in a passage giving advice to a *shi* setting out to persuade a powerful king to reform:

> Mengzi told Song Goujian, "Do you love traveling about advising rulers? I will tell you about such traveling. If people recognize your worth then be content and satisfied; if people do not recognize you then be content and satisfied." Song Goujian said, "How can one be content and satisfied like that?" Mengzi said, "By honoring virtue and enjoying rightness, one can be content and satisfied. Thus, leaders in adversity do not lose rightness, and in success do not leave the way. By not losing rightness in adversity, leaders attain it in their selves. By not leaving the way in success, the people do not lose hope in them. When the ancients attained what they had resolved (*zhì* 志) to do, kindness was bestowed on the people. When they did not attain what they had resolved to do, their self-cultivation was visible throughout their era. In adversity, they bettered themselves alone. Succeeding, they bettered the whole the world." (M 7A9)

Such resolve is the ultimate outcome of self-cultivation.

To be upset or not to be upset?

An unperturbed heart can only mean a heart that is not *improperly* perturbed. If the key to peace of mind is virtue and if virtue consists in greater sensitivity to the world, then peace of mind cannot mean freedom from commiseration for those in danger or freedom from sorrow when a loved one dies. For Mengzi, complete peace of mind is neither possible nor desirable. Here is the problem: the same factors that thwart our success also cause the suffering and exploitation of other people. If length of life and degree of poverty are controlled by fate, then accepting fate means accepting all negative events, including the death of loved ones and the oppression of the people. To mourn would be to fail to understand fate, as Zhuangzi says about the death of his own wife.

The problem goes beyond just acceptance and fatalism. When in a bad situation, should we feel indignation at the injustice of it or do we learn to enjoy it? The former compounds our suffering; the latter weakens our resolve to end it. We must find some balance of joy and suffering, but, as we have seen, how that balance works out depends on particular circumstances. Mengzi appeals to fatalism in a tactical way. Sometimes it is best to bring about resignation by recognizing fate. Other times resignation would be vicious. The Confucians are not concerned with putting forward a coherent *theory* of fate but rather with articulating practical viewpoints that support a way of life. That does not fit the academic discipline of philosophy, but it follows the way real people deal with the world. Sometimes we say, "Never give up!" or "Defeat is not an option!" Other times, we say, "There is only so much that you can do!" or "Sometimes you have to accept the inevitable and move on!" Which we say depends on the circumstances and the person.

Regarding the use of fate, we can discern common tactics. For example, the Confucians always advocate concern about self-cultivation. Mengzi explains:

> The noble have anxious concern until the end of their lives but are not troubled for a single morning. What they are anxiously concerned about is this: Shun was a person, I am also a person; Shun was a model the world could transmit to later generations, but I still cannot avoid being an ordinary fellow. This can be a concern. What kind of concern? To be like Shun, that is all. Now, there is nothing that troubles the noble. If not benevolent they do not do it; if not according to propriety they do not enact it. Even

if they have a morning's trouble, the noble are not troubled by it. (M 4B28)

If we are all equal in potential, then anyone can be a role model. As long as I fall short of the sages, I should be anxious about my development. Even Kongzi would not call himself a sage. Still, this anxiety or concern (*yōu* 憂) differs from the anxiety that comes from investing in real estate or wanting the approval of others, because we can always do more to cultivate ourselves. That is within our control. Regarding external success, we can only await fate and accept whatever happens. The last line plays on an ambiguity in the word *huàn* 患, which can mean objective troubles or feeling troubled. The noble have troubles, but they are not troubled by them.

Another common tactic is to advocate accepting our own troubles but resisting the troubles faced by others. We see our own death as a matter of fate, at least when we must choose between rightness and life. Regarding the death of a parent, though, we mourn, and regarding deaths brought about by war or poverty, we dedicate our lives to fighting it. This distinction between what happens to us and what happens to other people extends from the distinction between the concerns of the heart and the desires of the other senses. One tactic for maintaining the proper hierarchy is to see the objects of our sensual desires as outside our control. Mengzi describes this in a passage that makes his tactical approach explicit:

The mouth toward flavors, the eyes toward colors, the ears toward sounds, the nose toward scents, the four limbs toward peaceful ease: these are natural dispositions but they also involve fate. The noble do not speak of them as natural dispositions. Benevolence between father and son, rightness between sovereign and minister, propriety between guest and host, knowledge for the worthy, sagacity in the way of heaven: these are fated but they also involve natural dispositions. The noble do not speak of them as subject to fate. (M 7B24)

The connections of our mouth to food and the connections of our heart to people all express common human dispositions and desires. All are embodied responses to the world. How successfully we can act on these motivations is outside our control. In this way, all of our motivations have the same status—rooted in our dispositions but dependent for their results on fate—but the noble do not emphasize this sameness. In thinking about the things the senses desire, they attend to their instability and dependence on factors outside our control. That focus weakens the desire. With the feelings of the heart, the noble attend to the naturalness of the sprouts as part of our dispositions. Seeing the feelings as natural and inevitable encourages them. In other words, if I end up in trouble or in poverty, I should remember that such things are beyond my control and must be accepted as fate. But when I see suffering, I should do whatever I can to reduce it, knowing that this effort is a natural part of being human. In normal life, most people do the opposite. We will work and work to get the materials things we desire, striving no matter the odds, but then dismiss the problems of the world as something over which we have no control.

Doing what you really want

Human beings exist as a conjunction of forces set to respond to their environment in certain ways. These natural dispositions are based in our bodies. We should give precedence to the dispositions of the heart, which form our ethical relationships to other people: our feelings of concern (benevolence), our sense of shame and aversion (rightness), the ways we express our feelings (propriety), and our ability to distinguish what is so or not so (wisdom). Developing these tendencies is the task of self-cultivation. But we also naturally seek pleasure and joy. We must cultivate these dispositions too, channeling them into pleasures that are simple and supportive of community. Properly shaped, the eyes, mouth, and heart will each desire what is right. In those unfortunate situations where desires conflict, a cultivated person will more strongly desire whatever is most important, just as Mengzi chooses bear paw over fish and rightness over life.

The result of proper cultivation resembles the Daoist concept of *wúwéi* 無為, usually translated as nonaction. In Daoism, *wuwei* refers to actions done spontaneously, without being forced and without deliberation.[11] They happen by *ziran*, spontaneously, of themselves. That is the ideal for the Confucian sage as well. Even the Confucian most focused on hard work and deliberate effort, Xunzi, takes self-coercion as a sign of failure. He describes three exemplars of self-discipline—one who retreated to living in a cave in order to be free of distractions, one who would burn his palm in order to avoid falling asleep while studying, and Mengzi himself, who supposedly sent his wife away because of some infraction of propriety. All three are criticized for self-coercion. Instead, sagely people "indulge their desires and accept their feelings."[12] Whether or not Mengzi reached this ideal himself, he promoted it, distinguishing acting from virtue and acting according to virtue:

> Shun had insight into the multitude of things and observed human relations. He acted from benevolence and rightness, rather than enacting benevolence and rightness. (M 4B19)

Acting from virtue is spontaneous and unforced, different from forcing oneself do the right thing.

The similarity between these passages and Daoist *wuwei* follows because both Confucians and Daoists seek harmony with nature. But they conceive this harmony differently. Confucian *wuwei* involves internalizing social conventions. It follows years and years of study:

The master said, "At fifteen I resolved to learning. At thirty I took my place. At forty I had no confusion. At fifty I knew the mandate of heaven. At sixty my ears were attuned. At seventy I could follow what my heart desired without stepping beyond the proper measure." (LY 2.4)

Kongzi achieved the ability to do whatever he wanted, but only at the age of seventy. Most people never fully achieve it. A passage from the *Zhongyong* nicely illustrates the connection between education and *wuwei*. It begins by contrasting those who are authentic or fully integrated (*chéng* 誠) and those who must work at being authentic (*chéng zhī* 誠之, using *chéng* as a verb). The latter requires great effort:

Those working at being authentic select the good and firmly grip it. They study it broadly, question it carefully, think about it diligently, debate it with insight, enact it earnestly. If there is anything you have not studied or have studied but cannot practice, do not give up. If there is anything unquestioned or questioned but not known, do not give up. If there is anything not thought of or thought of but not attained, do not give up. If there is anything not debated or debated without insight, do not give up. If there is anything not practiced or practiced without earnestness, do not give up. If another person is able to do it with one try, do it a hundred times yourself. If another person is able to do it with ten tries, do it a thousand times yourself. By resolutely following this way, even the foolish will be bright, and even the weak will be strong. (ZY19–20)

That sounds exhausting, but in the end, the result is close to *wuwei*:

The authentic hit the center without effort and attain without thought, naturally and easily being centered in the way. They are sagely people. (ZY19)

Sages effortlessly and happily do the right thing. The question is, how do we reach this ideal? How is it possible to cultivate our natural reactions to the world so that we just want what is best?

4

Cultivating Feelings

Thou shalt not covet thy neighbor's house, thou shalt not covet thy neighbor's wife, nor his manservant, nor his maidservant, nor his ox, nor his ass, nor any thing that is thy neighbor's. (Exodus 20:17.)

Thou shalt love thy neighbor as thyself. (Matthew 22:39)

Being good requires that we do the right things. We hold people responsible for their actions, for things like whether or not they sleep with a neighbor's spouse. Not *coveting* or *desiring* a neighbor's spouse is trickier. Can we be blamed not just for our actions but for our desires? Do we have control over our desires? The imperative to love our neighbors runs into the same problems. It would be difficult enough to treat other people *as if* we loved them. Can we be expected to *feel* love for them as well? Christianity has developed many ways of addressing these questions. One response is to claim that changing our feelings and desires requires divine assistance in the form of grace. The immensely influential German philosopher Immanuel Kant (1724–1804) took a different approach. He argued that the biblical imperative to "love thy neighbor" cannot literally mean to *love* them but only to treat them lovingly. Kant calls this "practical love," concluding that "it resides in the will and not in the propensities of feeling, in principles of action and not in tender sympathy; and it alone can be commanded."[1] We cannot choose to feel love toward our neighbors, so we cannot be held responsible

Doing What You Really Want. Franklin Perkins, Oxford University Press. © Oxford University Press 2022.
DOI: 10.1093/oso/9780197574911.003.0005

for it. Because emotions are outside our control, morality cannot depend on them.

Kant's position on emotion gets something right. It does seem like you either love someone or you don't. Free choice would violate the very nature of emotions as responses to the world. And yet parents and teachers believe children can learn to become more compassionate or respectful. If someone sets a goal of becoming less angry or more caring, we do not take that as absurd. On the contrary, we would probably criticize someone who just resigned themselves to being greedy or ill-tempered. So, we do think emotions can be changed. The question is, how? There is no easy or simple answer, but if Mengzi places emotions at the center of a way of life dedicated to helping others and making the world better, he must offer some way of cultivating them.[2]

Immediate experience

The process of cultivation is not one of creating emotions from scratch. We exist through felt relationships to the world, and many of these feelings are social and constructive. The process of cultivation stimulates, extends, and refines these feelings. The first step is direct experience. Consider again the story of King Xuan of Qi and the ox (M 1A7). The king sees a frightened ox going to be killed in a sacrifice. He feels bad for the ox and orders that it be released, at the same time sending a sheep to be used in its place. The king does not *want* to have this feeling of concern. It disrupts the ritual. Substituting a less expensive animal for a more valuable one makes him look cheap. His feelings are also not based on reason. It is obviously irrational to substitute one animal for another when both will suffer equally. The king confesses that he did not understand his own feelings or actions until Mengzi clarified them: "I did this, but when I turned to search for it I could not grasp my own heart."

Mengzi's analysis begins with the importance of firsthand experience:

> This is the method of benevolence. You saw the ox but had not seen the sheep. The noble relate to birds and beasts such that seeing them alive they cannot bear to see them die; hearing their cries, they cannot bear to eat their flesh. Therefore, the noble stay far from the kitchen. (M 1A7)

The explanation exposes the limits of our control over emotions— if the noble live near the slaughterhouse they will feel bad eating meat, even if they do not want to feel that way. Mengzi does not fault this lack of control, but, on the contrary, says that it is the art or method of benevolence. That may make the way of benevolence appear ridiculous, but Mengzi gives an honest picture. From the perspective of reason, the sheep and the ox have no relevant difference, but that is not how we experience them. The king heard the cries of the ox and his heart reacted with pity. He did not have the same relationship to the sheep. Witnessing an animal being killed changes our relationship to it, but it is not a matter of gaining some new knowledge. No one needs to visit the slaughterhouse to know what happens there.

The importance of immediate contact appears in many illustrations of proper feelings. We have seen one on the origins of benevolence within the family: "Of children carried in arms and just old enough to smile, none do not know loving their parents. When they grow, none do not know revering their older brothers" (M 7A15). A child has this feeling for a parent and not for a stranger because of an embodied relationship to the one who carries the child in their arms. If someone other than a parent took their place, the child would love them instead. The "art of benevolence" originates within these kinds of direct relationships. Recall also the passage on the impulses behind funerals (M 3A5). That dialogue with Yizi illustrates the expression of emotions in the body and claims that this reaction of horror was provoked by seeing the body of not just any person but a parent. We can now note another striking point: throwing the dead bodies into a ditch was fine, until someone passed by and *saw* the half-eaten bodies. Seeing the bodies makes no difference to reason, but it makes a difference.

Let us return to the passage about King Xuan. Even though feelings are beyond deliberate control, the passage does contain an imperative. If the noble are unable to eat meat, that is their own fault.[3] He blames the king for his lack of concern for the people. It is not that the noble could choose not to feel for the animal or that the king could choose to feel for the people, but they can choose to avoid or seek out the experiences that give rise to these feelings. The feeling of compassion for the ox or the feeling of horror that leads to funerals can be attained or avoided by whether or not we witness the frightened ox or the corpse-filled ditch. This method is the other side of a strategy familiar to anyone trying to control their desires. We might not be able to resist temptation, but we can avoid those situations in which the temptations arise, something I learned well from many attempts to stop smoking. In the same way, the first step of self-cultivation requires exposing ourselves to circumstances that will evoke the proper feelings in us. That is one function of ritual and music: it creates a structured environment that stimulates the right feelings at the right moment.

The Confucian view of the self as a center of relations generates an imperative to witness suffering and injustice firsthand. This imperative is remarkably relevant to the contemporary world, where the powerful and privileged remain so distant from the victims of exploitation and suffering. We live in a world astonishingly segregated, most of all by national borders but also by region and neighborhood, even on social media, a world where realtors can promote a "gated-community" without a hint of irony or reproach. If Mengzi is right in claiming that our natural dispositions tend toward the good, then this distance is one of the things that allows us to tolerate such injustice and inequality. More of us would be pacifists if we were face to face with "collateral damage." Many more people would be vegetarians if it weren't so easy to keep far from the slaughterhouse. It is difficult to feel animosity toward a group of people when you live and work with them. The need for direct engagement with the problems of the world is another reason why the Confucians advocate self-cultivation through social action, rather than through self-help activities that draw together like-minded people with similar social positions.

Imagination, attention, and self-awareness

Direct experience most powerfully awakens our feelings, but personal experience is limited. Secondhand accounts and imagination offer more possibilities. Mengzi takes this route with kings, describing the suffering of their people in grim detail:

> When there is so much that dogs and pigs eat human food, you do not know to restrict and store grain. When those who are starving to death lie in the streets, you do not know to issue grain that has been stored. (M 1A3)

The story of the child at the edge of the well works in a similar way. Mengzi does not ask us to try it out as an experiment; it is enough to imagine it. When we do, we can awaken something of the feeling of concern we would have if we were actually there. The importance of literature for the Confucians also serves this awakening of feelings. Literature is one of our few points of access to the suffering of distant peoples. Those striving to change the world have long realized the power of literature not just to convey information but also to awaken feelings of concern. Film and photography do the same thing. Vegetarians present graphic images of animal suffering for the same purpose that Mengzi describes bodies in ditches, trying to make us *feel* what we already *know*. Like Mengzi, their ultimate goal is not to inform but to motivate.

Experience is not a mirror of the world. Two people can be in the same place at the same time but have very different experiences. Cultivating the right feelings requires proper attention. Most of us pass by those who are suffering in our day-to-day life, but we pay little attention and so they have little impact. Mengzi is well aware of this problem. After describing a king failing to make progress under his teachings, Mengzi says:

> Now as an art, the game of *go* is a minor one, but if you do not concentrate your heart and direct your intention, then you will not get it. Go Qiu was the best go player in the state. Imagine you have Go Qiu instruct two people. One person concentrates his heart and directs his intention, listening only to what Go Qiu says. The other person, although hearing him, with one heart considers a swan approaching and thinks of pulling his bow string and shooting it. Although he studies along with the other, he will not be as good him. Is it because his intelligence is not like that of the other? I say it is not that. (M 6A9)

The bad student hears the master but does not listen. Although he is no less intelligent, he fails to gain the skills. A contrast between perceiving and attending to our perceptions is made in several early Confucian texts:

> All people eat and drink, but few are able to know the flavor. (ZY2)

> If the heart is not engaged in it, then white and black can be in front but the eyes do not see them, thunderous drums can be in front but the ears do not hear them. How much more if the heart is engaged![4]

These lost perceptions sometimes come to us later, as when we realize that we heard a song earlier only because it is now an earworm.

In discussing the distinction between the great and the small of our body, Mengzi associates attention with the heart. We have seen Mengzi tell Gongduzi that what determines a person's character is whether they develop the greater organ of the body, which is the heart, or the lesser organs that are the other senses. Gongduzi follows up by asking why some people follow the greater part when others do not. Mengzi places responsibility with the heart:

> The offices of the eyes and ears are not to think and they are blinded by things. Things connect with other things, just drawing the senses along. The office of the heart is to think. If it thinks then it attains it and if it does not think then it does not attain it. (M 6A15)

The senses respond to whatever appears before them.[5] Mengzi uses the term *bì* 蔽, which is for one thing to block, screen, or hide something else. The eyes and ears get distracted by things that draw their attention away from everything else. They end up blindly pulled along by experience. The heart often reacts in the same way, but it has the ability to shift focus or attention. The key word here is *sī* 思, which means to attend to, to focus on, or to think about. Any moment of experience is infinitely complex. The world appears to us organized around whatever happens to draw our focus. By directing this focus, the heart indirectly controls what the body responds to. So, in walking through the city we can focus on the new products in the windows or the homeless person sitting on the sidewalk in front of them or the argument we had with a colleague two days earlier. Completely different desires and feelings will arise. Attention also determines *how* we see the things we notice. We can see someone as a person to be helped or as an obstacle to avoid.

One thing we must attend to is our own reactions. We could call this self-reflection, if we remember that the "self" is a dynamic center of relationships. When we turn our attention to our "self," we contemplate our embeddedness in a dynamic environment that defies a division into internal and external. We can look at a few examples:

> To desire honor is the common heart of human beings. All people have the honorable in themselves, only they do not attend to it. (M 6A17)

If we turned our attention to our felt relationships, we would see that we really do desire to be honorable and to be respected. When we act dishonorably, we contradict our own desires. If we pay attention, we can avoid this contradiction. A similar passage talks about care for the body or self (*shen*):

> With catalpa or paulownia trees small enough to grasp by hand, if people want to grow them, they all know how to nourish them. But when it comes to the body they do not know how to nourish it. Do they love their own body less than a catalpa or paulownia tree? Their failure to attend to it is deep. (M 6A13)

Even a foolish person knows that the self is more valuable than a tree. The problem is that they fail to attend to or think about this fact, and that failure to *si* is expressed in their actions. Mengzi tries to induce this kind of *si* in King Xuan when he draws his attention to the feelings he had for the sacrificial ox.

The power of self-reflection follows Mengzi's account of human dispositions. Given that human beings share ways of responding to the world that naturally lead toward virtue, vicious people are in some sense inauthentic. They have corrupted, distorted, or lost their heart:

> You cannot speak with those who oppress themselves. You cannot act with those who abandon themselves. Speaking against propriety and rightness is what I mean by oppressing themselves. Saying my body/self (*shen*) is not able to reside in benevolence

and follow rightness is what I mean by abandoning oneself. (M 4A10)

Denying our ability to become good means evading what we truly are. When applied to other people, it is like being a thief, stealing away their real potential:

> Blaming and challenging the sovereign is called respect. Expounding goodness to block his deviance is called reverence. Saying "my sovereign is not capable" is called thievery. (M 4A1)

Since all people have the same dispositions, no one can be dismissed as unable to become good. Doing so robs them of what is most basic in them.

When we consider how so many people live comfortably with luxurious houses and cars and gadgets while other people are literally starving to death, we might doubt Mengzi's claim that all have a heart of compassion. If most people have something they would die rather than do, why do those same people refuse to make small sacrifices for the good of others? Segregation is one reason, but it also comes from a failure to recognize our true priorities. This is described as losing one's heart:

> When people have chickens or dogs that go astray, they know to seek them. But when their heart goes astray, they do not know to seek it. The way of study and inquiry is nothing other than seeking this heart that has gone astray. (M 6A11)

As seen earlier, those who violate rightness for the sake of wealth are said to have lost the rooted heart. Mengzi gives an extreme example:

> Mengzi said, "How unbenevolent was King Hui of Liang! The benevolent take what they love and extend it to what they do not

love. The unbenevolent take what they do not love and extend it to what they love." Gongsun Chou said, "What are you referring to?" "King Hui of Liang, for the sake of land, devastated his people by sending them to war; after a great defeat, he did it again. Fearing he would not win, he then urged on his beloved son and younger brother, sacrificing them for it. This is called taking what one does not love and extending it to what one loves." (M 7B1)

Hui was king of the powerful state of Wei, known here by its capital Liang. Mengzi had a number of discussions with him, although with little success. What makes this anecdote profound and disturbing is that we can understand the king. If someone pointed it out to him, he would agree that he loved his son and brother more than the extra territory, yet when caught up in the path of ambition, he forgets what really matters. That is surprisingly easy to do, as anyone who has spent too much time in the office knows. This loss is possible only through lack of attention, lack of *si*.

Extending care

Mengzi's reliance on emotion is inevitably biased toward the local and immediate, exemplified in the primacy of familial relations. Mengzi says:

The way is in what is near but is sought in the distant. The work is in what is easy but is sought in the difficult. If everyone treats their parents as parents and their elders as elders, then the world will have peace. (M 4A11)

Kongzi makes the same point:

The master said, "Is benevolence far away? If I want benevolence, then benevolence arrives!" (LY 7.30)

Mengzi and Kongzi are not against seeking to change systems of power that are remote and distant. They traveled their world trying to do just that. The point is that we cannot leap over the place we inhabit. Without a basis in genuine care for those in our lives, desires for abstract reform amount to no more than personal ambition. Dedication to a cause serves as excuse for being a lousy person.

The amount we can experience is always limited in comparison to all "under the heavens." Even if we were to travel to areas where people suffer most, we would form connections to those particular places and people. This is how human beings and emotions work. It is the method of benevolence. While these immediate connections and emotional responses are the root of virtue, they are not enough. To have the virtues, we must extend these feelings to events that do not now move us. I have a friend who had been a vegetarian for a long time but went back to eating meat, until one day he was stuck behind a truck carrying chickens on the interstate. After witnessing the slow torture of chickens packed in wire cages open to the wind, he saw one chicken somehow escape and die a quick and violent death on the road. He returned to vegetarianism after that. For Mengzi, such experiences ground virtue. In this case, the sympathy aroused by immediate experience not only reached those particular chickens on the truck, but all chickens and even all animals. The immediate feeling extended beyond the immediate. We have already seen this process of extension in various examples. Even King Xuan extends his feelings somewhat—he does not substitute one ox for another but switches to a sheep.

Mengzi tries to initiate this process of extension by pointing out similarities. We discussed this earlier in chapter 2, when Mengzi compares the actions people take for the sake of wealth to begging leftovers from funerals (M 4B33) or accepting food offered in a humiliating way (M 6A10). With King Xuan he says:

Now your kindness is enough to extend to birds and beasts, but your accomplishments do not reach the people. Can they be the lone exception? (M 1A7)

He makes a similar extension with King Hui:

Mengzi replied, "Is there any difference between killing a person with a staff or with a blade?" The king said, "There is no difference." "Is there any difference between killing a person with a blade or with governing?" The king said, "There is no difference." (M 1A4)

To brutally kill an innocent person with a sword would evoke pity, guilt, and horror for most people. King Xuan had compared his feeling for the ox with his feeling at seeing an innocent person put to death. Murder has a visceral effect on us, and our aversion to it would be a prime example of the feeling Mengzi sees as the sprout of rightness. In contrast, being part of a power structure that leads to the death of innocent people does not evoke such strong feelings. Mengzi points out the similarity in order to shift the feeling of aversion aroused by stabbing someone to an aversion for bad governing. That is extending the sprout of rightness.

In a similar way, if we saw someone trying to physically harm a person on the street we would feel the need to stop it, even if just by calling for help. When the harm is far away from us or the cause is vague and systematic, we are less motivated. That is one reason why it is difficult to motivate people to take action on issues like climate change. For Mengzi, we must extend the feeling we have in some cases to cases that are more distant or obscure. Sages go further. We have already seen that Yi Yin was as concerned for people living in deprivation as he would have been if he were the direct cause of their suffering. Mengzi says something similar about Yu, the legendary tamer of floods, and Hou Ji, the founder of agriculture:

Yu thought that someone in the world drowning was he himself drowning them. Ji thought that someone in the world starving was he himself starving them. This is why they had such urgency. (M 4B29)

Most of us would find the act of drowning someone or starving them to death unbearable. We couldn't make ourselves do it. We don't feel the same way about letting someone drown or starve, at least if they are not immediately present to us. A fully cultivated person will feel the same way in both circumstances. By extending their aversion toward harming someone, these sages developed a feeling of responsibility for anyone in trouble.

From this idea of extension, we can understand Confucian *shù* 恕, which we might translate as empathy, reciprocity, or empathic understanding. It is explained in terms of treating others by analogy with oneself. The *Lunyu* has several versions:

Zigong said, "What I do not want other people to impose on me, I also want not to impose on other people." The master said, "Zigong, that is not something you have attained." (LY 5.12)

Zigong asked, "Is there one doctrine that can be practiced throughout one's life?"

The master replied, "It is *shu*! Do not impose on other people that which you yourself do not want." (LY 15.24)

The master said, "[. . .] As for the benevolent, in wanting to be established they establish others and in wanting to succeed they help others succeed. To be able to take what is near as an analogy for others can be called the technique of benevolence." (LY 6.30)

Virtue begins with what is near, our immediate relationships with other people. Empathic reciprocity, *shu*, is a means of extending from our experiences in these relationships to what is more distant.

Similarities with the "Golden Rule" are striking, and the intent is the same: to overcome selfish desires. We too easily get caught up in our own wishes and plans; reciprocity turns our attention to others. But these Confucian versions of the golden rule must be read within the context established so far. *Shu* is not a logical rule but a technique. By attending to our similarities with others, the feelings with which we regard our self can extend to how we feel about others. This method is familiar. One common tactic in teaching children is to say, "How would you feel if someone did that to you?" If I see an elderly man struggling to get on the bus and I think of him as someone's grandfather and thus like my own, I can awaken some of the feelings of concern I would have for my own grandfather.

The versions of *shu* given by Kongzi speak not just of action but of what we want. The difference is subtle but significant. The Golden Rule can take the form of self-denial. You will want certain benefits for yourself, but you should act according to the rule instead. The Confucian version requires extending feelings from within our own realm of concern to people outside of it. We must develop our relationships to our family, but then extend those feelings to other families. We must develop our sensitivity to the suffering around us, but then extend this sympathy to those suffering at a greater distance. To truly enact reciprocity would mean to want for others in the same way that we want for ourselves. That is not something we can just choose to do. It requires a process of self-transformation, but a transformation that extends our self rather than denying it.

This process of extension responds to the Mohist idea of impartial or inclusive care (*jiān ài* 兼愛). In discussing the two roots (M 3A5) in the previous chapter, I noted that Mengzi rejects the Mohist appeal to heaven's impartiality or inclusivity. One reason is that the objective view taking all people as equally valuable has no direct connection to our actual feelings and concerns. It cuts off and undermines what Mengzi takes as the only reliable root for dedicated effort to help others. As an alternative, Mengzi presents care for strangers as growing from our embodied emotive responses to the world. That process of extension relies on recognizing relevant similarities but not the application of an abstract rational principle. It is too irregular and inconsistent. If based on rational inference, the king would move from this particular frightened ox not just to other oxen but all animals that would be similarly frightened. That is obvious. Rather than being an argument by analogy, this process of extension follows a kind of association of imagination and attention, so that when my vegetarian friend saw a cooked chicken he was drawn back to that experience on the road. The issue is not uniting two sources of morality—one based on our subjective feelings and another on an objective or rational perspective—but rather extending a rationality embedded within our natural emotional responses to the world.

Mengzi's approach avoids another problem with the Mohist appeal to heaven. Mozi assumes that heaven is anthropocentric, considering all human beings equally but going no further. Otherwise, heaven would turn out to be too inclusive, equalizing human beings with other animals and even life with death (since death is as natural as life). That is the conclusion reached by Zhuangzi. By relying on extension, Mengzi can justify a concern that goes beyond human beings, to other animals and the natural world. This extension is most famously expressed by a later Confucian, Wang Yangming 王陽明 (1472–1529), who writes:

> Great people regard heaven, earth, and the myriad creatures as a single body. They look upon the world as one family and China as one person within it. Those who, because of the space between their bodies and other physical forms, separate themselves from others are petty people. The ability great people have to form one body with heaven, earth, and the myriad creatures is not deliberate; the benevolence of their hearts is originally like

this. How could it be that only the hearts of great people are one with heaven, earth, and the myriad creatures? Even the hearts of petty people are like this. It is only the way in which such people look at things that makes them petty. This is why, when they see a child falling into a well, they will surely have a heart of alarm and compassion for it. This is because their benevolence forms one body with the child. The child is of the same kind as us, but when people hear the anguished cries or see the frightened appearance of birds or beasts, they will surely have a heart that cannot bear it. This is because their benevolence forms one body with birds and beasts. Birds and beasts still have awareness, but when people see grass or trees uprooted and torn apart, they will surely have a heart of sympathy and distress. This is because their benevolence forms one body with grass and trees. Grass and trees still have life and vitality, but when people see tiles and stones broken and destroyed, they will surely have a heart of concern and regret. This is because their benevolence forms one body with tiles and stones. This shows that the benevolence that forms one body is something that even the hearts of petty people necessarily possess.[6]

Even when this extension reaches as far as broken roof tiles, there remains a hierarchy of differentiated care. That differentiation is precisely what allows for greater reach. Rather than drawing a clear line between human beings and all other things, the Confucians have a continuum that starts from the family and extends all the way to trees and rocks.

The limits of individual effort

On the level of the individual, the most common explanation for why someone fails to develop virtue is lack of attention. We ignore the reactions of our heart, usually because we are distracted by the drives of the lesser parts of the body, pursuing wealth and success while ignoring our social feelings. Like any other physical process, the reactions of our various organs strengthen with practice and weaken without it. The more we stimulate our sensory desires and ignore the concerns of the heart, the more difficult it becomes to restore the proper balance.

Mengzi's full explanation for how people become bad is different. It is not about individuals but environment. He describes the process of losing the spontaneous reactions of the heart in a story about Ox Mountain:

> "The trees of Ox Mountain were once beautiful. But it is on the outskirts of a large state, so axes and hatchets came and cut them down—could it stay beautiful? Even then, with the rest given day and night and the nourishing moisture of the rain or dew, it was not without the growth of sprouts and buds on it. Cattle and sheep then followed and grazed on it, and by this it has a barren and bald appearance. People see its barrenness and consider that it never had woods: but how is that the natural dispositions (*xing*) of a mountain! As for what is maintained in human beings, how can they be without a heart of benevolence and rightness? That by which they let their good hearts go astray is like the axes and hatchets going to the trees. Cutting them day after day—can they be beautiful? Even then, with the rest given day or night and the vital energy [*qi*] of the dawn, what they love and detest is still not far from that of other people. But what they do in the light of day again and again shackles and destroys it. Shackling it again and again, the vital energy of the night does not suffice to maintain it. If the vital energy of the night does not suffice to maintain it, then their distance from birds and beasts is not far. People see their being like birds and beasts and consider that they never had ability: but how is that the genuine feelings [*qíng* 情] of a human being! Thus, if it attains its nourishment, nothing will not grow. If it loses its nourishment, nothing will not die. (M 6A8)

The growth of the plants is driven by the power of nature, described through vital energy, *qi*. The genuine emotions arising from our natural dispositions channel the very same vital energy. In either case, whether plants or emotions, the vital power of nature can be thwarted by external factors.

People need a stable environment free from anxiety about their basic needs. In the same dialogue that discusses the king's compassion for the ox, Mengzi says:

> Only a leader [*shi*] can have a constant heart without having a constant livelihood. For the people, if they lack a constant livelihood, then they lack a constant heart. Without a constant heart, they will become dissolute, crooked, deviant, and excessive. There will be nothing they do not do. To set a pitfall that drops them into crime, and then to follow that up by punishing them—this is to entrap the people. When there is a benevolent person in power, how can there be the entrapment of the people! (M 1A7)

Those raised in poverty or exploitation have little chance of developing virtue. We have seen Mengzi say that all people have things they will not do (M 7B31). Here, he admits that this can be lost. Suffering and desperation dehumanize.

A more common problem is not the direct destruction of the concerns of the heart but rather external forces that encourage the growth of sensual desires. Those desires are natural as well, and if encouraged they spread like weeds, choking out the reactions of the heart. Our entire economic system is based on the creation of a culture that does just that, constantly drawing our attention to the next step up in comfort, prestige, or convenience, so that those kinds of desires are continually strengthened and extended. Mengzi would say that in such an environment, our hearts have little chance.

In needing the right environment, we depend on others. The plant metaphors reveal this dependence on other forces. Can the trees on Ox Mountain be blamed for their own destruction? The loggers and shepherds are the ones to blame. Consider Mengzi's account of a king who fails to develop:

> Don't wonder at the king's not being wise! Even the most easily growing thing in the world, if you give it one day of warmth and ten days of cold, cannot grow. I rarely see the king and when I withdraw, those of the cold arrive. Though I succeed in bringing out some buds, what of it? (M 6A9)

In comparing the king's development to a plant, Mengzi points to the limits of what the king can do for himself. Plants have an internal drive toward growth, but without the right environment they cannot live at all. The king is presented in the same way. Mengzi does not blame him. He could do better if he had wisdom, but the development of wisdom is precisely what is in question. The king is caught in a vicious circle: he lacks the wisdom needed to determine which influences would help him become wise. His only way out is to happen upon the right teachers. This dependence on external help makes it essential for good people to actively shape the broader culture and to seek pupils. Mengzi must pursue the king. As Yi Yin says, those first to realize the way must awaken those who have yet to realize it. Without someone to help us, we have little chance of becoming virtuous, so much so that if someone is virtuous, we know they must have had a good teacher (LY 5.3).

The right environment includes contact with the right people. As with other experiences that stimulate our feelings, the most important factor is direct contact. That is another reason people depend so heavily on their families:

> If your own self does not enact the way, it will not be enacted by your wife and children. If you command other people without using the way, you cannot have it enacted by your wife and children. (M 7B9)

Remember that the word for self refers to the body: *shēn* 身. It is something public that literally walks (*xíng* 行) with or against the path (*dào* 道). The only way to influence other people is through action. The position of the wife and children in this passage, however, is striking. If the father does not follow the way, how are the wife and children responsible for their lack of virtue? The situation of the wife reflects the patriarchy of Mengzi's time, but everyone was once a child.

The transformative effect of the people around us fits the Confucian worldview that highlights direct relationships. Just as we respond to suffering with sympathy, we respond to the people around us with emulation. Events in the world stimulate spontaneous motivations to help someone in danger or to avoid a shameful act, but insofar as we are motivated to become a *good person*, we must be drawn toward people we consider good. That is the only place we see a model for how our various emotions and desires can be integrated with each other and with a concrete position in the world. I draw this point from Amy Olberding's excellent study of exemplars in the *Analects*.[7] Olberding argues that theoretical understanding of what is good is secondary to our experience of specific people as good. She takes Confucian moral theory as derived primarily from the attempt to understand and theorize the function and power of role models.

Ideally, we should be surrounded by virtuous people. Mengzi compares it to learning a language, using the example of someone from the state of Chu wanting their son to learn the language of Qi:

If one person from Qi teaches him but many people of Chu chatter around him, even if you whip him every day trying to get him to speak Qi, it cannot be done. If you take him and plant him for several years in the Zhuang and Yue [areas of Qi], even if you whip him every day trying to get him to speak Chu, it cannot be done. You say that Xue Juzhou is a good officer (*shi*) and you have him residing next to the king. If those who are next to the king, old and young, noble and lowly all are like Xue Juzhou, with whom will the king be not good? If those at the king's side, old and young, noble and lowly all are not like Xue Juzhou, with whom will the king be good? What can one Xue Juzhou alone do for the king of Song? (M 3B6)

In acquiring a language, we need a shift in how we think, act, and move. This transformation comes about from immersion with speakers of the language, not just from a transfer of information. Language teachers call this language acquisition, in contrast to language learning. Virtue acquisition requires a similar change.

We do not choose the place or the time in which we are born, nor do we choose our parents. Things outside our control have the deepest impact on who we become. As with extending feelings, though, we can take some control by choosing our environment. Selecting friends is of utmost importance:

Kongzi said, "There are three types of friends that are constructive and three types of friends that are destructive. Befriending the upright, befriending the trustworthy, befriending those who have learned much—these are constructive. Befriending panderers, befriending charmers, befriending flatterers—these are destructive." (LY 16.4)

Good friends inspire us to become better people. Bad friends tell us how great we are. Our circle of good friends can expand further and further. We can even form a kind of friendship with people of the past by learning about their lives and reading their books (M 5B8).

The greatest people are distinguished by their power to influence others. The effect of the cultivated person is almost magical:

Now where the noble pass is transformed and where the noble stay it is like magic. Above and below flowing in union with heaven and earth—how can one say it is but a small help! (M 7A13)

Sages and the noble have the deepest impact on those who know them immediately, but their power to influence extends further over time. Mengzi explains:

> Sagely people are the teachers of a hundred generations. Bo Yi and Liuxia Hui are like this. When the greedy hear the ways of Bo Yi they become frugal, and the timid gain resolve. When the stingy hear the ways of Liuxia Hui they become generous, and the narrow become tolerant. These arose a hundred generations ago and in a hundred generations from now, it will still be that case that any who hear of them will be stimulated to rise up. Could it be so if they were not sagely people? How much better for those who learned directly from them! (M 7B15)

The sages and worthies of the past provide role models that are open to anyone, or at least anyone with access to education. Mengzi's own path of study illustrates that:

> The influence of the noble goes for five generations and then is cut off. The influence of petty people goes for five generations and then is cut off. I never attained becoming a disciple of Kongzi. I gathered it from other people on my own. (M 4B22)

The power of sages, transmitted through legend and literature, makes us somewhat less dependent on the contingencies of our immediate family.

Who is responsible?

Although we have some ability to choose our influences, how can we recognize good friends and teachers unless we already have some wisdom? We depend on other people, we need a little luck, and the distribution of virtue isn't fair. Contemporary philosophers have come to call this "moral luck." For people born into a bad environment, their lack of virtue may be *ming*, fate. This is a disturbing conclusion, but hard to deny. Moral luck is a problem because it undermines inherited ideas of blame and punishment. We think that bad people deserve to suffer, but you can't punish someone for having bad luck. That is one reason why Kant argues that morality, blame, and punishment can only be based on freely chosen actions, not emotions or dispositions. Kant formulates this position under the influence of Augustine. In a dialogue called *On Free Choice of the Will*, Augustine derives free will from the need to rationalize the eternity of Heaven and Hell.[8] Each person is responsible for his or her own actions, and if I go to hell, it must be my fault alone. That means a person's chances for salvation cannot depend on other people or on chance. It demands an ideology of the "self-made man." The individualism implicit in this orientation is clear if we just imagine an alternative account of divine justice. For example, imagine how differently it would work out if it were not individual souls that were judged but the human race as a whole.

Given the obviousness of our dependence on a social environment, how could such an individualistic account of responsibility be taken seriously? To make sense, this individualism requires belief in a robust human nature. Each of us must have an innate ability to understand the world, sufficient to make fair decisions regardless of our education or socialization. That is our ability to reason, which is taken as universal and a-cultural. It also requires belief in a "free will," an ability to make choices that are not determined by education, circumstances, social relationships, or history. These assumptions are inseparable from our concept of morality. As Henry Rosemont Jr. puts it:

> Every culture has a vocabulary denoting core concepts for describing, analyzing and evaluating human conduct, long ago as well as today. In contemporary English that vocabulary tends to cluster around the term "morals" and includes such other terms

as "freedom," "ought," "rights," "liberty," "reason," "obligation," "choice," "dilemma," "evil," "objective/subjective," "right/wrong," "individual," "duty," "rational," and several related terms. Without these terms a contemporary discussion of moral issues in English could not take place.[9]

The whole cluster of terms and problems around the idea of morality is foreign to Mengzi. His system is not a *moral* system in this sense, which of course does not mean he gives up norms. To borrow Nietzsche's terms, Mengzi distinguishes between good and bad. That is different from the moral distinction between good and evil.

If the self is a center of relationships, then virtue cannot be my own achievement but something also accomplished by my family, teachers, and culture. That is why we owe so much to those who raised us. Similarly, the viciousness of other people is not entirely their own fault; we all bear some responsibility for it. Because becoming good depends on so many factors outside our control, we must be cautious in judging others. We do not know what advantages and disadvantages they had. While Mengzi employs a concept similar to a human "nature," *xing* refers to a center of patterned reactions, relations, and developments. It is a point of interaction among vital forces, including the forces of desires and habit and the forces of our relationships to other people and the natural world. Our "nature" is to influence and be influenced by what happens around us. While wisdom sometimes functions like reason, it is not an innate possession but the result of cultivation and learning. Thinking and knowing are modes of responding to the world, not an independent power of arranging and ordering abstract ideas. No early Chinese word corresponds to will, in the sense of a free self-determining will. The closest word is *zhì* 志, which refers to having a fixed intention and can usually be translated as "committed" or "resolute." If we take the heart as a center of felt relationships, then *zhi* describes the stable direction of these relationships. It must be cultivated over time.

This dependence on others may seem to conflict with Mengzi's many exhortations to take responsibility for ourselves:

The benevolent are like archers: archers correct themselves and then shoot. If they shoot but do not hit the center, they do not grumble against those who beat them. They just turn and seek it in themselves. (M 2A7)

We are even held responsible for finding role models, since Kongzi suggests we can learn from anyone:

The master said, "On seeing the worthy think of equaling them; on seeing the unworthy, turn inwards and examine yourself." (LY 4.17)

All of these passages imply that virtue is within our control.

On the issue of responsibility, Mengzi wants to say that we bear responsibility for our actions, but he also wants to admit that we depend on others, and they depend on us. These two sides appear contradictory, but as with appeals to fate, they should be understood within the context of a way of life. When encouraging someone, Mengzi says that they must take responsibility for themselves. What else could he say? If you find yourself lacking virtue, blame your parents? The Confucian imperative—"do not blame heaven or complain against other people"—is based on this practical approach. At the same time, Mengzi wants to persuade us that we should not just abstain from causing harm; we must also actively care for and teach others. So, he emphasizes how much human beings depend on other people. His tendency is to say, "You can take care of yourself, but others cannot. You must take care of them as well." The same tactical divide appears with peace of mind—be ready to accept your own death and poverty, but not that of others.

We have seen the dangers of assuming a dichotomy between activity and passivity. As a living center of relationships, our lives are an integration of our motivations (the internal) and the world around us (the external). There are limits to our abilities to control the world and our reactions to it, but also some power and activity to change things. Simply put, we always bear some responsibility and always have excuses. The relationship between these varies. At an early stage, everyone depends on others. Children have this dependence, and in a bad environment they may have little chance of becoming virtuous. At a certain stage, however, we may achieve a level of wisdom that allows us to begin cultivating ourselves. We gain the ability to attend to the appropriate situations and to recognize those whose virtue exceeds our own. If we act on this recognition, we can put ourselves into the right circumstances to develop further.

At a certain level of development, we become responsible for ourselves. We can then speak of a something like autonomy or will. This process is described in the first line of a recently discovered text, *Dispositions Come from What Is Allotted* (Xing zi ming chu 性自命出):

> Although each person has natural dispositions, the heart lacks a fixed resolve (*zhi*). It awaits things and then moves, awaits being pleased and then acts, awaits practice and then is fixed.[10]

All human beings have the same basic ways of reacting to our environments, but our heart has no fixed intention because it responds to whatever appears before it. I see the ox so my heart responds with compassion; I don't see the sheep so my heart does not respond. This is the heart "waiting on things and then moving." The heart only goes beyond this immediate responsiveness through repeated practice, after which it can have a fixed and steady direction.

When properly cultivated, this resolve allows us to stay on course no matter what challenges, dangers, and temptations arise. Mengzi describes such a person:

They reside in the broad home of the world, stand in the correct place of the world, enact the great way of the world. If they attain what they have resolved, the people follow them; if they do not attain what they have resolved, then they enact their way alone. Prosperity and honor cannot make them lascivious; poverty and dishonor cannot make them change; awesome military might cannot make them bend. These are what we call great people! (M 3B2)

This will is not something free. It is not something we all have by nature. It is forged through our environment, experience, and education. The *Dispositions Come from What Is Allotted* explains:

Within the four seas, their dispositions are one. It is in using their hearts that each becomes different. Education makes them so.[11]

The heart makes each of us different, but our hearts become what they are through education and experience, that is, through other people.

5

Learning

The right feelings are not enough. No matter what your mother told you, it is not the thought that counts, not if our goal is to change the world. We need to know how the world works, which means we need to understand political power, family dynamics, what will persuade people and what will tempt them, and so on. Self-cultivation itself requires knowledge—our dynamic motivations and spontaneous responses are too complex to sort out on our own. We need guidance on how to adjust, express, and harmonize them. As much as Mengzi talks about the goodness of our dispositions, he remains fully within a Confucian tradition that prioritizes learning, education, and self-cultivation.[1] We cannot just trust our intuitions or go with our gut, at least at first.

According to the *Lunyu*, even good motivations become dangerous if pursued in ignorance:

> Loving benevolence without loving learning: its blindness is foolishness. Loving knowing without loving learning: its blindness is indulgence. Loving sincerity without loving learning: its blindness is causing harm. Loving uprightness without loving learning: its blindness is intolerance. Loving valor without loving learning: its blindness is unruliness. Loving firmness without loving learning: its blindness is rashness. (LY 17.8)

If we love benevolence but do not learn about the world, we will be naïve and easily taken advantage of. Benevolence requires some understanding of the social structures that cause suffering, of how real change can be enacted, and of who is most in need. The causes

Doing What You Really Want. Franklin Perkins, Oxford University Press. © Oxford University Press 2022.
DOI: 10.1093/oso/9780197574911.003.0006

of suffering are almost always systematic but acts done from compassion tend to treat symptoms rather than causes, sometimes
doing more harm than good. Mengzi gives several illustrations of
how compassion can lead astray. One describes a king who appears
to be exceptionally compassionate toward his people, going so
far as to use his own chariots to ferry them across a flooded river.
Mengzi says that this king is indeed kind but he does not know how
to govern. Someone who knew governing would have bridges built
at the proper times. Then the people would not need his chariots
(4B2). All of the virtues are like this. If we love sincerity without
learning about human relations and political realities, we will be
too candid and insensitive, causing harm. If we love correctness
without understanding the complexity of human experience, we
become intolerant. A strong sense of shame and moral righteous-
ness is one of the most dangerous qualities a person can have, if
coupled with ignorance.

Love of learning

Learning is not opposed to or isolated from natural feelings. Mengzi
sees wisdom as arising from a heart that affirms and negates; Kongzi
sees it as coming from the love of learning. The term "philosophy"
itself appeals to a feeling: the love (*philo*) of wisdom (*sophia*). Plato
calls this longing a form of divine madness, because it is not itself
based in reason. For Plato, the longing for wisdom reveals a felt
connection to something beyond the self. Its ultimate object is the
realm of the eternal and divine.[2]

The belief that the object of philosophy is eternal concepts rather
than the concrete world around us partly explains the most basic
contrast between *haoxue* (love of learning) and *philosophia*, particularly in how they developed. The primary concern of philosophy
has been independent thought. A philosopher justifies all premises
and takes nothing on faith or authority. Philosophy has tended to

be iconoclastic and antitradition, at least in its rhetoric, focused on questioning and critique. As Socrates says, "the unexamined life is not worth living."[3] Learning as *study* plays a relatively minor role in comparison to reflection, reason, and argument.

This tendency was most pronounced in the birth of modern European philosophy. René Descartes (1596–1650) sets out to demolish all he has learned in order to build a foundation based solely on his own thoughts and judgments. At the start of the *Meditations on First Philosophy*, he writes:

> Some years ago I was struck by the large number of falsehoods that I had accepted as true in my childhood, and by the highly doubtful nature of the whole edifice that I had subsequently based on them. I realized that it was necessary, once in the course of my life, to demolish everything completely and start again right from the foundations if I wanted to establish anything at all in the sciences that was stable and likely to last.[4]

John Locke (1632–1704), another founding figure of modern European philosophy, takes up Descartes's metaphor:

> But in the future part of this Discourse, designing to raise an Edifice uniform, and consistent with it self, as far as my own Experience and Observation will assist me, I hope, to erect it on such a Basis, that I shall not need to shore it up with props and buttresses, leaning on borrowed or begg'd foundations: Or at least, if mine prove a Castle in the Air, I will endeavour it shall be all of a piece, and hang together.[5]

Even if his conclusions are wrong, at least they are an expression of his own thought, not something borrowed or begged from others.

In contrast, the love of learning centers on study. As Kongzi says: "Loving knowing without loving learning: its blindness is indulgence." The term translated here as indulgence, *dàng* 蕩, has a range of senses difficult to convey with a single English word. It can mean unstable, overwhelmed, or dislodged. It also has a sense of letting loose or indulging. One who wants to be knowledgeable but does not want to learn from others will lack discipline. Their beliefs will be self-indulgent and unstable. Kongzi contrasts *xue* (learning) with *si*, the word that means to think, reflect, or attend to:

> The master said, "I once spent the whole day without eating and the whole night without sleep in order to think. It was of no benefit. It's not as good as learning." (LY 15.31)

It is not that *si* as reflection has no value. Kongzi also says:

> The master said, "Learning without thinking gets lost. Thinking without learning is dangerous." (LY 2.15)

The contrast for Kongzi here is not between study and rational analysis but between learning from others and trying to reflect for oneself. If you study others without reflecting for yourself, your knowledge will be fragmentary, incoherent, and difficult to apply to your own life. You will be lost. If you reflect without learning from others, your ideas will lack a broad enough grounding in reality, and that is dangerous.

We should not exaggerate cultural differences on this point: reflection and learning are important in both Confucianism and Western philosophy. Many Western philosophers, such as Aristotle, Leibniz, or Hegel, have been extremely learned. Whether or not Descartes really believed he had freed himself from all cultural presuppositions, anyone now can see how much he remains bound by his early modern European context and scholastic education. The contrast between philosophy and the love of learning is one of emphasis and self-presentation.

This contrast can be explained in a few ways. One is through a difference in goals. Although what the Confucians did overlaps with what has been called philosophy in Europe, they are not identical projects. The goal for modern European philosophers has tended to be solving conceptual problems and forming coherent and defensible conceptual systems, all modeled on science as the pursuit of truth. Confucianism is a way of life directed toward enacting social change, particularly from within government. That difference in goals brings a difference in methods. Descartes's idea of doubting everything and starting from scratch and Locke's wish to avoid borrowing are absurd for anything that requires knowledge of the world. That applies even to relatively abstract fields. As Philip J. Ivanhoe points out, a well-educated person now comes out of secondary school knowing more mathematics than many of history's greatest mathematicians. Why? Because they learn from the past.[6] If the issue is natural human dispositions, isolated reflection and abstract argumentation have little to contribute. We need wide learning about human behavior. If the goal is to understand familial relations, I cannot just reflect on my own limited experience. Much more effective is the approach recommended by Xunzi:

> I once went to the end of a day thinking [si], but that is not as good as a moment of study [xue]. I once stood on my tiptoes and looked into the distance, but that is not as good as climbing high to see far. In climbing high and waving, one's arm is not made longer but it can be seen far away; in calling out with the wind, one's voice is not made quicker but it can be heard more clearly. One who borrows a horse and carriage does not improve their feet but reaches a thousand miles; one who borrows a boat does not gain abilities in water but still crosses rivers. The noble are not different by birth; they are good at borrowing from things.[7]

We can reach into new territory, but only by learning what has already been done.

The difference between philosophy and love of learning also expresses a deeper contrast. Descartes's ideal of doubting everything he has learned and then using his own reason alone makes sense only if culture and language play no constitutive role in rationality. If rationality is inescapably cultural and linguistic, then our thinking is never free from its placement in a particular cultural setting. Descartes doesn't consider the possibility that his reliance on French and Latin might threaten the universality of his conclusions. That seems naïve, but he believed that reason has a transcendent basis in the mind of God, distinct from any particular culture or language, a position with roots going back to Plato's theory of divine forms or ideas. On this view, (human) concepts are in the structure of the universe. Such a view is foreign to early Chinese philosophers, who took human beings to be just one of the myriad living things. Knowledge and concepts result from the cumulative effort of human beings driven by a natural desire to make distinctions and learn. Learning, the cultivation of the sprout of wisdom, lays the foundations for individual reflection. As Xunzi says before the passage just quoted above:

> Thus, if you do not climb a high mountain, you do not know the height of heaven; if you do not descend into a deep valley, you do not know the thickness of earth; if you do not hear the remaining words of the early kings, you do not know the greatness of study and inquiry. The sons of the Gan, Yue, Yi, and Mo peoples are born with the same sounds but grow up with different customs— it is education that makes them so.[8]

The ability to reason is not isolated from language and culture, all of which must be learned. That language plays a constitutive role in thinking became widely accepted among European philosophers only in the twentieth century, a change sometimes called the "linguistic turn."

The humanities

What might make this Confucian emphasis on learning less plausible as a way of changing the world is the kind of learning they promote. The Confucians had little interest in studying nature, even by comparison with other thinkers of their time. The Mohists sought to attain objective criteria based on natural patterns, using the metaphor of the compass and square. Later Mohists created a kind of logic for evaluating statements and they had interests in science and mathematics. Another source for the systematic analysis of nature in early China was through correlating relationships between natural phenomena, a process associated with *yinyang* thinking.

The Confucians had little involvement with these lines of inquiry, although they did investigate human psychology. We have already seen reasons for their orientation. While Mengzi advocates harmony with nature, that harmony is based primarily on the natural reactions within human beings, not the patterns of nature. This view is nicely expressed in a poem from the *Xunzi*:

Magnifying heaven and thinking longingly of it—how can this compare with fostering things and regulating them?

Following heaven and singing its praise—how can this compare with regulating what heaven mandates and using it?

Looking off toward the timing and waiting for it—how can this compare with responding to the time and making it serve?

Following along relying on things and considering their multiplicity—how can this compare with intensifying their abilities and transforming them?

To think longingly of things and take them for granted as things—how can this compare with integrally ordering things and not losing them?

To yearn for that by which things are generated—how can this compare with having that by which things are completed?

Thus, to discard the human and think longingly of heaven is to lose the genuine characteristics of the myriad things.[9]

For Xunzi, what matters most is not the basic processes of nature but what we human beings can do with them. In retrospect, we can see that Xunzi was mistaken. Studying how nature itself works turns out to be immensely useful for determining what human beings can do with it. Any modern Confucian would have to add some role for science within learning.

The Confucians were dedicated to investigating human relations, but they had no experimental method or statistical studies that would resemble what we call the social sciences. That is hardly surprising given that they were writing two millennia before such disciplines appeared. Instead, they rely on is what we would now call arts and humanities. Already by the Warring States period, the Chinese saw themselves as part of a culture that had been developing for thousands of years. Kongzi considered himself a protector and transmitter of this inherited culture (LY 9.5), which had been passed down through legends and stories and in written documents. While the tradition that Kongzi personally edited the classics may be false, his close connection to them is certain. The *Lunyu* records:

> The master's frequent themes of discussion were the *Songs*, *Documents*, and grasping the rituals. These are what he frequently discussed. (LY 7.18)

One recently excavated text buried around 300 BCE lists six classics along with their functions:

> Ritual transmits the art of acting in interaction with others.
> Music sometimes inspires and sometimes instructs.
> The *Songs* is that by which to gather together the commitments of the past and present.

[The *Documents* is . . .]¹⁰

The *Changes* is that by which to gather together the way of heaven
and the way of human beings.

The *Spring and Autumn* is that by which to gather together the
affairs of the past and the present.¹¹

The *Songs* (now known through the *Classic of Songs*) is a collection
of poems. Some of these celebrate great historical leaders but others
describe regular life, containing love poems, descriptions of social
turmoil, and even criticisms of war. A few laments from the *Songs*
were quoted in chapter 1. Another recently discovered bamboo text
from around the same time includes comments from "the master"
on various *Songs*.¹² The *Documents* (transmitted as the *Shang
Documents* or *Classic of Documents*), is a collection of speeches pur-
portedly from transitional moments in Chinese history, drawing
ethical and political lessons. The rituals and music mentioned here
might refer to particular texts or to the practices passed down over
time. The *Changes*, known as the *Yijing* 易經 (*Classic of Changes*,
often written as *I Ching*) or the *Zhouyi* 周易 (*Zhou Changes*), is
difficult to summarize, but is popular as a method for divination,
recognizable by its use of 64 hexagrams. These are meant to represent possible configurations of events based on natural patterns
(the way of heaven). The advice then tells how to act appropriately
in that situation (the way of human beings). A copy of the *Yijing*
was found in the same collection of bamboo strips as the master's
comments on the *Songs*.¹³ The *Spring and Autumn* (*Chunqiu* 春秋)
was a historical record of the time leading up to Kongzi, supposedly
arranged by Kongzi himself with the purpose of illuminating good
and bad historical models. As a historical text drawing contemporary lessons, it brings together the affairs of the past and the present.

Why were they so focused on these humanistic texts? History
was their source for information on what works and what fails in
terms of political practices. One could draw models from the successful sage kings and analyze the failures of the bad ones. Mengzi

calls learning the tool of the leader (*shi*), the "compass and square" by which they measure the world:

> Now there are those with benevolent hearts and benevolent reputations, but the people do not receive their generosity and they cannot be models for later generations. This is from not walking the way of the early kings. Thus it is said, "Goodness alone does not suffice for governing; the models alone cannot enact themselves." The *Songs* says, "Not erring, not forgetting, following the ancient models." To respect the standards of the early kings but still err—that never happens!

Mengzi then says that sages did what they could by eye but went beyond that by inventing the compass, square, and level. They did what they could by ear but went beyond that by introducing a system of pitches. He then turns to governing:

> Once they reached the limits of the thinking of the heart, they continued with a government that could not bear the suffering of others, so that benevolence covered the world. Thus, it is said, "To make something high you must rely on a hill, to make something low, you must rely on streams and ponds." To govern without relying on the way of the early kings—how can that be called wise? (M 4A1)

One can govern "by ear" but politics is not a good arena for trial and error. The stakes are too high and the errors take too long to appear. For the Confucians, the thousands of years of their history demonstrated a process of trial and error that had already been worked out. Ignoring that history and speculating on one's own would be reckless. Better to learn from other people's errors than make them ourselves. Our situation now is not so different, but we have the advantage of considering the histories of many different cultures.

Another key role of the humanities is the transmission of role models, which inspire emulation and provide concrete guidance:

> If one wants to be sovereign, fully implement the way of a sovereign; if one wants to be a minister, fully implement the way of a minister. These two follow the models of Yao and Shun and that is all. Those who do not serve their sovereigns with what Shun used in serving Yao do not revere their sovereign. Those who do not manage the people with what Yao used to manage the people rob their people. (M 4A2)

The ability of role models to influence us has already been discussed, and it is still a common way in which literature and history are used today. A passage on friendship explains:

> If befriending the good leaders of the world is taken as insufficient, reach back to examine the people of the past. If you chant their songs and recite their documents, it can be done without knowing them in person! For this reason, one examines that era. (M 5B8)

If you ask someone to list the people that have inspired them, they will almost surely mention some they have known only through stories.

The classics provide more than just information about the past. They work as a collection of wise sayings and advice that can be applied in different contexts. They provide ritualized ways of expressing emotions and making criticisms, conveying messages politely and indirectly. They stimulate feelings in the proper ways. Kongzi summarizes the many functions of the *Songs*:

> The master said, "My children, why do none of you study the *Songs*? They can be used to inspire or as a point of view; they can be used to bring people together or to express complaints.

Brought in close, they help serve your father; at a distance, they help in serving the sovereign. They give broad knowledge of the names of birds, beasts, grasses and trees." (LY 17.9)

Learning from the past

The Confucians downplay their own innovations. Just as Xunzi says the noble are merely good at borrowing, Kongzi says:

The master said, "I am not one born knowing it; I love the ancients and diligently seek it." (LY 7.20)

Two of the most famous sayings from Kongzi highlight his close connection to the past:

The master said, "Warming up the old so as to know the new, one can be considered a teacher." (LY 2.11)

The master said, "A transmitter and not a maker, sincere and loving the ancients, I humbly compare myself to our Old Peng." (LY 7.1)

These claims cannot be taken at face value. They are a form of self-presentation, the opposite of Descartes's attempt to present himself as utterly original. The Confucians advocate a feeling of reverence and gratitude toward origins, first toward parents, then toward the elderly in general, and then toward ancestors. Their reluctance to directly criticize the past makes them appear more conservative than they really are. Almost all early Chinese thinkers appeal reverently to the past, but they justify divergent and conflicting positions. Inherited cultures always contain such plentitude that many contradictory views have some precedent. Choosing role models and practices worthy of emulation requires critical and creative thought. This critical attitude is implied in Kongzi's warming up the old while acquiring the new. Mengzi even says, regarding the *Documents*:

> It would be better to not have the *Documents* than to fully trust it. In the "Completion of the War," I take two or three lines, and that is all. A benevolent person has no enemies in the world. When the most benevolent attacks the least benevolent, how could blood flow so much that threshing sticks float away! (M 7B3)

The "Completion of War" (Wu cheng 武成) chapter of the *Documents* describes King Wu's overthrow of the Shang dynasty. Given Mengzi's view of human dispositions, people will flock to a ruler who is benevolent, and flee one who is not. If the two come into conflict, the bad ruler will lack the support needed to put up a real fight. When the virtuous King Wu fought the evil last emperor of the Shang, how could there be so much violence that things floated in the blood? Mengzi trusts his reasoning about the world more than the literal words of the classics.

Even if the Confucians were more innovative than they present themselves as being, they certainly place great trust in the relevance of the past. In part, confidence in the past follows from seeing time as repeating certain cycles and patterns. Whether based on creationism or evolution or a universe expanding from the Big Bang, we tend to see change as moving from a certain beginning and heading toward an end or goal. If history is linear and progressive, then the old becomes less and less relevant. What do our grandparents have to tell us about twitter or cloud computing or anything else? We live in a different world (so much so that any example I choose will be outdated by the time you read this). Doesn't artificial intelligence present genuinely new problems? Of course it does, and the rapid pace at which our lives now change is different from the situation in early China. But the Warring States period also was a time of great social and technological change. Consider this story, which is not from a Confucian text but from the *Zhuangzi*. Upon seeing an old man hauling pitchers of water to irrigate his field, a passing wise man tells him about a new technology that pumps water into the fields with much less effort.[14] The farmer responds:

> I heard from my teacher that where there are mechanized devices there must be mechanized work, and where there is mechanized work, there must be mechanized hearts. When a mechanized heart exists inside the chest, then what is pure and simple is not maintained. When what is pure and simple is not maintained, then spirit and vitality are unsettled. The spirit and vitality being unsettled is something the way does not support. It is not that I do not know about this invention—I would be ashamed to use it.[15]

Out of context, it would be difficult to believe this passage was written more than 2,000 years ago. We can easily imagine someone making the same response when told about all the things a new phone will allow them to do.

Technology changes fast, but our narrow focus on technology and progress is part of the ideology of modernity. Think about what has changed and what has not. The movements of the sun and moon and stars are the same for us as they were for Mengzi, as is the changing of the tide. The problem is that few of us understand or even notice these patterns. Living in Chicago or Singapore, it was rare to even see stars. Social life also repeats patterns, even through changes in its material and institutional conditions. In theory, the technology that continually progresses is not meant to define our lives but rather to help us live better lives, and what counts as better has not changed much over time. The vast majority of people in the world still base their ethics on texts thousands of years old. Many people who consider themselves "radical" or "progressive" find inspiration in ancient writings from Buddhism, Daoism, Christianity, and so on. That ability of the distant past to speak to us now supports Mengzi's claim that we all share common dispositions.

If our goals are in business and worldly success, then as social and economic conditions change, the past becomes less relevant. But these kinds of concerns are for profit and stem from those parts of our body that, if poorly cultivated, just seek luxury. That way of life is consistently attacked by the Confucians. The focus should be on cultivating the heart in immediate human relations and directing our other desires toward simple pleasures. If our problems are how to resolve familial conflict, how to cultivate the ethical responses of the young, how to deal with suffering in the world, and how to enjoy a simple life, the past has more relevance. These are the kinds of things on which we might ask an older relative for advice (perhaps while showing them how to use their new phone). The classic texts of the Confucians record the actions and sayings of wise people, so that, facing the same kinds of situations, we do not have to begin from scratch.

Vices of learning

The idea that the humanities have no value is part of the same ideology that draws our attention exclusively to technology, materialism, and progress. If making more money is all that matters, the humanities are difficult to justify. Our salespeople have to argue that the ability to "think outside the box" ultimately brings greater success in commerce, or that skills in writing and analyzing arguments will pay off in the end. Did you know that in terms of midcareer salaries, philosophy majors make more than majors in chemistry, political science, or business?[16]

These arguments already give up the game, because if the question were about how to live a happy and fulfilling life, the importance of the humanities would be obvious. Beyond a minimum level, increasing wealth does not increase happiness. The arts and humanities are an intrinsic source of joy for almost everyone (if not literature and art, at least film and music). They contain many models and discussions of what constitutes a good life. What if our question were about the kinds of knowledge and skills needed to make wise decisions as an active citizen of a democracy? Technical skills will be helpful once in a while on specific issues, but overall one needs the ability to make and criticize arguments, a knowledge of history, and some understanding of other cultures. It is no coincidence that enemies of democracy are almost always also enemies of the humanities. Whatever those people with power might say to the rest of us, we need only look at the education they choose for their children and grandchildren. Small expensive liberal arts colleges are filled with the children of the top 1 percent. Technical schools, not so much.

Even if my defense of the arts and humanities is right, there are problems with the humanities. On the one hand, they are bound to elitist systems. "Great books" education has served to reinforce privileges based on race, gender, and class, both in terms of who gets to read and who gets to write the books that count as great. Knowledge of the humanities is one of those things that distinguish those with cultural capital from those without it. On the other hand, academia has become so narrow and specialized that our work very often is trivial.[17] I remember a disturbing bit of advice I got when I was a graduate student doing research at the archives of the German philosopher Wilhelm Gottfried Leibniz. A slightly more senior colleague who already had a decent job told me that I had a golden opportunity, because the key to a successful career was to find something really obscure in the archives and then keep writing about it. I was horrified at the suggestion, since pumping trivial minutiae for publications was not what I had in mind when I fell in love with philosophy. As practical advice, I can't say he was wrong (and I do cite some obscure handwritten letters in my first book).

Confucianism drifted into similar vices, but Confucian learning provides a powerful criticism of academic life, not a justification. The Ming dynasty Confucian scholar and statesman who talked about extending compassion all the way to trees and rocks, Wang Yangming, diagnoses the problem with precision:

> Those who concentrate on self-cultivation every day see where they are lacking; those who concentrate on broad learning every day see where they have extra. Those who every day see where they are lacking will every day have extra. Those who every day see where they have extra will every day lack more.[18]

The continued progress we can make in studying easily leads to complacency and a sense of superiority. That might gain us a little prestige but it makes us worse as people.

For the Confucians, learning is justified only as part of a way of life dedicated to action. That is why labeling them as "philosophers" in the contemporary sense is misleading. Kongzi had a number of topics that he would not discuss because they were irrelevant to effective action. He avoided questions about death, ghosts, or omens. One passage explains:

> Zilu asked about serving ghost and spirits. The Master said, "You are not yet able to serve other people—how could you serve ghosts?"
>
> "May I ask about death?"
>
> "You do not yet understand life—how could you understand death?" (LY 11.12)

Kongzi does not say whether he believes that the spirits of the dead exist. We have enough to worry about without speculating on such things. For the same reason, he would discuss culture and ethics but not abstract metaphysical concepts:

There were four things that the master taught—cultured refinement [*wén* 文], practice, dedication, and trustworthiness. (LY 7.25)

Zigong said, "The master's models for cultured refinement could be heard, but his doctrines on natural dispositions and the way of heaven could not be heard." (LY 5.13)

Kongzi did not talk about life after death, or about dispositions (*xing*) or *tian*, because such speculation is irrelevant for living a good life. The same approach is expressed in the Buddhist parable of the arrow. A disciple of the Buddha named Māluṅkya asks him a series of speculative questions, threatening to give up his practice if he receives no answer. Is the cosmos eternal and infinite? Are the soul and body separate or one? Will the Buddha still exist after death? Buddha compares him to a person who has been shot with a poisoned arrow and before allowing treatment demands to know what kind of person shot the arrow, what feathers were on its shaft, and what type of bowstring was used. That person would die.[19] The point is that we know the source of human trouble and we know how to treat it. Other questions are irrelevant.

I have been discussing just the kinds of topics Kongzi refused to bring up. That isn't just my bias as a philosopher. By the time of Mengzi, rival philosophers had theories that undermined the foundations of Confucianism as a way of life. Some people accused Mengzi of liking to argue, but he denies it—he only argues because he must. He explains:

The doctrines of Yang Zhu and Mo Di fill the world. If the doctrines of the world do not go back to Yang Zhu then they go back to Mo Di. Mr. Yang advocates being for oneself, which is to lack a sovereign. Mr. Mo advocates impartial caring, which is to lack a father. To lack a father and lack a sovereign—such are the birds and beasts! Gongming Yi said, "The kitchens have fat meat, the stables have fat horses, the people have a starved look, the wilds have those who have starved to death: this is to lead animals to eat people." If the way of Yang and Mo is not stopped and the way of Kongzi manifested, then deviant doctrines will fool the people and block up benevolence and rightness. When benevolence and rightness are blocked up, animals are led to eat people and people even will eat each other. I am afraid for this. I protect the way of the early sages to resist Yang and Mo, so reckless words and deviant doctrines are unable to arise. Arising in their hearts, it harms their work; arising in their work, it harms their governing. If sagely people rise up again, they will not alter my words. (M 3B9)

Words and doctrines have a powerful effect on the world. Yang Zhu undermines public service by teaching self-interest and Mozi undermines care for the family by teaching equal care for all. When people become convinced of such beliefs it affects their actions, and that impacts the whole community. The ultimate consequence is disorder and the suffering of the common people. Philosophical debate is justified because it affects practice, a conclusion ultimately reached by Buddhist philosophers as well, who often discussed the kinds of questions Buddha refused to answer.

The Confucians have little appreciation of learning for its own sake:

The master said, "Though a person recites the three hundred songs, if he does not succeed when entrusted with tasks of governing or he cannot give answers on his own when sent on a mission to the far corners, although he has much learning, what of it?" (LY 13.5)

The *Lunyu* goes so far as to define learning in terms of proper actions:

Zixia said, "If people honor the worthy instead of alluring looks, can exhaust their strength in serving their mother and father, can devote their lives to serving the sovereign, and keep their word in interacting with friends—even if people say that they have not learned, I will certainly say that they are learned." (LY 1.7)

This passage is striking in contrast to the traditional discipline of philosophy and even more to contemporary academic learning. Would any Western philosopher say that if one cultivates the right feelings, has good familial relations, serves the public, and is sincere with friends, then he is a philosopher? Not since the Romans. It certainly won't get you tenure.

The need to practice what you learn is a central Confucian concern. It is easy to assent to good ideas, hard to put them into practice:

The master said, "When one is rebuked with exemplary words, who can avoid going along with them? What is valuable is reforming. When one is praised with respectful words, who can avoid being pleased? What is valuable is drawing them out in practice. If a person is pleased but does not draw it out in practice, or goes along but does not reform, I really can do nothing with him." (LY 9.24)

Kongzi worried about this even in relation to himself:

The master said, "To have virtue without cultivating it; to learn but not analyze it; to hear rightness but not be able to follow it; to find what is not good and be unable to change it—these are things I worry about." (LY 7.3)

The master said, "In cultured refinement there are none like me, but personally putting nobility into practice is something I have not yet attained." (LY 7.33)

We can distinguish learning and practice, as some of these passages do, and then say that both are essential. But we could also say that those who do not practice what they learn have not truly learned. Living well is a skill, and in skill, learning is inseparable from doing. If someone had studied how to play guitar for years but had never actually touched a guitar, we would not say they had learned to play guitar.

The benefits of literature, history, and philosophy for self-cultivation do not necessarily come from long detailed study. Spending six years writing a dissertation on Leibniz or Milton (or Mengzi) will not necessarily make one a good person. It might have the opposite effect. The Confucians were well aware of the temptations of a life of leisurely study and the way that book learning can lead to unjustified pride and empty talk. *Xue* involves more than just book learning. We must be willing to consult others:

> Zigong asked, "Why was Kong the Cultured called the 'cultured?'" The master said, "He was diligent and loved learning, and he was not ashamed to ask those below him. That is why he has been called 'the cultured.'" (LY 5.15)

Kong Wen got the title "Cultured" (*wén* 文) from loving to study, but also because he was willing to learn from everyone, even those of a lower status. The love of learning also requires self-awareness:

> Zixia said, "Each day to be aware of what you lack, and over a month to not forget what you can do—that is just what it means to love learning." (LY 19.5)

We must attend to what we lack but also remember what we are capable of. The effort involved with learning is itself a form of self-cultivation:

> The master said, "The noble in eating do not seek being full and in residing do not seek comfort. They are diligent in work and

cautious in speaking. They approach those with the way and are corrected by it. That is just what it means to love learning." (LY 1.14)

Working hard, associating with the right people, and not caring much about material comforts are intrinsic aspects of the love of learning. Learning must be part of a way of life.

As these statements suggest, *xue* should be done along with other forms of action:

> The master said, "A younger brother or son, when inside should be filial and when going out should be respectful to elders, should be conscientious and trustworthy, should broadly care for the masses and cherish the benevolent. When he has spare energy in doing this, he should use it to study cultural refinement." (LY 1.6)

> Zixia said, "Officers (*shì* 仕) with leisure should learn; learners with leisure should take office." (LY 19.13)

If while reading books and talking about ideas we were also engaged in service, both activities would be transformed. The meaning of what we read would appear in terms of how it shed light on our work, and our work would be interpreted in terms of what we read. That is the ideal behind what is known as service learning. Similarly, if humanistic learning goes along with respect toward elders, with trustworthiness, with cultivating feelings of care, and with the influence good people, different concerns would emerge than if one were engaged all the time with solitary study or associated only with people who do little more than research.

Breaking the rules

Learning requires teachers. Of all the early Confucians, Xunzi gave the greatest priority to self-transformation through rigorous study and learning, but he says it does no good without the right person to guide it. The rituals and music contain appropriate models but they are not sufficiently explained. The *Songs* and *Documents* present the past but not how they should be applied.[20] Teaching requires careful adjustment to the particular situation of the student:

> Zilu asked, "On hearing it, should it be immediately enacted?" The master said, "There are your father and elder brothers—how could you immediately enact what you hear?"
>
> Ran Qiu asked, "On hearing it, should it be immediately enacted?" The master said, "On hearing it, it should be immediately enacted."
>
> Gongxi Hua said, "Zilu asked whether he should immediately practice what he heard, and you said, 'There are your father and elder brothers.' Qiu asked whether he should immediately practice what he heard, and you said, 'On hearing it, it should be immediately enacted.' I am perplexed. May I ask about it?"
>
> The master said, "Qiu holds back; so I urged him forward. Zilu wants to excel others, so I hold him back." (LY 11.22)

Different people need different advice. The close and personal connection between teacher and student is one reason these early Confucian writings are difficult to interpret. Each saying was meant for some particular context, but we no longer know what that context was. This passage again shows how Confucians use comments tactically, not with the direct goal of presenting consistent arguments but as a way of promoting self-cultivation.

The goal of self-cultivation is not to learn a set of general rules or commandments, but to shift our feelings, desires, and actions so that we live in a certain way. There are many methods for teaching, as Mengzi says:

> There are five means by which the noble teach. There is transforming them like timely rain. There is bringing their virtue

to completion. There is releasing their talent. There is answering questions. There is setting a model they can select from on their own. These are the five means by which the noble teach. (M 7A40)

Teaching still has many methods. When I consider someone unworthy of teaching and instruction, that also is just a way of teaching and instructing them. (M 6B16)

For some students, the best way to teach them may be to tell them they are not yet ready to be taught.

My last chapter ended by describing how a person with properly cultivated dispositions will spontaneously feel the right responses in any situation. At the highest level, they simply want to do what is best. That spontaneous ability to do what is right is inseparable from the highest levels of learning, as we must not only have the right feelings but also see how to enact these feelings effectively. We must apply the rules and models we learn to unfamiliar and changing circumstances. This requires flexibility, creativity, and attention. Those who rely on fixed rules fall short:

Yangzi chooses to be for himself. If he could benefit the world by plucking out one hair, he would not do it. Mozi impartially cares. If he could benefit the world by rubbing all the hair off his body, he would do it. Zimo grasped the center. Grasping the center is close, but grasping the center without weighing and balancing is still grasping just one position. What I detest is grasping one position, because it robs the way, elevating one while casting off a hundred. (M 7A26)

Holding the mean is better than holding one of the extremes, but even the mean is bad as an absolute. Some moments call for extreme action.

This ability to apply knowledge with attunement to the singularity of different contexts is one of the things that distinguished

Kongzi's love of learning. Kongzi had no absolutes in what he would or would not do, so he could adapt to any situation. Mengzi explains:

> When Kongzi left the state of Qi, he dried the rice he was about to cook and walked off. When he left the state of Lu, he said, "Slowly, slowly, I go. That is the way of leaving the state of one's father and mother." If it was proper to go quickly he went quickly. If it was proper to take a long time, he took a long time. If it was proper to stay and reside, he stayed. If it was proper to take office, he took office. That was Kongzi.

Mengzi concludes with a comparison:

> Bo Yi had the purity of a sage. Yi Yin had a sage's sense of responsibility. Liuxia Hui had the harmoniousness of a sage. Kongzi had the timing of a sage. (M 5B1)

The word translated as "timing" is shí 時, which contains an image of the sun rì 日 and has the root meaning of season. It does not refer to abstract "time" but to the requirements brought by a certain moment in a process. Having or not having the opportunity to succeed can be referred as having or not having the right shi, timing. The same term refers to the ability to act according to the configuration of the moment. Thus, Mengzi says that Kongzi is the one who acts not by preconceived rules, but according to the shi, to the season. The culmination of studying the actions of past sages, of exposure to role models, of learning about human relations, of understanding the world and social institutions, and of cultivating the right feelings is the intuitive ability to act appropriately. It is the consummation of Confucian cultivation:

> The noble occupy their position and act. They do not want to go outside it. Residing in wealth and honor, they act according to

wealth and honor. Residing in poverty and low position, they act according to poverty and low position. Residing with the Yi or Di peoples, they act according to the Yi or Di. Residing in sorrow and difficulty, they act according to sorrow and difficulty. There is no place the noble enter and are unable to be content in themselves. (ZY8)

6

Ritual, Music, and Embodied Emotions

One particular moment stands out to me in my early thinking about ritual. I always felt somewhat out of place as a first-generation scholarship kid at a university with a large proportion of wealthy southerners. On this particular occasion, I was attending a banquet with various students and their parents after some academic ceremony. I walked in with a classmate of mine and we found seats next to each other at a long table, across from our parents. She stood by her seat looking at me, clearly waiting for something. I was confused and stood by my seat, waiting for her to sit down. After what felt like a very long awkward pause, she sat down and then I sat. I was into the appetizer when I realized she had been waiting for me to pull out her chair for her. I was mostly amused by my own ignorance, but I knew my lack of proper manners had given me away as an outsider. Etiquette is inseparable from class and the enforcement of its boundaries—you can tell who belongs where by what they wear, how they sit, and how they eat. We recognize those who do not belong to our group because they do not know the proper rituals. This exclusionary role of ritual is so strong that the university I attended for graduate school—a large state university—offered a seminar for students from disadvantaged backgrounds on proper etiquette (something I obviously should have attended earlier in life).

My distaste for ritual and etiquette is not unusual. Most of us, at least in the United States, are profoundly antiritual. People say they are religious or spiritual but they do not believe in organized religion. They attend no regular religious rituals and they see no need

Doing What You Really Want. Franklin Perkins, Oxford University Press. © Oxford University Press 2022.
DOI: 10.1093/oso/9780197574911.003.0007

for them. The common view is that ritual is only empty form, a way of standardizing what should be a spontaneous, personal relationship based on genuine feeling. We attend a weekly ritual and feel we have taken care of the spiritual side of life. We turn at a certain point in the ritual, shake hands, and say "peace be with you." This substitutes for a friendly conversation. Attitudes toward organized religion are just one example of a rejection of ritual we find in many other areas. The classroom has lost much sense of propriety as my students eat snacks in class and I debate if I must wear shoes or can get by with sandals. Don't get any teacher started on the emails students send.

This suspicion of ritual and manners comes from two attitudes deeply engrained in American culture. One is an ideology of authenticity and individuality. What matters is that I be "true to myself" and engage in genuine "self-expression." Ritual is a hindrance to that. These are the people who think you should not greet someone with "How are you?" unless you really want to know the answer. The other attitude is egalitarianism. It is not just that people in different social positions have different etiquette but that rituals themselves instantiate hierarchies. Calling someone "Doctor . . ." marks an inequality. There are some people to whom we must be more formal and polite, because they are more senior, more prominent, or more powerful. We Americans tend to find that distasteful. It makes me uncomfortable when someone outside the context of the university calls me Professor Perkins.

To dismiss ritual in the name of individual expression and egalitarianism is naïve at best. Our lives are full of inequalities and hierarchies—eliminating ritual markers does not change that but allows us to live in denial. As much as one might make a classroom look egalitarian, in the end, someone is giving grades and everyone else is being graded. Ritual marks that imbalance of power; obscuring that inequality just makes the abuse of power easier. As for the idea of an individual engaging in pure self-expression, that is based on an illusory idea of the self. The very feelings we would like to express arise as responses to the world around us, the social world most of all. In spite of what some people might say, we almost always hope the thoughts and feelings we express will be acknowledged and understood by someone else. Otherwise, we would just keep them to ourselves. Even my cat speaks only when he thinks someone is around to hear him.

Mengzi takes one of his four main virtues as *lǐ* 禮. In its broadest sense, *li* refers to the conventionalized embodied ways we express ourselves to others. It includes ritual, ceremonies, and manners, but is broader than these. The value given to ritual and propriety is one of the most difficult aspects of Confucianism to explain in a plausible way.[1] Part of the problem is that we usually recognize behaviors as rituals when they have ossified and lost their meaning. We identify rituals only when they become *mere* ritual. If we extend our perspective beyond the things we notice as ritual or etiquette, we can see that we dwell in *li* in many ways that we would not want to give up.

Consider greeting or meeting people. When I first meet someone, I introduce myself. That conveys information, but I do it even if they already know my name, because it is a ritual that opens an engagement with someone. A handshake can be an empty ritual, but it usually conveys some similar meaning of engagement or welcoming. It would be difficult to translate into words, particularly since its precise meaning varies depending on the grip, movement, duration, and so on. Meeting an old friend with a hug is a standardized ritual, but genuinely expressive. Funerals can be empty formalities, but attending a funeral conveys something that goes beyond words. When I say to someone, "I'm so sorry for your loss," that is a ritualized way to communicate complex feelings, of sorrow, empathy, and care. Facing those feelings, we fall back on ritual formulations. We say "I don't know what to say."

Our interactions with other people are always structured by *li*. Imagine navigating a city street. We maintain a certain distance from other people, we stick with the flow of movement, we yield and are yielded to, we hold the door for the person behind us, we stand in lines, we don't stare. When we mess up in this complex order, we say, "Excuse me," or, "Sorry." If you think about any form of social interaction you will find a similar structure underlying it, from conversations at a dinner party to how people take turns speaking at a meeting. This level of *li* remains largely invisible in the way that fish do not notice water. It is rarely codified and is usually enforced only by disapproving stares or gossip. Consider the significance of calling someone rude or inappropriate. It means they have disrupted the otherwise smooth flow of interactions. Their actions become noticeable in a way that they should not. This flow of propriety becomes most obvious when one goes to a different place and feels, as we say, like a fish out of water. We become unsure of ourselves. We struggle not to see those people as rude, rather than just different.

Something like propriety exists in any community of people, and that makes it important for thinking about social change, but it is not a common topic for philosophers. There are many reasons why Confucian philosophers took it up as a concern, but the foundation is their vision of the world as interconnected dynamic processes. We are always embedded in a complex web of influences. Since the body is an organic whole, what happens in one part naturally spreads to the others. It is not that the *mind* must be expressed through the *body*. The heart, *xīn* 心, is part of the body. The reactions and movements of the heart extend to the limbs, to the eyes, to the skin (and vice versa). When Mengzi describes people's reaction to seeing the corpse of a parent eaten by animals and insects, it is not just their heart that is moved: perspiration starts on their foreheads and their bodies are forced to turn away (3A5). When emotions project through our body, they become visible and inspire reactions in the people around us, stimulating their emotions as well. A continuous line of expression runs from our heart into the broader community and back again. These lines of mutual influence encompass almost all of the meaningful aspects of our lives.

A holistic approach to the body is common in many traditions. Forms of bodily practices meant to calm the heart or mind are central in Buddhism, Hinduism, and Daoism. All these traditions share a belief that harmony between our heart and the movements of our body comes through learning and discipline, and all see intrinsic value in that cultivated control. As in so many other ways, the Confucians turn this commonality toward relationships with other people. Without much distortion, we could call *li* a yoga or *zazen* (sitting meditation) of being with others. That makes it inherently political.

Ritual and music as expression

Several early Confucian texts derive ritual from the need to express feelings, a function also attributed to music.[2] The earliest known statement is in one of the Guodian bamboo texts, which says: "Genuine feelings (*qíng* 情) are born from natural dispositions, and ritual is born from genuine feelings."[3] We have feelings of love, sympathy, and respect, but we also feel a need to *show* love, sympathy, and respect. A chapter on music in the *Xunzi* begins:

> Now music is joy, something genuine human feelings certainly cannot avoid. Thus, human beings cannot be without joy, and joy must issue out through sounds and tones and take form through movement and stillness. The human way and the methods by which dispositions [*xing*] change are fully contained in sounds and tones, movement and stillness. Thus, humans cannot lack joy and joy cannot lack form, but if the form is not guided by the way, there will surely be chaos.[4]

The passage once again plays on the meaning of 樂 as both music (*yuè*) and joy (*lè*), but joy is just one example of emotions that naturally and necessarily arise and take form. Proper forms of music and ritual originated from these spontaneous expressions, which were then systematized and adjusted by sagely people over a long period of time.

Since feelings naturally move toward expression, someone who subtly observes other people can judge their character. Mengzi says that if you listen to someone's words and look into their eyes, what they have in their hearts can be determined (M 4A15). Those who dissemble, who try to convey an emotion or intention that is not genuine, are usually betrayed by their appearance:

> People who love their reputation can decline a state of a thousand chariots, but if that is not who they really are, then in relation to a basket of food or bowl of stew, it can be seen in their appearance. (M 7B11)

> Zixia asked about filial piety. The master said, "The difficulty is with the appearance. When there is work, sons and younger brothers dedicate their labor to doing it; when there is wine and food, the elders eat it. Is that really enough to be considered filial?" (LY 2.8)

You can make yourself take care of elders, but filial piety requires a feeling of respect. That is the difficult point and it appears in the physical expression, most of all in one's face. Music and the voice are particularly expressive. In one passage in the *Lunyu*, someone hears Kongzi playing a stone chime and from that alone criticizes his stubborn pursuit of reforming the world (LY 14.39).

Highlighting the importance of ritual for expressing emotions was a radical departure from what would have been its most obvious justification: that performing proper sacrifices and ceremonies is required by the gods, spirits, or ancestors. None of the

Warring States Confucian philosophers we know of argue that gods or spirits will be angry if the rituals are not performed properly. That would have been a common belief at the time and was the view in the early Zhou period that the Confucians drew so heavily upon. Xunzi explicitly opposes this justification:

> We do the rain dance and then it rains. Why is this? There is no reason. It is just like when we don't do the rain dance and it rains. When the sun or moon are eclipsed and we [ritually] rescue them, when the skies (*tiān* 天) are dry and we do the rain dance, when we uses shells or sticks to prognosticate before deciding great affairs—these are not done as means of attaining what we seek but are for the sake of cultured form (*wén* 文). Thus, the noble consider them as cultured form but the people consider them as for spirits. Considering them as cultured form brings good fortune; considering them as for spirits brings ill fortune.[5]

Unlike Xunzi, Kongzi and Mengzi take no explicit stance on the role of spirits in relation to rituals, but they only justified ritual in naturalistic ways. This shift is an excellent example of how Confucian traditionalism hides radical reforms.

Regulating and refining

The need for embodied forms of expression is easy to justify, but why worry so much about proper forms? The Confucians paid remarkable attention to the consequences not just of *what* we express but *how* we express it. There are several reasons for their concern.

Insofar as we exist in a community, our expressions impact other people. We must express our feelings accurately and appropriately if we are to live well with others. Compassion for a friend is of doubtful value if our words only upset them more. The ability to put people at ease is a valuable skill, we might even say an ethical skill. Feeling hurt can be expressed so as to bring about a solution or to make a person defensive and hostile. The success of a relationship depends on how each person expresses annoyance and anger. It is not just a matter of what we say. Only a fraction of how we interact with others is through words. We relate through how we walk, dress, and gesture. Descriptions of the specificity of Confucian *li* reveal an intense awareness of bodily communication. For Kongzi, the nuances of his facial expressions, his posture, even the movements of his feet, all function as subtle forms of communication. The importance of nonverbal communication is crucial in close relationships and in conveying emotion. We almost always know when someone we love is upset before they start to tell us about it. Ideas might be adequately expressed in words, but emotional connections are not. We need tears and hugs and smiles. Try to imagine a verbal substitute or "translation" for holding hands, or for touching someone's arm when they are upset. These ritual gestures cannot be replaced with words or objective descriptions. Signing off an email with "hugs" is just not the same thing. In fact, the disembodied nature of online communication is part of what makes it so easy to come off as rude or offensive. The rules of etiquette required to address that are still in the process of formation, making courteous and effective communication even more challenging.

Music and *li* create a common framework of meaning. This communicative function means that they must be learned as part of a community and that we can talk about proper and improper forms. Improper forms convey something other than what we intend. We can now begin to see why spontaneous expressions of emotion might lead to chaos, as Xunzi says. If *li* is to be a common language, an individual cannot just make it up. Moreover, it is extremely difficult to know what impact words and gestures will have. Even the most skillful communicator sometimes gets it wrong. You can't figure it out from scratch. Rituals and music evolve over time to become effective forms of expression. *Dispositions Come from*

What Is Allotted describes this progression. The rituals emerge from the genuine feelings that arise from our natural dispositions, but what makes them so effective was their gradual modification as sages ordered, arranged, and refined them.[6] The Xunzi passage on music quoted earlier goes on to describe how sages created specific forms of music that could express emotions without excess or deficiency and would encourage good feelings while blocking harmful ones. A passage from the *Lunyu* explains that each dynasty inherited rituals from the previous one but added and subtracted. Kongzi follows the Zhou as the culmination of that process (LY 2.23). We have seen Mengzi's explanation for the origins of burial practices (M 3A5). Another passage describes a further moment in the evolution of funerals. When a disciple worries that the coffin Mengzi used for his mother's funeral was too extravagant, Mengzi explains:

> The ancients had no set measure for the inner and outer coffins. In mid-antiquity, the inner coffin was seven inches and the outer coffin matched it, from the son of heaven down to regular people. This was not just to see its beauty, but because doing so fully expressed the human heart. If people could not attain it, they could not be content. If they lacked the resources, they could not be content. If it could be attained and they had the resources, the ancients all used this—how could I alone not do so? Moreover, doesn't keeping dirt away from the skin of the one decomposing give some comfort to the human heart? I have heard this: the noble, even for all the world, will not be stingy toward their parents. (M 2B7)

When this passage is put together with the one on the origin of burials, it illustrates the evolution of ritual over time. The initial feeling of horror at an exposed body was eased by covering the bodies with dirt, but eventually that was not enough and people began to use coffins, then coffins with two layers.

Ritual and music as shaping emotions

I have so far discussed ritual and music as expressing emotions, but they also influence emotions. That comes partly from their external effect. As emotions are expressed into the world, those expressions stimulate new emotions, in ourselves and in others. The *Dispositions Come from What Is Allotted* says: "For any sound, if it comes out from genuine feelings, it is sincere, and then it enters and moves people's hearts thoroughly."[7] The form of expression also has an internal effect, channeling the emotion that it expresses. Xunzi argues that we might mourn a great loss indefinitely without rituals that help bring grief to an end.[8] Even so, later in life we are sometimes disturbed by thoughts of the people we have lost. The periodic sacrifices to ancestors arose to direct and release these feelings.[9]

Imagine you are attending a friend's wedding in a distant city. Your plans are all arranged but the day before leaving you lose your wallet. You have to miss your flight, hassle with the DMV, and spend extra money for a new plane ticket. You arrive tired, annoyed, and frustrated, not the right feelings for a wedding. Then the ritual kicks in. Our very association of the rituals with happy feelings cheers us up, as do all of the particular elements—the flowers, the music, the words of the ceremony. The joy felt by others is contagious. All of this works together to create a setting in which everyone shares the same positive feeling. A funeral does the opposite, bringing everyone into communal grief and solemnity.

The evocative function of ritual and music goes back to a question from chapter 4: how we can control our emotions? We cannot directly choose to feel happy or sad, but we can put ourselves into circumstances that will elicit the correct feelings. I don't think I am unusual in using music to change my mood, playing certain songs to cheer myself up, to feel nostalgic, or to be inspired. The effects are physical, as I truly seem able to run faster and further with the right

music. On a social level, think of the inspirational function of protest songs, or what is intended by singing the national anthem. The
Dispositions Come from What Is Allotted lists specific effects from
different forms of music:

> In hearing the sounds of laughter, one feels refreshed and this is
> pleasing. In hearing singing and chants, one feels happy and this
> is exciting. In hearing the sounds of the lute and zither, one feels
> thrilled and this causes sighs. In observing the "Lai" and "Wu,"
> one feels solemn and this is stirring. In observing the "Shao" and
> "Xia," one is encouraged and this is restraining. In nurturing
> thought and moving the heart, one sighs deeply.

We don't know what these types of music sounded like, and the
terms for their effects are hard to decipher, but the point is clear.
Most of us could make a similar list coordinating certain songs or
types of music with the way they make us feel.

The stimulating power of music and ritual goes beyond the moment. The passage continues:

> If one resides in their rhythm for long, they return to what is
> good and begin again. This is delightful, and their going out and
> coming in follow smoothly. This is the beginning of virtue. As for
> the music of Zheng and Wei, people condemn the sound but still
> follow it. In general, ancient music swells the heart, and extrava-
> gant music swells appetites. Each teaches the people it affects.[10]

Regularly evoking emotions makes lasting changes in our character.
If one resides in the music for a long enough time, the process will
be transformative. Michael Puett describes rituals as creating an "as
if" space.[11] In the ritual, we put ourselves in a situation that evokes
the proper feelings in us, as if we were virtuous people. The hope is
that regularly doing so will affect the feelings we have outside of the
ritual as well, so that we become virtuous people. Ritual and music

are forms of self-cultivation. According to *Dispositions Come from What Is Allotted*, music is the most effective form: "Following what is to be done is close to attaining it, but that is not as good as using the speed of music."[12] We can make progress in self-cultivation by forcing ourselves to do the right actions in the right circumstance, but the goal is to have the right feelings, and music directly engages feelings. The power of ritual and music to shape people is difficult for us to evaluate, because so few of us live within coherent systems of ritual and music. Two examples to consider would be those who join religious orders and those within the military. In both cases, people inhabit a highly ritualized life that inculcates certain attitudes, feelings, and behaviors.

Ritual and music stimulate proper feelings, but they also block improper ones. Mengzi gives an example:

Gongsun Chou said, "Why do the noble not teach their own sons?" Mengzi replied, "The circumstances do not work. One who teaches must use correction and if correction does not bring about action, they go on to use anger. That then turns back to cause hurt. [The son thinks:]'My master teaches me with correction, but my master does not act from correctness.' By this, father and son hurt each other. When father and son hurt each other, that is bad. The ancients exchanged sons to have them taught. Father and son do not demand goodness from each other. Demanding goodness leads to alienation, and nothing is more unfortunate than alienation." (M 4A18)

The proper feelings of a teacher and the proper feelings of a father conflict, as a teacher can get angry with a pupil in a way that a father should not. These feelings arise naturally in context, so the context must be controlled. In this case, a tradition evolved in which people would exchange sons in order to teach them. I have heard of people using this same strategy for teaching children how to drive.

One final value of ritual and music is that they can be a constructive source of joy. A passage in the *Mengzi* puts ritual and music as the final stages of development:

> The core of benevolence is serving parents. The core of rightness is following elder brothers. The core of wisdom is knowing these two and not abandoning them. The core of ritual is to regulate and refine [wén 文] these two. The core of music is to enjoy these two. Enjoying these two, joy/music then grows. If it grows, how can it be stopped? If it cannot be stopped, then without knowing, the feet skip to it and the hands dance to it. (M 4A27)

Ritual refines, adorns, moderates, and harmonizes. Music (*yuè* 樂) expresses joy (*lè* 樂). This joy permeates the body—we dance with joy. The joy reinforces our activity, so that the flourishing of our familial relationships cannot be stopped. As we have seen, when Kongzi and his disciples were in desperate conditions between the states of Chen and Cai, Kongzi strummed the zither while Zilu danced. That expressed their joy, but surely also helped to cheer them up.

The connection between music and pleasure appears in many places in early Confucian texts. Kongzi had a particular fondness for music:

> When the master was in the state of Qi, he heard the Shao music and for three months he did not recognize the taste of meat. He said, "I did not think that music could be as perfect as this." (LY 7.14)

The pleasures of music are particularly good because they are communal. The *Lunyu* contains another simple claim about music, emphasizing singing together:

When the master was together with people who were singing well, he would always have them repeat it and only then would he join in harmony with it. (LY 7.32)

This passage beautifully indicates how music brings people together through harmony and common pleasure. Another illustration of this communal aspect is the passage discussed earlier, in which King Xuan of Qi confesses his love of popular music. While, from a Confucian perspective, that is not as good as loving the proper music of the ancients, it is still good, because the pleasure of listening to music is social. He would prefer to listen with others rather than listen alone (M 1B1).

Tradition and reform

Because rituals evolve over time and serve so many interdependent functions, they are difficult to evaluate. Even Mengzi's disciple did not know the reason for the exchanging of sons. That complexity creates a tension between two problems. On the one hand, rituals tend to stay the same while conditions change. That means we need to continually examine and evaluate them to ensure they are still relevant and are not doing something we no longer support (like reinforcing gender inequality). On the other hand, we have to be cautious in altering rituals. Since we might not grasp all of the roles that a certain ritual plays, the consequences of a change are difficult to foresee. If changes in rituals are not coordinated, so that some change while others do not, the ritual itself can become a marker of division and conflict.

For me, Confucians err on the conservative side, but they do allow compromise and change. One passage challenges Mengzi on the absoluteness of ritual:

Chunyu Kun said, "Does propriety require that men and women not touch hands when giving or receiving?" Mengzi said, "Propriety does." "If your sister-in-law is drowning, can you pull her out with your hand?" Mengzi said, "To not pull out a drowning sister-in-law is to be like a wolf. Men and women not touching hands when giving or receiving is ritually proper; pulling out a drowning sister-in-law with your hand is a matter of balancing and weighing." (M 4A17)

We could take this as a conflict between the demands of two virtues. Benevolence requires that we save our sister-in-law, while ritual requires that we not touch her. The dilemma is solved through *quán* 權, a term that literally refers to a balance scale. We must weigh the importance of each action or rule. As Mengzi's comparison to the wolf suggests, letting our sister-in-law drown would go so deeply against our natural dispositions that it would be almost inhuman. A similar process of weighing appears in the dialogue discussed in chapter 2, where Mengzi says that relatively minor issues of ritual can be compromised in order to avoid starvation or to get married (M 6B1). Both passages exemplify how, at the height of learning and cultivation, a person should have the ability to adapt the models and rules to particular circumstances. Absolute obedience to ritual (or any rule) would lead us to do unacceptable things.

Change in ritual is allowed for the sake of reducing waste:

The master said, "The linen cap is ritually proper. Nowadays it is silk. That is frugal and I follow the majority. Bowing below the stairs is ritually proper. Nowadays, the practice is to bow above it. That is arrogant. Even though it is far from the majority, I follow bowing when below." (LY 9.3)

One passage suggests that ritual extravagance was an innovation promoted by those who claimed to be "noble":

The master said, "Those who first approached ritual and music, were still rustics. Those who later approached ritual and music, were nobles [*junzi*]. If I had to use one, then I would use those who came first." (LY 11.1)

Compromising rules of propriety to avoid wasting resources was part of a broader reaction against excessive and extravagant ritual practices. Mozi had argued that funerals and musical performances should be radically reduced or eliminated because they wasted resources. The Confucians see rituals as essential to orderly human relations and to the expression of natural feelings. They needed to be maintained, but moderated when possible.

The allowance for simplicity weakens the connection between propriety and wealth. Given the likelihood that a good person will end up poor, proper ritual must be compatible with poverty. The concern with appearances and form might lead one to be ashamed of poverty, but that would be a mistake:

The master said, "A leader (*shi*) who is intent on the way but ashamed of poor clothing and poor food is not worth engaging in discussion." (LY 4.9)

The master said, "To be unashamed wearing a tattered robe while standing with those wearing fine furs—that is Zilu!" (LY 9.27)

Cultivation and discipline

Since rituals and propriety function in a communal and historical context, they require study and training. Part of cultivation is the shaping of our body, bringing it into harmony with our heart on one side and with our community on the other. We might ask, if ritual is just an effective expression of our feelings, why does it take discipline? Why speak of it as restraint? In the beginning, any new form of expression feels unnatural. Consider learning a foreign language. It takes great discipline and feels extremely restrictive. Speaking a foreign language makes it more difficult to express oneself, not the opposite—and not just in the beginning but for a long time. I have had few experiences more miserable than immersive language learning, which requires spending months speaking like a child. Eventually, though, someone who is multilingual increases their expressive power, as they can rely on expressions from multiple languages and can communicate with more people. In the same way, learning a proper form of dance at first is awkward and less expressive than just freely jumping around, but eventually the learned dance can express even more. And if we want to dance with others in certain settings, we have to learn their ways of dancing. If expression is always expression to others, it requires a degree of subjection to the community.

Ritual unifies form and feeling. Both sides require cultivation. Kongzi explains the basis of propriety:

Lin Fang asked about the roots of ritual. The master said, "A great question indeed! In ritual, it is better to be frugal than extravagant. In mourning, it is better to be sorrowful than meticulous." (LY 3.4)

One of Kongzi's contributions to the traditional system of ritual may have been this shift from the external aspects of ritual propriety to their grounding in emotions. The need for ritual to come from genuine feeling is repeated in many passages:

The master said, "To reside in a high position but without generosity; to perform ritual but not feel reverence; to conduct mourning rites but not grieve—how could I look upon such a person?" (LY 3.26)

The master said, "If a person is not benevolent, what have they to do with ritual? If a person is not benevolent, what have they to do with music?" (LY 3.3)

Xunzi describes the ideal:

> Generally, ritual begins in release, is completed in cultured form, and ends with affirmation and pleasure. Thus, at its most complete, genuine feelings and cultured forms are fully expressed together. Short of this, feelings and cultured forms dominate in turn. Short of this, it reverts to feeling, thereby going back to the great oneness.[13]

Ritual is formed when the spontaneous expression of emotions is shaped according the proper forms, and the result is complete satisfaction. One can deviate from this ideal in either direction, expressing feelings without proper form or practicing rituals without proper feelings. The failure to align feelings and form is a sign of a poorly cultivated person. We see this in a passage in which Zai Wo proposes to reduce the three years of mourning to only one. Kongzi responds that if he does not feel sorrow after one year, then he should indeed stop at one year. It is better to change the ritual than to do it without genuine feeling. But that is still bad. When Zai Wo walks away, Kongzi criticizes him for lacking the feelings he should have (LY 17.21).

In some cases, the form can be modified. This flexibility is expressed in a long passage in which the son of the ruler of the small state of Teng must plan a funeral for his father. He sends Ran You to ask Mengzi for advice. Mengzi praises the king for being so earnest and for seeking help from others. He then gives this advice:

> I have never studied the rituals of the feudal lords, but I once heard this: for three years of mourning, wear coarse and simple

clothing and eat congee—from the son of heaven all the way down to the common people, the three dynasties all had this in common.

The prince goes to implement Mengzi's suggestions, but his family and ministers resist, saying that it does not fit the traditions established by their own ancestors. The prince is unsure of what to do and again sends Ran You to Mengzi:

> Mengzi said, "That is so. He cannot seek for it in others. Kongzi said, 'At the death of a sovereign, one listens to the high ministers, eats congee with a darkened complexion, takes the proper position and cries. The hundred officers have their duties and none dare not grieve, because he does it before them. What those above love, those below must deeply support. The virtue of the noble is like the wind; the virtue of lesser people is like grass. When the wind blows above the grass, the grass must bend.' It is all up to the royal heir." Ran You reported his mission. The royal heir said, "That is so. It truly lies with me." For five months, he resided in a small hut. He issued no commands or admonitions. The officials and his clan members could say that he understood. When it came to the burial, people arrived from the four corners to observe. With misery in his appearance and grief in his tears, those coming to pay condolences greatly approved." (M 3A2)

If the prince's people practice a certain tradition, he should follow it even if it diverges from the model of the ancient sages, because it is most important to express feelings within that community. This passage also provides guidance for how to be concerned with propriety. In one sense, the prince's approach is good—he recognizes the limits of his learning and asks others for advice, including Mengzi, his ministers, and his elders. In another sense, the prince's approach is wrong. He is so worried about the details that he misses the crucial element, which is the feeling the rituals express. For that feeling, he must turn to his own heart. Once he does so, his ritual propriety is excellent.

With this discussion of *li*, we now have all of the main elements in the complex process of Confucian cultivation. We cultivate the feelings of the heart, awakening emotions like compassion. At the same time, we channel other desires into simpler pleasures, so that our felt connections to the world harmonize. We also learn about the concrete conditions of the world and which actions are proper to which circumstances. This process of learning is not a separate step, because it flows from one of the tendencies within our nature, the "heart of affirming and negating." As we cultivate the right feelings and learn about the world, we train our body and its movements, so that we sincerely express ourselves as part of a community. The result can be compared with playing music. Music brings people into harmony and allows them to act together. Each musician is distinct but participates in a greater whole, creating beauty. Feelings are expressed genuinely and in forms that are meaningful and constructive. Order emerges without the need for rewards or punishments, sometimes without any effort at all. The result is the harmonious coordination of complex human activities without coercion or conformity (*hé ér bùtóng* 和而不同).[14]

Mengzi describes this ideal:

Broad land and a multitude of people are what the noble desire, but what they enjoy is not in this. Standing in the center of the world and stabilizing the people of the four seas are what the noble enjoy, but what they have by their dispositions is not in this. What the noble have by their dispositions is not added to by great actions or diminished by residing in adversity, because they make firm distinctions. What the noble have by their dispositions is the benevolence, rightness, propriety, and wisdom rooted in the heart. It generates a pure and luminous appearance that is manifest in the face, fills the torso, and spreads through the four limbs. The four limbs do not speak but people understand. (M 7A21)

One who reaches this ideal achieves a harmonious integration of thoughts, feelings, body, action, and community. This harmony is situated in nature itself through dispositions that come from *tian*.

We have now seen the main elements of Mengzi's account of self-cultivation and the ideal person, but how does a cultivated person deal with the actual problems of the world? What is involved in this way of life dedicated to change? The next two chapters will take up Mengzi's account of the specific challenges and strategies involved with striving to make the world a better place.

7

Temptations, Excuses, and Putting Ideas into Practice

Mengzi presents us with a philosophical vision of the meaning of human life, but he hoped to do more. His aim was to get people to act and to act effectively, which requires more than just philosophical theories. Confucian texts contain a wealth of concrete advice, practical guidance, and helpful sayings.[1] That makes the texts different from works of academic philosophy but it aligns with the kinds of materials written by Stoic and Epicurean philosophers or Buddhist and Hindu philosophers, all of whom see philosophy as a way of life. The primary audience for Kongzi, Mengzi, and the other Confucians were those people with some education, leisure, and power who genuinely want to be good people. That would describe most students I teach and most readers of this book. One key problem is translating those motivations into action. With their sophisticated understanding of self-cultivation and long experience promoting social change, the Confucians gained insight into the temptations and distractions good people face, and the ways people can be co-opted by a corrupt system. Ideally, we would have some wise person to give us the right advice at the right moment. Books don't work that way. The Confucian strategy was to throw together all kinds of advice by gathering quotations, short dialogues, and wise sayings from many different contexts, hoping each reader finds what they most need. I regularly ask my students to pick the two passages from the *Lunyu* that they find most significant and explain why. There is surprisingly little overlap in their choices. I think the compilers of the texts would be pleased.

Doing What You Really Want. Franklin Perkins, Oxford University Press. © Oxford University Press 2022. DOI: 10.1093/oso/9780197574911.003.0008

Confucian texts contain advice for many situations, but I will concentrate on those most directly related to the core goal of inspiring people to dedicate themselves to changing the world for the better. We have already seen many of the dangers and temptations facing a capable, well-intentioned person. One is the temptation of academia. Those with some privilege and a love of learning are easily channeled into irrelevant scholasticism and the prestige of being exceptionally learned. If the goal was to neutralize the impact of such people, one could hardly do better than our current academic system. Another temptation is to consider only genuine self-expression, without considering how our expressions impact the communities in which we live. In both of these cases, the errors come from an imbalance in which something good goes too far. It would be worse to reject learning entirely or ignore genuine feelings and just conform to those around us. These dangers were as present in the time of Kongzi and Mengzi as they are now. In this chapter, I will discuss six other points of concern. We might call them temptations. We might call them excuses.

The temptation of wealth

The main thing that keeps caring, educated people with some privilege from dedicating themselves to making the world a better place is the desire to make money. If survival is at stake, that orientation is sensible and necessary. The temptation is the pursuit of luxury. Much of the Confucian program of cultivation is directed against this threat, discussed through the contrast between the love of benefit and the love of virtue and rooted in the danger that the lesser desires will dominate the feelings of the heart. We have already seen many passages criticizing the pursuit of wealth. In one passage Kongzi allows for wealth, but only if the people also are well off:

The Master said, "[. . .] When the state has the way, poverty and low status are shameful in it. When the state is without the way, riches and honors are shameful in it." (LY 8.13)

If the people do not have enough and the state is poorly run, it is shameful to profit from that. If the country has the way, then the state provides a good route for positive change. In that situation, poverty and obscurity would be something to be ashamed of.

We have already seen several strategies for avoiding the temptation of wealth. One is the cultivation of simple pleasures. To deny the eyes, ears, and mouth would be unpleasant, unnatural, and unsustainable. The choice is not between an ascetic, miserable life and a life of comfort, but between a life of joy in friends, music, and plain rice, on one side, and a life of joy in a giant house, fancy car, and lots of toys on the other. That our tastes evolve and can be deliberately cultivated is undeniable. It's just that we are usually encouraged to develop a taste for the finer things in life, when what we need is a taste for the simpler things. As the environmental philosopher Arne Naess puts it: "The development of sensitivity toward the good things of which there are enough is the true goal of education."[2] Instead, people are brought up in an environment focused on profit and excess, so much so that people will actually take pride in their inability to enjoy common things. In our environment, like that of Mengzi, cultivating the proper balance of desires is difficult and countercultural.

Another strategy we have seen for shifting desires away from material things is to distinguish what is and what is not within our control. The uncertainty of material goods always brings some level of anxiety. Even if we could avoid anxiety about losing what we already have, the path of gaining more and more stuff never ends. There is always something finer or more precious. One can never be satisfied following that route. This a point on which philosophers (and religions) across cultures agree. Mengzi draws a contrast between concern [yōu 憂] and being troubled [huàn 患] (M 4B28).

Good people have constant concern about their own virtue and relationships, but they are not troubled by the events that happen to befall them.

Aside from strategies, Mengzi provides a coherent philosophy that explains why an exclusive concern for wealth and luxury is not ultimately satisfying. If Mengzi's account of natural human dispositions is even partly true, then to concentrate only on the pleasures of the senses is to be inauthentic, like the king who sacrificed the life of his son for the sake of expanding his territory (M 7B1). What people care most about are relationships, expressed through the four sprouts of the virtues. Pursuing wealth as the primary goal leaves us divided against ourselves. Our feelings and desires can be integrated and expressed, but only by taking the heart as the root.

The temptation of prestige

As Mengzi's account of dispositions would lead us to suspect, few people are motivated solely by the desire for luxury and comfort. The lure of wealth is largely for the sake of prestige, which is why people are often more concerned with appearing wealthy than with enjoying the sensory pleasures that wealth allows. The desire for prestige is not as bad as the desire for wealth. Wealth appeals to the desires of the other senses. Prestige draws on connections to other people. The desire for respect is a distortion of the feeling of shame that, if directed properly, leads to rightness. In an ideal culture, prestige would attach to goodness and thus would motivate self-cultivation. Teaching, nursing, and social work would be high-prestige professions. In our world, as in Mengzi's, the desire for prestige is a force that often tempts people away from making the world better.

One strategy for dealing with this problem is to distinguish recognition from worth. Kongzi contrasts fame (*wén* 聞, literally, being heard of) with *dá* 達, a broad term that has a sense of succeeding, attaining, and penetrating through without obstruction (LY 12.20). In a similar way, Xunzi contrasts the honor or glory (*róng* 榮) of rightness with honor that depends on power and recognition:

> There is right honor [yìróng 義榮] and circumstantial honor [yìróng 埶榮]; there is right shame and circumstantial shame. When one's commitments and intentions are cultivated, one's virtue and conduct are deep, and one's knowing and deliberating are insightful—this is honor that comes from one's own center. This is called right honor. When one's title and rank are respected, one's salary and rewards are deep, one's position and situation are overpowering, at the top being the son of heaven or the lord of a state or below being a chief minister or great official—this is honor that arrives from outside. This is called circumstantial honor.[3]

The same strategy appears in many traditions. As Socrates says, we should not worry about the opinions of the majority but rather those who are most wise.[4] Kongzi agrees:

> Zigong asked, "What about one whom all in the village love?" The master replied, "That is not enough." "What about one whom all in the village detest?" The master replied, "That is not enough. It is not as good as considering one whom all the good people in the village love or that the bad people detest." (LY 13.24)

Caring about the opinions of good people is helpful, as it leads us toward being good.

Aside from distinguishing honor from fame, the main Confucian strategy is close to the strategy around wealth. The pursuit of prestige is never satisfied. Even the very wealthy and very famous envy those who are slightly higher in status. Ultimately, fame and wealth are both outside our control, making us vulnerable. We should concentrate on being worthy of respect rather than on attaining it:

> The master said, "Do not be troubled about having no position; be troubled about being ready to hold a position. Do not be troubled that no one knows you; seek to be one who should be known." (LY 4.14)

The Confucians do not say that we should ignore the opinions of other people, advice that follows from a one-sided concern for self-expression. That would not be possible or even desirable. When Kongzi says one should seek to be ready to take office or worthy of being known, he acknowledges a concern with recognition, even if it is a desire to be recognized by someone yet to come.

Taking wealth and prestige together, we can add one more warning. The dedicated person should not be awed by the wealth and power of others:

> Mengzi said, "Those who persuade powerful people should disdain them and not gaze at their majestic appearance. High halls with immense beams—if I got what I intended, it would not be that. Huge spreads of food with hundreds of attendants and concubines—if I got what I intended, it would not be that. Music and wine, and the thrill of the hunt with thousands of chariots following after me—if I got what I intended, it would not be that. Now, these are all things that I would not want. What I have in me is the system of the ancients. Why should I stand in awe of them?" (M 7B34)

Wealth and power do not coordinate with true worth. On the contrary, to have more than one needs when others have less than they need reveals a lack of virtue. Remember that what Mengzi truly wants follows from the social feelings of the heart. He would prefer to die rather than act against rightness. This desire reflects something common to all human hearts. Someone who takes pride in their wealth and prominence not only displays their poor level of cultivation. They are to some extent inauthentic.

The temptation to compromise

Mengzi is almost obsessed with worries about "selling out." One of the greatest threats to a caring person is to be co-opted by a corrupt system, to try and reform things "from the inside." With the first two temptations, the answer is simple even if hard to live up to—disregard wealth and fame. With compromise, there is no easy answer. The extension of our heart requires that we take positions that allow our abilities to have the greatest impact but it also requires us to not participate in exploitation. When power structures are corrupt, these imperatives collide.

Willingness to compromise and refusal to compromise each has its own dangers. If we remain too pure, we exclude ourselves from influence and leave power in the hands of the unvirtuous. It gives us the easy role of the critic, who can sit back and feel superior without any exertion or risk. It is also disingenuous, since it is impossible to fully withdraw from systems of power. If, instead, we participate in a corrupt system, we give it our consent and reinforce those corrupt structures. Participation usually poses the greater danger, because it brings wealth and prestige. It is an easy way to evade a hard choice between prosperity and doing the right thing. A fully cultivated person free of attachment to wealth and prestige would clearly see when to compromise and when not to. The rest of us have to be wary lest our desire for ease distort our judgment.

The issue of compromise is almost always addressed through particular cases, and Mengzi opposes any rigid principle that would determine all cases, but he gives some general guidance. Choice of career is crucial:

Isn't the arrow maker less benevolent than the armor maker? The arrow maker only fears that people will not be harmed; the armor maker only fears that people will be harmed. The shaman-healer and the coffin maker are also like this. Thus, one must not fail to be cautious in choosing their trade. (M 2A7)

The main way we impact the world is through our job, so the choice of career largely determines what kind of influence our life has. That is yet another point that appears across cultures. In Buddhism, "right livelihood" is one step in the eight-fold path.

There must be things that one will not do. The previous passage reflects Mengzi's opposition to war, employing a distinction used by the Mohists between offensive and defensive warfare. Kongzi refused to support military aggression:

Duke Ling of Wei asked Kongzi about battle formations. Kongzi replied, "I have heard all about affairs involving sacrificial vessels, but I have not studied military affairs." He left the next day. (LY 15.1)

Just as one should not assist those who support violence, one should not increase the wealth of the powerful (LY 11.17), nor assist those solely concerned with benefit and power. As Mengzi says:

Those who serve sovereigns today say, "For the sovereign, I can expand the agricultural lands and fill the treasuries and granaries." Those called good ministers now would have been called robbers of the people by the ancients. If the sovereign does not turn toward the way and is not intent on benevolence, then to seek to enrich him is to enrich a Jie. "For the sovereign, I can form alliances with other states and be certain of victory in war." Those called good ministers now would have been called robbers of the people by the ancients. If the sovereign does not turn toward the way and is not intent on benevolence, then to seek to strengthen the military for him is to aid a Jie. (M 6B9)

Appealing to a ruler's desire for more land or military victories feeds that motivation, giving form to their bad tendencies rather than supporting the good. Jie was a paradigmatically evil emperor, the last ruler of the Xia dynasty. Mengzi again uses a method of extension: you wouldn't work for Jie, but to encourage a powerful person to accumulate more wealth or use violence against others is to do the same kind of thing.

The personal consequences of refusing to take office could be devastating. The most famous examples were the brothers Bo Yi and Shu Qi. They refused to serve the evil last Shang emperor but were also unwilling to join the rebelling forces of King Wu. Cutting themselves off from all sources of power, they starved to death in the wilderness. We have seen Mengzi list Bo Yi as an exemplar of purity (M 5B1) and as a sage whose reputation still influences people (M 7B15). Kongzi often brought great trouble on himself by declining the offers of a corrupt leader. That was how he and his disciples ended up trapped without supplies between the states of Chen and Cai:

When Kongzi was cut off from provisions in Chen, his followers became so ill that they could not get up. Zilu, with evident dissatisfaction, said, "Do even the noble have adversity like this?" The master said, "The noble firmly endure adversity; petty people are swept away by it." (LY 15.2)

Here we see how freedom from excessive material desires supports Kongzi's ability to leave office. We need the ability to enjoy simple things. Anyone can end up in a desperate situation. Great people will not respond with desperate acts. In the version of this episode discussed in chapter 3, Kongzi and Zilu end up dancing and playing music.

Mengzi allows taking a position in a corrupt government in order to avoid starvation. In that case, one should assume a low-level office, should receive only the pay needed to survive, and should do the duties of the office as well as possible (5B5). He gives the example of taking a position as gatekeeper. Even so, you cannot personally act against virtue. Compromise on that level is not acceptable:

> Chen Dai said, "Not meeting with any of the feudal lords seems to rely on a minor point of appropriateness. Now, if you met with one, a great one would become a true king, and a lesser one would become an overlord. Moreover, the *Records* says, 'Bend the foot to straighten the yard.' In terms of appropriateness, it seems it could be done." [...]
>
> Mengzi said, "'Bend the foot to straighten the yard' is said with reference to benefit. If benefit is the goal, then, isn't it also acceptable to bend the yard to straighten the foot? [...] Moreover, you are mistaken. Bending oneself can never straighten other people." (M 3B1)

Mengzi here criticizes a simple form of consequentialism. If we only care about direct benefits, then it is fine to compromise our principles to attain that benefit, but on that principle, any increase in benefit would justify any unethical action. On a deeper level, long-term benefit comes from getting people to be virtuous. Compromising our own virtue, even with good results, encourages others to compromise as well. It is not a matter of putting principles before consequences, but of attending to the power implicit in our social relations. As we have seen, people follow what we do, not what we say.

Another example describes Liuxia Hui, a minister in the state of Lu who was earlier (M 5B1) mentioned as a model of a sagelike harmony:

Liuxia Hui, acting as a minister of justice, was dismissed three times. Someone said, "Is it not yet time for you to quit?" He replied, "If I serve other people with an upright way, where shall I go and not be thrice dismissed? If I serve other people with a crooked way, why would I need to leave the country of my parents?" (LY 18.2)

Liuxia Hui follows a subtle principle. He will serve as a judge even for an imperfect ruler, but he will never compromise how he decides cases. The result is that he is frequently fired, but always willing to come back again if given a chance. He thus can exemplify virtue while having some impact on the world.

The ultimate reason for taking office is the hope of having a positive effect. Since this hope gives us the wealth and prestige of a good job while also allowing us to feel like a good person, it must be viewed with suspicion. One check on false hopes of making a difference comes after taking a position. If you find that you are not making much of a difference, you have to resign. Giving up a comfortable position is even harder than refusing one in the first place. Mengzi gives numerous examples of people leaving office, as the frequent loss of position is a reality for anyone set on promoting benevolence. In a few passages, Mengzi directly advises people who are having little effect to give up their position:

Mengzi went to Ping Lu and spoke to the chief minister, saying, "If one of your spearmen in a single day broke ranks three times, then would you get rid of him or not?"

"I would not wait for the third time."

Mengzi said, "But you have broken ranks even more. In years of famine with bad harvests, there are thousands of the king's people who are old and weak and turn up in ditches and ponds or who are adults and are scattered off to the four corners."

"That is not something I can do anything about."

Mengzi replied, "Now if there is a person who accepts another's cattle and sheep in order to raise them for him, he certainly will seek out pasture and grass for them. If he seeks pasture and grass but cannot get them, then will he return them to the person? Or will he stand there and watch them die?"

The minister said, "In this, I am at fault." (M 2B4)

If one keeps a position, they become responsible for the actions of their boss, even if these actions are not what they themselves would want. Mengzi's analogies provide further examples of extending feelings. The minister sees the wrongness in the examples Mengzi gives but needs to see his own actions in a similar way. At the same time, Mengzi's vivid account of the suffering of the people is meant to stir the minister's natural feelings of compassion.

In another case, Ran Qiu and Zilu were serving as ministers to the Ji family that held power in the state of Lu. They report to Kongzi that the Ji family plans to attack the region of Zhuanyu. Kongzi says that is unacceptable and the two disciples agree. It is what their boss wants, not what they want. Kongzi replies:

Zhou Ren had a saying—"When he can exert his strength, he takes his place in the ranks; when he finds himself unable to do so, he stops." Of what use is an assistant who cannot give someone support when they are about to collapse or give a lift when they have fallen? Moreover, you speak in error. When a tiger or rhinoceros escapes from its cage, when a tortoise shell or piece of jade is injured in its case—whose fault is that? (LY 16.1)

Since Ran Qiu retained his position, with considerable benefits, he is responsible for restraining his sovereign. If incapable of doing so, he should have resigned. Ran Qiu starts offering excuses, explaining why Zhuanyu might actually be a threat. Kongzi replies:

The noble are sickened by those who avoid saying they want something and yet always make excuses for it. I have heard that when one has a state or a district, they are not troubled by scarcity of people but are troubled by discontentment. They are not troubled by poverty but are troubled by unequal distribution. That is because with equal distribution there is no poverty, with harmony there is no scarcity of people, and with contentment there is no conflict. Since this is so, if distant people do not obey, then get them to come by cultivating cultured refinement and virtue. Once they come, then make them content. Now, the two of you assist your master but when distant people do not obey you cannot make them come. When the state is fragmented, on the brink of collapse and dissolution, you cannot protect it but rather scheme to move shields and spears to the center of the state. I am afraid the trouble for the Ji family is not in Zhuanyu but within its own walls. (LY 16.1)

Kongzi's explanation reflects his opposition to war and his vision of how political power works. These themes will be discussed in the next chapter. As a rebuke to Ran Qiu, Kongzi first points out his hypocrisy—he says the invasion is wrong but then offers justifications for it. Kongzi also shows how Ran Qiu places the blame on the people of Zhuanyu rather than considering how his own failures have caused the conflict to arise in the first place.

The temptation to blame others

The first three temptations relate primarily to choosing among different actions or career paths. The psychological tendency to blame others has a more intimate connection to the whole project of self-cultivation. As such, it receives frequent criticism in many traditions. Here is a sampling of Confucian passages on this topic:

The master said, "The noble seek it in themselves. Petty people seek it in others." (LY 15.21)

[The master said]: "To attack our own badness but not attack the badness of others—is this not the way to correct our hidden faults?" (LY 12.21)

Mengzi said, "The trouble with people is in their liking to be teachers of others." (M 4A23)

Blaming others and telling them what they should do is a temptation because it requires little effort and yet allows us to feel morally superior. That is why straight Christians tend to obsess more about homosexuality than adultery, and why everyone would prefer to march in a protest or occupy a park than to volunteer at a community center or tutor struggling children. To counteract this tendency, the Han dynasty Confucian Dong Zhongshu 董仲舒 says that we should apply benevolence to other people but apply rightness to ourselves:

The model for benevolence is in caring for other people, not in caring for myself. The model for rightness is in correcting myself, not in correcting other people. If I do not correct myself, then even if I am able to correct others it cannot be considered rightness. If other people are not cared for by me, then even if I care deeply for myself it cannot be considered benevolence.[5]

Dong Zhongshu's approach is tactical: he knows that we tend to care for ourselves and harshly judge others, so he advised us to do the opposite.

Criticizing others rarely does much good, but criticizing oneself leads to improvement. For the Confucians, we always have room for self-improvement. When in conflict with other people, our first response should be not to dismiss them or determine what they are doing wrong, but to question our own contribution to the situation:

> If you care for other people but they do not cherish you, turn back and examine your benevolence. If you manage other people but they are not orderly, turn back and examine your wisdom. If you treat other people with propriety but they do not respond, turn back and examine your reverence. When actions do not attain results, always turn back to seek it in yourself. If the self is correct, the world will come home to you. (M 4A4)

When we encounter people who are difficult to deal with or seem to mistreat us, our first response should be to take the responsibility, not just to see what we can do to improve the situation but also to see where we might be part of the problem. Once again, Mengzi takes a tactical approach meant to counteract our usual reaction, which is to complain about how terrible the other person is.

Aside from being useless, blaming others is usually off track, because people are formed by social forces outside their control. Consider this description of the noble from the *Zhongyong*:

> In a high position, they do not bully those below. In a low position, they do not cling to those above. They correct themselves and do not seek in others, so they have no resentment. They do not resent heaven above or blame other people below. Thus, the noble are at ease in awaiting fate, while petty people walk into danger looking to get lucky. The master said, "The archer is like the noble. When archers miss the center of the target, they turn back and seek the reason in themselves. (ZY8-9)

The saying that the noble do not grumble against either heaven or other people is attributed to Kongzi in the *Lunyu* (14.35) and is quoted in the *Mengzi* (2B13). It gives the people the same status as heaven, as something we must accept. It is natural (i.e., according to heaven) that in corrupt times, most people will be corrupt. It is difficult to lay blame in that context. Mengzi's response is not fatalistic resignation. We can take responsibility for our own position, like Yi Yin leaving his fields, saying those who are first to realize must go and teach those who are later to realize (M 5A7). Ranting at how bad or ignorant other people are distracts from analyzing the causes of their behavior and how we might address systematic factors that leave people unvirtuous.

Another tendency of those with good intentions living in a largely exploitative culture is to blame the system and those with power. In a sense, Mengzi agrees. Those with power exert the most influence and are the main cause for the mistreatment of the people and of nature. We can rightfully attribute injustice to systems of power and those who dominate them. Criticism is one tactic for enacting change. A dialogue between Kongzi's disciple Zisi and the ruler of the state of Lu, found among the texts excavated at Guodian, says that criticizing the ruler is the most important role of a dedicated or loyal (zhōng 忠) minister:

> Duke Mu of Lu asked Zisi, saying, "What is a dedicated minister like?" Zisi said, "One who constantly names his sovereign's faults can be called a dedicated minister."[6]

When Mengzi is accused of disrespecting a king, he explains that the real disrespect comes from those who do not criticize him. It is not that they approve of his action but that they do not believe he can do better (M 2B2).

The danger of focusing only on those with power is that it takes pressure off of well-intentioned individuals, who get caught up in pointing out how the system is wrong rather than looking for what they can do. One response to this danger is the Confucian emphasis on the local. We exert the most influence through our personal connections to family, friends, and those nearby who are suffering. This route to influence is always open.

This aspect of political power will be discussed more in the next chapter.

The temptation of hopelessness

Seeing change as depending entirely on those with power makes change seem hopeless. That may be the most dangerous temptation of all—the sense that nothing we do will make a difference anyway. That is why you see at rallies and demonstrations the same simple phrase: "Another world is possible." It is why "hope" can be an effective campaign motto. The Confucians saw this danger long ago, and they address it in several ways.

The claim that change is hopeless is usually made not at the conclusion of a life of effort, but as an excuse to avoid making an effort at all. Kongzi calls out Ran Qiu on this point:

> Ran Qiu said, "It is not that I do not approve of your way, but my strength is insufficient." The master said, "Those whose strength is insufficient collapse along the way; now you limit yourself." (LY 6.12)

The limits of the possible are only known by crashing into them. On avoiding discouragement, Mengzi writes:

> Benevolence overcomes what is not benevolent as water overcomes fire. With those who practice benevolence today, it is like they use a cup of water to save a cartload of burning firewood. When it is not extinguished, they then say that water does not overcome fire. This contributes greatly to those who are not benevolent. In the end, all will surely be lost. (M 6A18)

The limited power of benevolence might be discouraging, but Mengzi addresses one with a little benevolence set on changing the whole world. That will not happen. The person then gives up and concludes that change is impossible. For someone in this situation, two options remain open. If the person cultivated great benevolence, they might accomplish great things. Or, if the person shifted their attention to the more immediate, they might accomplish smaller things with small benevolence.

The problem is the impatience of one who makes some effort but wants success to come easily. Such impatience leads to failure:

> Having something to accomplish is like digging a well. To dig a well to a depth of nine fathoms but not go on to reach the spring is the same as giving up the well. (M 7A29)

On the surface, the passage just means that to pursue virtue and then give up without success is to throw away all the previous effort, but it also reveals something about the power of benevolence—great success can come at any moment, even after a long period without any results. One should think of this in hopeless times.

Besides giving bits of advice, the Confucians argue that better things are possible. One temptation on a personal level is to think that while it would be good to dedicate one's life to helping others, only extraordinary individuals do those kinds of things. Against this, Mengzi argues that any person can achieve virtue. The argument is based on human commonalities. In one passage, Mengzi's philosophy is summed up with two slogans: human dispositions are good, and, follow Yao and Shun (M 3A1). The former emphasizes our common potential; the second presents what that potential can become.

Here we have one of the most significant consequences of the humanity of the Confucian cultural heroes:

> Chuzi said, "If the king sent someone to observe you, master, would there really be something that makes you different from

other people?" Mengzi said, "How would I be different from other people? Yao and Shun were the same as other people." (M 4B32)

Asking what Shun would do is not like asking what Jesus would do. Jesus could raise the dead, know the future, and save a party by turning water into wine. Anyone can be like Yao or Shun. Mengzi explains:

> Just do it and that is all. There is a person here whose strength is not enough to lift a chicken, so he is considered a person without strength. If today he lifts a hundred *jun*, he is considered a person with strength. So then if one lifts a weight like the strongman Wu Huo did, they are considered a Wu Huo and that is all. Now, how can people be troubled by not being able? It is just they do not do it. Walking slowly behind elders is called respect. Walking hurriedly ahead of elders is called disrespect. Now walking slowly— can that be something a person is unable to do? It is what they do not do! The way of Yao and Shun is filial piety and filial respect and that is all. If you wear the clothes of Yao, repeat the words of Yao, enact the actions of Yao: that is just what is means to be Yao. If you wear the clothes of Jie, repeat the words of Jie, enact the actions of Jie: that is just what it means to be Jie. (M 6B2)

Human beings are what they do. Being a great person just means doing the things a great person does. Since human beings have the same dispositions, anyone can do great actions. At the same time, accomplishing what Yao or Shun did depends on circumstances not fully within our control. Not everyone can become emperor. What everyone can do is cultivate themselves and their relationships to other people. Acting like Yao or Shun lies in simple things like respecting elders. This local orientation grounds the belief that a better world is possible. It may be impossible to radically reform the existing power structures, but we can surely improve our own community and relationships. The way lies in what is near and easy. Perhaps the greatest danger of blaming the system—of looking exclusively at what is far and hard—is that it leads to hopelessness and inactivity. It takes only a few minutes of looking at community news to find opportunities for constructive action. Reading about the presidential election or the latest news from congress mostly just generates frustration and despair.

Just as we have the ability to do better, so do other people. They just need the right experiences and the right support. The duty to be the person who awakens others cannot be avoided, because the possibility of that awakening cannot be given up. This follows from the tendencies toward goodness that all people have. Mengzi makes this point when he is accused of lingering too long after resigning his position with King Xuan of Qi:

> I came a thousand miles to see the king because it was what I wanted to do. To find him unreachable and thus leave—how could that be what I wanted? It was forced upon me. I stayed three nights and then left Zhou, but in my heart, it still seemed too fast. The king almost reformed things. If the king had reformed them, then he would surely bring me back. Now when I went from Zhou and the king did not pursue me, only then did I fully commit to returning home. Even so, could I abandon the king? The king has what he needs to become good. If the king used me, then would it lead to peace for the people of Qi? The people of the world would also be at peace. The king almost reformed things—every day I hope for it. How could I be like one of those petty fellows? When the sovereign does not accept their admonishment they get angry and their indignation appears in their faces. They take off and exert a full day of effort before stopping for the night. (M 2B12)

Mengzi traveled so far not to make a pointless gesture but because he had hope that the king could become good. That would not only relieve the suffering of his people but might influence the whole world. He thought he was making progress, as we see in his dialogue with the king about the ox going to slaughter. In the end, though, the king did not change. Mengzi resigned his position, as the Confucians advise. He did not storm off but sacrificed his pride in leaving slowly. His decision to leave was probably itself a tactic meant to prompt the king to action. Mengzi gives up only when the king makes no gesture to call him back.

So far, we have seen how the Confucians fight hopelessness by arguing that change is possible, but even if change were not possible, a good person would work for it. Two consecutive passages in the *Lunyu* describe encounters with recluses who had withdrawn from public life. In one, a farmer tells Kongzi that instead of running from one prince to another, he should run away from them all, as the recluse himself had done, now farming the land on his own. Kongzi does not respond by saying: "Don't be so cynical! It'll work one of these times!" Instead, he says with a sigh:

> It is impossible to flock together in unity with birds and beasts. If I do not associate with these people, then with whom? (LY 18.6)

Whether or not success is possible, the human heart is entangled with other people, and if the heart is properly developed, we are driven to try to end suffering and exploitation. Kongzi continues:

> If the way prevailed in the world, there would be no need for me to work for change. (LY 18.6)

When times are bad, we try to change them. Success or failure is up to fate.

The second passage describes a similar encounter, between a recluse and Kongzi's disciple Zilu. The farmer criticizes him for not doing manual labor. Zilu stands there respectfully and takes it, but later he says to Kongzi:

To not lead [*shì* 士] is to lack rightness. If the relations between young and old cannot be abandoned, how can one abandon the rightness between sovereign and minister? In wanting to purify his own self, he disrupts that great relationship. The noble take office to enact their rightness. As for the way not being enacted, they already know about that. (LY 18.7)

Zilu recognizes that change might be impossible. The key to his response lies in the comparison between family and political power. It is within families that we see the strongest examples of people who struggle even when it seems hopeless, as parents will continue to try to help a child who is having (or causing) trouble or a child will persist in trying to make their parents content and comfortable even in the worst circumstances. That level of commitment needs to be extended beyond the family into politics and our community. The need to try in spite of the likelihood of failure follows from the belief that the best life extends from the feelings of the heart. If properly cultivated, we will want to help others and find our pleasure in a simple life compatible with that pursuit. This life is worth living in itself, not for the sake of its consequences.

The temptation of having done enough

How do we know when to be satisfied? We vote, recycle, donate some money here and there, maybe stop eating meat, and feel fairly content. Stopping too soon is particularly easy in a profit-oriented culture, where such minimal actions are uncommon enough to be praiseworthy. The previous passages on fame already entail that we disregard the opinions of the many and worry only about the opinions of the good. Our models for comparison should be those who have changed the world, not the guy down the street with the big SUV. Mengzi addresses this point in another conversation with

King Hui of Liang. The king complains that his efforts to benefit the people are not producing any results:

> In relation to my state, I put my heart fully into it. If the harvest is bad in the area inside the river, I move people to the east of the river and move grain to the land inside. If the harvest is bad on the east side of the river, I do likewise. On examining the government of the neighboring states, there are none who use their hearts like I do. And yet the people of the neighboring states do not decrease, nor do my people increase. Why?

Mengzi responds with an analogy:

> Mengzi replied, "Your majesty likes war—let me offer a military analogy. The drumming fills the air to advance the soldiers, but once their weapons engage, they throw down their shields and run away, dragging their weapons behind them. Some go a hundred paces and only then stop. Some go fifty paces and then stop. How would it be if those who ran fifty paces laughed at those who ran a hundred?"

> The king said, "Not acceptable—though they did not run a hundred paces, they still ran away!"

> "If your majesty knows this, then do not look for the people of your state to be more numerous than those of neighboring states." (M 1A3)

We do not want to be like those who pat themselves on the back because they only fled fifty paces. Mengzi takes an extra jab at the king by pointing out his fondness for war.

In general, Confucians say we should never think that we have done enough. Even Kongzi and Mengzi were not satisfied, and we should always be "anxious at not being Shun." We should try to completely withdraw from exploitative and harmful activities. In one dialogue, a minister in the state of Song says he knows he should tax only 10 percent and eliminate tariffs on the market, but since he cannot afford that, he will lighten the demand a bit now and correct it later. Mengzi replies:

> Now imagine there is a person who every day snatches some of his neighbor's chickens. Someone tells him: "That is not the way of the noble." He replies, "Please allow me to reduce it. I will snatch one chicken a month and then wait for next year to finally stop." If you know an action is not right, then quickly stop doing it. How could you wait until next year? (M 3B8)

Mengzi makes a similar comparison in relation to mourning:

> King Xuan of Qi wanted to shorten the mourning period. Mengzi's disciple Gongsun Chou said, "To have a year of mourning is still better than stopping completely, isn't it?" Mengzi replied, "That is like someone twisting the arm of their elder brother and you saying to him, 'For now, just do it more gently.' Teach him with filial piety and fraternal respect. That is all." (M 7A39)

These are excellent examples of extension—if the issue were harming our brother or stealing from a neighbor, we would not accept stopping halfway. When the harm we cause is less direct, we don't feel the same demands. In our world, the imperative to stop causing harm would itself lead to unceasing effort. Could we ever withdraw from practices and systems that harm the environment? Could we ever withdraw from systems that exploit labor? Perhaps not, but for the Confucians, until we do, our involvement should be a source of concern and effort.

Mengzi addresses complacency in a long analysis of types of people who fall short of the Confucian ideal (M 7B37). The discussion interprets and integrates several comments from Kongzi that also appear in the *Lunyu*. Mengzi's disciple, Wan Zhang, begins by asking about Kongzi's description of his students as "wild" or "crazy" (*kuáng* 狂) (LY 5.22). Mengzi replies:

> When Kongzi did not get those who hit the center of the way, he always went with the wild or the fastidious. The wild advance to take it; the fastidious have that which they will not do. How could Kongzi not want those centered in the way! When he could not necessarily get them, he thought of those who were next best.[7]

Wan Zhang asks Mengzi for more explanation of these two types. The wild set high ideals for themselves and praise the ancients, but in practice they do not reach those ideals. They were Kongzi's second choice. If he could not get them, he went with those who were cautious and uncompromising. These are the ones who have what they will not do, a feeling connected with the sprout of rightness. In relation to the temptation to compromise, they are so uncompromising that they would refuse to engage in politics at all. The ideal, of course, is those with the right balance, those who hit the center (*zhòng* 中) of the way (*dào* 道), but such people are rare. They must be cultivated and the wild and the fastidious at least have the motivation to set on that path.

The group that Kongzi wanted nothing at all to do with he calls the "fine people of the village." The phrase is difficult to translate because the key term (*yuán* 原, read as *yuàn* 愿) is positive, meaning cautious, respectful, or precise. When Wan Zhang asks about them, Mengzi starts with what the "fine people" say about the Confucians:

> What blowhards! Their words ignore their actions and their actions ignore their words, so they say "The ancients! The ancients!" Why do they act in way that is so stand-offish and cold! We are born in this era, we act in this era, and that goodness is alright.

As descriptions of those Confucians who are wild or fastidious, it doesn't seem like an unfair criticism. Wan Zhang doubts these fine people are really so bad. Why would Kongzi call them thieves of virtue? Mengzi explains:

> When you oppose them you find no point to raise; when you criticize them, you find nothing to critique. They conform to common customs and fit in with a corrupt era. When they reside, they seem to be dedicated and trustworthy. When they act, they seem to be honest and pure. The masses all approve of them and they consider themselves to be right but with them you cannot enter into the way of Yao and Shun. Thus, they are called the thieves of virtue. Kongzi said: "I detest that which seems to be but is not: I detest weeds, fearing they will be confused with sprouts of grain; I detest flattery, fearing it will be confused with rightness; I detest glibness, fearing it will be confused with sincerity; I detest the sounds of Zheng, fearing it will be confused with genuine music; I detest purple, fearing it will be confused with vermillion; I detest the fine people of the village, fearing they will be confused with virtue." (7B37)

The wild and the fastidious are not ideal students, but they set high ideals and take action seriously. In contrast, the "fine people of the village" rest content with the minimal demands of the time. Rather than seeing them as striving toward an ideal, they mock the wild Confucians who call for such idealistic standards and the fastidious Confucians who are so particular. These Confucians make everyone uneasy. They disturb the status quo by appealing to great people of the past and by appealing to the deepest concerns of the human heart. These appeals threaten the self-satisfaction and prestige of the fine people of the village. We might say that these fine people achieve a harmony of the body, but with the wrong balance. They are not like the ill-intentioned who have destroyed the connections of the heart through the pursuit of benefit, but they minimize the demands of the heart, allowing for the pursuit of profit. Because they do not extend their hearts, they can rest content in a world of suffering and exploitation. Kongzi calls the fine people of the village "thieves of virtue" (LY 17.13). We have seen thievery used several times for those who steal away the real potential of the heart by saying that such ideals are impossible to realize.

But why are the fine people of the village *the worst*? The ill-intentioned invigorate the well-intentioned. Perhaps they are the worst, but not the most dangerous. The fine people of the village entice the well-intentioned, allowing them to be self-satisfied without answering all the demands of the heart. The danger is that those who desire virtue will be lured in by this model. The fine people of the village succumb to all of the temptations discussed in this chapter. Because they set low standards and conform to the time, they readily compromise with unjust power structures. They succeed in pursuing wealth and prestige. They rest content with themselves and turn their attention to criticizing others. At bottom, the low standards are based on a lack of hope that things could be different than they are.

The moral burden of Confucianism with its endless demands to cultivate ourselves and extend our concern may seem too much to bear. We cannot forget that the Confucians still enjoy life, even in difficult circumstances. The division between our own private enjoyment and the call of caring for others follows a false opposition between egoism and altruism. Our "private" enjoyment should not entail accumulating heaps of luxury goods but the simple pleasures of being with friends or making music. In these situations, we contribute to the growth of community and we exert influence as a role model, while also having fun. As Mengzi says, it is better to enjoy music with other people rather than alone. These kinds of enjoyments are not separate from "public" duty. "Public" duty should be a source of joy, driven by what the heart really wants. The greatest model for ceaseless concern was Kongzi, but in the *Lunyu* he appears to be a happy person.

8

Power, Politics, and Action

Up until a few centuries ago, no one would have thought Christianity was more compatible with democracy, rights, or gender equality than Confucianism. On many contemporary political values, China was ahead of Europe for most of history. China has always been more pluralistic and tolerant in relation to other religions, including not just Daoism, Confucianism, and Buddhism (imported from South and Central Asia), but also Islam, Christianity, and Judaism. For centuries, high political positions in China were held by Muslims or Christians, an openness to other religions that is still rare in Europe or the United States. This difference was recognized at the start of the modern European encounter with China. Matteo Ricci (1552–1610), the key figure in establishing the Jesuit mission in China, opposed China's practice of religious tolerance, arguing that Daoism and Buddhism should have been banned long ago.[1] More progressive European philosophers, such as Gottfried Wilhelm Leibniz (1646–1716) and Pierre Bayle (1647–1706), used China's greater tolerance to criticize Europe.[2] Leibniz points out that while the Qing dynasty emperor Kang Xi issued a proclamation allowing the free practice of Christianity in China, Louis XIV made Protestantism illegal in France.[3] Bayle was one of the hundreds of thousands of Protestants (known as Huguenots) forced to flee. His brother died in a French prison.

Philosophical thinking was also far less restricted than in Europe. There were some attempts to control philosophical speculation in China, the most notorious example coming at the

Doing What You Really Want. Franklin Perkins, Oxford University Press. © Oxford University Press 2022.
DOI: 10.1093/oso/9780197574911.003.0009

founding of the Qin dynasty, but these were rare, particularly in contrast to Europe. If anything is unique about the European context, it is that for well over a thousand years one would have been killed for deviating from the dominant religious philosophy of the time. This contrast also was recognized early on. Haun Saussy quotes an early Chinese convert to Christianity, Yang Tingyun 揚 廷筠 (1574–1659), who criticized China for allowing books to be freely published. China, he argued, should emulate Europe, where the death penalty was applied to anyone publishing without government approval.[4]

This history sets a more expansive context for considering contemporary discussions of Confucian political philosophy, which focus almost entirely on how Confucianism relates to democracy, human rights, and gender equality.[5] Some dismiss Confucianism as conflicting with modern values. Some defend Confucianism by arguing that it is compatible with or perhaps even supported by democracy and rights. A growing number of Confucians respond instead by criticizing contemporary Western forms of government, advocating Confucian alternatives. This orientation has been forced on the rest of the world by the global power of the West, and I don't want to diminish the significance of these debates, which have real-life consequences in East Asia. Yet the focus is misleading, because philosophies and religions are broad enough to generate diverse political systems. Confucianism is no more bound to monarchy than Christianity was to the divine right of kings. History also warns us against taking for granted our contemporary system of capitalism, voting for government leaders, and the enforcement of negative human rights. Political values change radically over time. It would be provincial and egotistic to think we will be the one exception. To ask about the compatibility between Confucianism and democracy is to ask the wrong question. The question should be: What can Confucianism contribute to the formation of a politics yet to come?

What counts as political?

A deeper problem comes with the very focus on government structures and policies. This way of framing discussions of Confucian politics imports a narrow conception of the political that misrepresents both Confucianism and the nature of political power. In its broadest sense, all of Confucianism is political, because the self is fundamentally social and cultivating the self involves influencing and being influenced by others. Confucianism as a way of life is entirely based in extending that influence in order to change the world. Confucian philosophers had political theories and ideas about the ideal state, but that was not their primary concern. In a sense, there is no need to add a chapter on Confucian "politics"—that has been the theme of every chapter of this book. Here, I will show how those earlier themes are integrated with and through a particular vision of political power.

The focus on forms of government misrepresents not just Confucianism but also the nature of power. Think about the various ways in which power is exerted over you in your day-to-day life. The most immediate power comes through personal relationships. Within the family, we do chores and compromise our desires, we get upset depending on other people's actions and moods, and we worry about each other. Mengzi would say we do these things because they express our deepest concerns, but that doesn't change the power these relationships exert on us. Beyond the family, I feel obligated to take care of my students, do my share of administrative work, help my friends when they need it, and try to live in a way that is more sustainable. I do these things because I care about them. On another level, power works through customs (li), educational institutions, the media, and culture in the broad sense. These shape our actions and decisions in ways we are hardly aware of. The main source of visible power over us is economic—money determines what we do most of our days (work), where we live, our education, the leisure activities we have access to, and so on. These are the forms of power that dominate our lives, and democracy has little relationship to them. That is the point of the "right to private property"—it removes control of property from democratic control. It is no coincidence that governments went under the control of citizen votes at the very same time that power shifted from government to capital.

Narrowing the political to theories of government hides the real sources of power over our lives. It makes us feel far more free and autonomous than we really are. It is bound up with many of the temptations discussed in the last chapter: it leads us to criticize the government rather than make best use of our power, it minimizes our responsibility (as if all we need to do is vote), and it leaves us with a feeling of hopelessness. This focus on government and democracy expresses an ideology of depoliticization that obscures forms of power beyond government.[6] That ideology draws support from another ideology: individualism.[7] The British philosopher Thomas Hobbes (1588–1679) based his political theory on a hypothetical state of nature in which every individual struggled for their own benefit against every other. He explains:

> Againe, men have no pleasure, (but on the contrary a great deale of griefe) in keeping company, where there is no power able to over-awe them all. [...] Hereby it is manifest, that during the time men live without a common Power to keep them all in awe, they are in that condition which is called Warre; and such a warre, as is of every man, against every man.[8]

By nature, we each try to take as much as we can for ourselves. The only way to avoid constant conflict is to institute a power great enough to keep us all in line. That is the origin of the state. If we assume that individuals are self-made, then it is the origin of the political as well. From this perspective, individuals first exist on their own and then decide to enter into relationships with other people.

Hobbes presents this state of nature as a thought experiment rather than a historical account. As history, it is obviously false. Human beings have lived within a matrix of social power from the start. Even the species from which we evolved were social, never living in a condition of a war of all against all. In Mengzi's terms, as soon as there are human beings there will be relationships of care (*ren*), rules motivated by shame and disgust (*yi*), rituals and customs (*li*), and collected wisdom (*zhi*). A situation of individuals looking out only for their own self-interest would be extremely unnatural, coming about only through active destruction of our natural dispositions.

Confucians believe we are political all the way down. We can say that they bridge the gap between the personal and the political or between ethics and politics, but in their own context, there was no gap to overcome.[9] There is just a continuum of degrees of power and influence. Although we naturally have certain dispositions as human beings, living is an ongoing integration of internal and external. The external is social and suffused with relationships of power. As we would expect, Mengzi's political thought does not focus on the origins of the state but on the evolution of culture. The key question is how to harmonize all of the different relationships in which a person is already embedded. How can the naturally arising needs, desires, and concerns of human beings be integrated? How can the communities that naturally arise (on the level of family and village) support each other rather than harming each other? How can they be integrated into greater units of organization, culminating in a global political order? How can this political order work with nature in a way that is sustainable and allows for human flourishing?

Mengzi sees a continuum between nature, family, and broader political structures. All emerge naturally from human beings living together. The greatest expression of this vision of the political is in a chapter of the *Record of Rituals* known as the *Greatest Learning*

(*Daxue* 大學). We have encountered it in short quotations here and there, but the text itself is tightly organized into a progression leading to the highest ideal of leadership. That explanation is interwoven with quotations from the *Songs* and *Documents*, and over the millennia, as one of the "Four Books," it has accumulated many more commentaries and explanations.[10] Its integrative approach to power and action make it a suitable conclusion for this book.

The greatest learning and the highest ideal

The *Greatest Learning* begins by describing the highest ideal for leadership:

> The way of greatest learning lies in making the brightness of virtue shine, in cherishing the people, and in coming to rest in the utmost good. Knowing where to come to rest, one can be steady. When steady, one can be still. When still, one can be at peace. When at peace, one can deliberate. With deliberation, one can succeed. Things have roots and branches; affairs have beginnings and ends. Knowing what is first and last comes close to the way. (TX1)

The density of this passage explains why so many people have written explanations of it. The first line presents three interdependent goals: leading by example, caring for the people, and resting in the highest good. The first is "making the brightness of virtue shine." The Chinese uses the same character first as a verb and then as an adjective. That character is *ming* 明, mentioned earlier as combining images of the sun and the moon. The ideal is not just to have virtue but to make virtue known through one's own example. The next passage equates it with bringing peace to the world.

Caring for the people (*qīnmín* 親民), the second item in the list, is the foundation of the Confucian vision for a good society. Mengzi explains:

> The people are most valuable, the spirits of earth and grain come next, and the sovereign is the lightest. [. . .] If a lord endangers the spirits of earth and grain, then depose him. Suppose the sacrificial animals are complete, the offerings of grain are pure, and the sacrifices accord with the time. If this is so and yet there are droughts and floods, then depose the spirits of earth and grain. (M 7B14)

Not only should ministers and rulers who fail to support the people be demoted or deposed, the same even applies to spirits. If they don't benefit the people, fire them! The root of caring for the people is the benevolence that grows from natural feelings of compassion. The term used for cherishing the people, *qīn* 親, is usually reserved for feelings toward parents or relatives. Its use here emphasizes the continuity between love of family and concern for other people.

The third aspect of the ideal seems disappointingly obvious: you need to be good. The emphasis, though, is not on goodness but on how one relates to it. Zhu Xi explains the character for stop or rest (*zhǐ* 止) as meaning to dwell or be at home in (*jū* 居). Being at home in the good allows one to be calm and steady. That state of mind enables one to make correct decisions and thereby to succeed. This aspect of the ideal is explained with a series of quotations from the *Songs*. One says:

> The *Songs* says: "The little yellow bird comes to rest on the branch on a hill." The master said, "In coming to rest, it knows where to rest. Can one be human but not be equal to a bird?" (TX6)

The bird illustrates the naturalness of finding a proper resting place. Human beings should rest in the highest good in that same genuine and spontaneous way. This naturalness also appears in the metaphor of the root and the branches. It is not just that the root is more important but that if the root is cultivated, the results naturally and easily follow. The next lyric describes King Wen:

> The *Songs* says: "Illustrious King Wen, in continuing splendor he revered coming to rest!" In being a leader, he came to rest in benevolence. In being a minister, he came to rest in reverence. In being a son, he came to rest in filial piety. In being a father, he came to rest in parental care. In dealing with people from other states, he came to rest in trustworthiness. (TX6)

We exist in specific relationships and circumstances and what counts as good depends on the context. At the highest level of cultivation, one has the flexibility to be at home in the proper actions no matter where one ends up, whether in the family, in the halls of power, or in another country.

These three ideals are different aspects of one goal. The power of being a role model comes from being at home in goodness, making goodness seem natural. That is why Mengzi says that the influence of a sage extends further than that of other people (M 7B15). The root of utmost goodness is cherishing the people. That is what one must come to rest in. Making the brightness of virtue shine is itself a way of caring for the people by providing guidance for their own cultivation.

The description of this ideal is followed by a longer progression showing how to reach it. The progression is given from two directions. The first starts at the ideal and shows the conditions that enable it. The other goes from the bottom up, showing how each stage expands into the next. I will begin with the whole passage and then consider each step in more detail:

> The ancients who wanted to make the brightness of virtue shine in the world first managed their states. Those wanting to manage

their states first aligned their community. Those wanting to align their community first cultivated their body/self. Those wanting to cultivate themselves first corrected their hearts. Those wanting to correct their hearts first made their intentions authentic. Those wanting to make their intentions authentic first extended their knowledge to the utmost. The utmost extension of knowledge lies in dealing with things. When things are dealt with, then knowledge is at its utmost. When knowledge is utmost, then intentions are authentic. When intentions are authentic then the heart is correct. When the heart is correct then the self is cultivated. When the self is cultivated then the community is aligned. When the community is aligned then the state is ordered. When the state is ordered then the world is at peace. From the son of heaven all the way down to commoners, all must take cultivating the self as root. It is impossible for the branches to be in order while the root is in chaos. It should never be that what is important is treated lightly while what is light is treated as important. This is called knowing the root. This is called the utmost of knowing. (TX2)

The *Greatest Learning* portrays a continuum in which power gradually grows, starting in immediate relationships and extending to the whole world. This extension begins with self-cultivation. The remainder of the text explains each step of this progression.

Cultivating authentic reactions

The explanation starts with making one's intentions authentic. That is the pivot of the whole process. The word I've translated as "authentic" is *chéng* 誠. In normal usage, it means to be genuinely so. As a philosophical term, it has connotations of integrity, in the sense of being fully integrated, and of creativity or the power to support the development of things. The *Greatest Learning* illustrates it with a line we have already seen in chapter 2:

What is called making one's intention authentic and avoiding self-deception is like being disgusted by a disgusting smell or like loving those with alluring appearances. This is called being satisfied in oneself. (TX3)

Recall smelling a horrible smell. That one moment of experience unites perception, evaluation, and action. That is, as we become aware of the smell we simultaneously are disgusted by it and we recoil from it. That is what it means to authentically detest something. Mengzi describes similar experiences. When we see a child in danger, the very perception of that event fills us with anxiety and prompts us into action. The same goes for seeing the corpse of a parent eaten by insects or contemplating kidnapping a neighbor's daughter. The character translated here as "being disgusted by" and "disgusting" (*wù* or *è* 惡) is the same term found in the sprout of rightness, translated there as "aversion." The problem is that most people react in this authentic way only in extreme or vivid cases. Much of the time, we say and perhaps believe that something is bad and yet we do not have this visceral aversion toward it. That kind of self-deception or inauthenticity prevents us from being fully satisfied. For Mengzi, we must extend the feelings we have in the more extreme cases to those for which we currently lack the feelings.

The passage continues with another marker of authenticity:

Thus, the noble must certainly be cautious when alone. Petty people when relaxing at home do things that are not good; there is nothing they will not do. When they see the noble, with shame they cover up their badness and present their goodness. (TX3)

When our behavior is known to other people, we conform to their expectations. We want other people to think that we are good. That is one of the reasons we will *say* something is good or bad even when we do not *feel* it as good or bad. It is when we are alone that we can recognize our genuine feelings. Mengzi might add two more observations. First, shame is part of the sprout of rightness. The very fact that petty people try to hide their bad actions shows that they still have the sprouts of goodness. Second, it is not just that we do good things in public and bad things in private. It can also be the opposite. It is when we are out in the world that we are lured into pursuing wealth, fame, and success. When alone, we can get a glimpse of the things we truly care about.

The final part of the description points out the difficulties of sustaining deception:

> When people look at them, it is as if they see through to their lungs and liver. So what gain is there in it! This means that authenticity in the center must take form on the outside. Thus, the noble must certainly be cautious when alone. Zengzi said: "What ten eyes look at and what ten fingers point to—how awesome!" As wealth fills the halls, virtue saturates the body, making the heart broad and the body stout. Thus, the noble must certainly make their intentions authentic. (TX3)

Deception sometimes works, but it is difficult to consistently fake emotions. The internal cannot be isolated from the external. For Chinese philosophers, emotions, desires, and physical health are explained through one system of vital energies, *qi*. Integrating the feelings of the heart, the desires of the senses, and the actions of the body has a visible effect. That is how one makes the brightness of virtue shine by resting in the utmost good. The integration of the self leads toward the integration of the broader community as well.

Cultivating proper emotions and caring for the community

We can now turn to the other steps of self-cultivation. Making our intentions authentic is rooted in gaining knowledge:

Those wanting to make their intentions authentic first extended their knowledge to the utmost. The utmost extension of knowledge lies in dealing with things. (TX2)

Neither of these stages is given much explanation in the *Greatest Learning*. We have seen the importance of study and knowledge in chapter 5, but the meaning of "dealing with things," *gé wù* 格物, has been a key point of contention among later Confucians. "Things" (*wù* 物) should be taken in the loose sense that we might say we have "things" to do. The character *gé* 格 has many meanings, but as the root of extending knowledge, it must involve some sense of examining or learning from events in the world. Zhu Xi stresses study and investigation. Since our individual experience is not enough to understand the world, investigating things requires studying history and literature. Study alone, though, does not necessarily lead to authenticity. For the progression to make sense, we must investigate the world as it evokes responses in us. I said earlier that when we examine the self we are really examining the self's engagement with the world. Similarly, investigating the world investigates the self. This focus on the self is emphasized by Wang Yangming. Either way, rooting the whole progression in dealing with things shows that self cultivation is not individualistic. There is no self isolated from personal relationships, responsibilities, and tasks. Attention to the way things evoke our responses and the way our responses change the world is the root from which knowledge extends, and that knowledge leads us to become authentic.

Authenticity lays the foundation for responding appropriately to the world:

When intentions are authentic then the heart is correct. When the heart is correct then the body/self is cultivated.

As we have seen, the key to the cultivation of the whole self or body (*shēn* 身) is the heart. Authenticity comes from the natural reactions of the heart, and it lays the foundation for making the heart correct. With the heart correct, emotions will be appropriate:

> What is meant in saying that cultivating the body/self lies in correcting the heart is this:
> If the self hates or resents something, then it does not attain its correctness;
> If the self is afraid or terrified of something, then it does not attain its correctness;
> If the self loves or enjoys something, then it does not attain its correctness;
> If the self is anxious or troubled about something, then it does not attain its correctness. (TX8)

The biases of the embodied self skew its responses to the world. This passage does not oppose emotions but warns against the way emotions can distort our perceptions. They do that partly by directing our attention, determining what it is that we notice. The explanation continues:

> If the heart is not present to it, then we look but do not see, listen but do not hear, and eat but do not know the flavor. This is why cultivating the self lies in correcting the heart. (TX8)

As discussed in chapter 4, we can exert some indirect control over our emotions by controlling our focus, but our attention isn't simply under our control. When the self has particular things that it resents or fears or loves, those things automatically pull in its attention, shaping how the world itself appears. Someone afraid of spiders will enter a basement noticing where spiders might be, perhaps even seeing a tangle of string as a spider. Someone who likes to be the center of attention will see ways of gaining the spotlight. Cultivating emotions and cultivating attention are two sides of the same project.

Extending influence

It may seem like the progression so far has been on the personal level without any relation to politics, but that is not true. Our emotions are always already involved with the world and with other people. Every stage of self-cultivation is social and thus involves power and relationships. So, it is not that after self-cultivation one starts to take on a broader role in the community but that self-cultivation is what allows us to lead successfully. Leadership is the next step in the progression:

> When the self is cultivated then the community is aligned.

The term for community is *jiā* 家, which can refer to a district but more likely refers to a household or extended family. For most people at the time, their community would have consisted largely of more or less distant relatives. The term I've translated as align is *qí* 齊, which means to even out, bring into line, or harmonize.

There are many reasons why taking a constructive role in our community requires self-cultivation, but the *Greatest Learning* continues with the concern for bias:

> What is meant in saying that aligning the community lies in cultivating the body/self is this:
> People approach what they cherish and love by comparison with themselves;
> They approach what they disdain and detest by comparison with themselves;
> They approach what they revere and hold in awe by comparison with themselves;
> They approach what they mourn and pity by comparison with themselves;
> They approach what they scorn and dismiss by comparison with themselves. Thus, there are few in the world who can recognize

the faults in what they love and recognize the fineness in what they detest. Thus, a saying has it: "No one recognizes the faults of their children; no one recognizes the greatness of their sprouting grain." This is why aligning the community lies in cultivating the embodied self. (TX9)

We encounter the world from our own perspective and our focus determines how the world appears to us. We don't even see the faults in the people we love. No matter how rich, no one views their "sprouting grain" as sufficient. Our evaluations of other people are relative in several ways. They depend on social positions: we love those closest to us; we befriend those like us; we feel awe toward those above us. They also depend on our values and beliefs: we like those who agree with us and dislike those who contradict us. The passage describes what we would now call confirmation bias: we overlook the faults in what we like and the strong points in what we oppose.

Overcoming this tendency lies in correcting the heart and cultivating the self. Without that cultivation, we cannot treat others fairly and we cannot determine who should be given what responsibilities. Bias also inhibits self-cultivation. We learn through our interactions with other people, particularly those around us. As Kongzi says in the *Lunyu*:

When I walk together with two other people, I certainly have a teacher among them. I select their good qualities and follow them and their bad qualities and reform them. (LY 7.22)

Kongzi does not necessarily categorize people as good or bad. Bad people have good points we can learn from, and good people have flaws. In fact, those we see as bad may not be bad at all. They may just be different. Our biases blind us to this complexity. As we have seen, one method for extending our emotions is empathic reciprocity, *shù* 恕. Rather than judge someone by how they relate to our own views, we try to see that other person as having the same standing as we do. Trying to look from the perspective of the other is one way to overcome our own biases. This connection shows how the various stages of the greatest learning are interdependent rather than chronological. Leading in our community depends on correcting the heart but also allows us to further correct our biases.

The progression next takes a big leap from leading one's community to ruling a state:

> When the community is aligned then the state is ordered.

The *Greatest Learning* was not primarily written for princes waiting to become kings. This step is really from taking a leadership role within a community of people with whom we have personal connections to taking a broader role in shaping society. As we would expect, dedication to improving society extends from our community concerns. The explanation begins:

> What is meant in saying that managing a state lies in aligning the community is this: It never happens that one who cannot educate their community will be able to educate other people. Thus, the noble establish education in the state without even going outside their family/community. Filialness is that by which one serves the sovereign; fraternal respect is that by which one serves seniors; parental concern is that by which one moves the masses. The "Announcement of Kang" says: "Like protecting an infant." If the heart authentically seeks it, then even if you miss the target it won't be far off. What woman marries only after she knows how to raise a child! If one community is benevolent, benevolence rises up in the state; if one community is yielding, yielding rises up in the state; if one person is greedy and corrupt, chaos arises in the state. (TX10)

This passage highlights the continuity across the family, community, and society at large. That continuity takes at least three forms.

One line of continuity is in what brings success. Someone who cannot act within their community has even less chance of succeeding in a broader arena. Without self-cultivation through correcting the heart, a person will be driven by their own biases. They will form poor alliances, make bad hiring decisions, and fail to see their own weaknesses. They will attract flatterers and manipulators rather than frank advisers. Those who work with them will either despise them or emulate them, with bad results either way. Such a person might still succeed in the world, perhaps even become leader of a powerful nation. Many people with power are jerks, but that is not success for a Confucian and it will not lead to a happy or fulfilling life. The goal is to have a constructive influence on the world. Why does that depend on starting with the community? Working within our community is difficult because the feedback is immediate. We see how others are affected not just by our decisions but by our way of life. We realize that helping other people is challenging because each person is unique and every context is different. All of this is true for any attempt to change the world, but these difficulties are easier to ignore when those we affect are more distant. That is why one must begin with what is near.

The second point of continuity is in motivation. The feelings that are the sprouts of the virtues are awakened in response to the environment around us. For Mengzi, any normal person will interact with their community through feelings of care, shame and disgust, reverence and deference, and a love of learning. When these feelings are properly cultivated, they naturally lead us to increase our sphere of influence. One paradigm for authentic motivation is caring for a small child. If people only had children after they were sure how to raise them, there would be no children at all. Love for a child drives us to figure out what we need to do. One reason for this effectiveness is that care requires attention to the desires of others. Kong Yingda (574–648), a Confucian scholar from the Tang dynasty, explains:

> It says that in loving this infant, the inner heart is pure and authentic in seeking what the infant desires and wants. Even if one cannot exactly get what it desires, it will not be very far off. It says that getting close to what the infant desires and wants is just like the way of managing other people. (TX10, 1.4)

A good person has this kind of genuine and intense care for other people. Knowledge is important, but extending that motivation is the key point. We will sometimes miss the target, but if we care and pay attention, we will at least get close.

The third point of continuity is in influence. Virtue tends to spread, from individual to individual and from community to community. The second part of the explanation emphasizes this theme:

> Yao and Shun led the world with benevolence and the people followed them. Jie and Zhou led the world with cruelty and the people followed them. If what is ordered contradicts what is loved, the people will not obey. For this reason, the noble must have it in themselves before they seek it in others. They must lack it in themselves before they condemn it in others. If what they hold in themselves is not empathic reciprocity, they can never be a model for others. (TX10)

People are always influencing others and being influenced by them. A leader can influence people by getting them to do what they want, but people are less likely to listen to someone they see as a hypocrite or phony. Moreover, stability and long-term success depend less on getting people to *do* constructive things and more on getting them to *want* to do such things. As Kongzi says:

The noble give form to what is good in other people and not what is bad in them. Petty people do the opposite. (LY 12.16)

We don't just influence people's actions but also their desires, emotions, and ideals. We do this through the example we set in our own actions, and that power increases as we become more and more of a leader. It does not require a political position:

Someone said to Kongzi, "Why are you not engaged in governing?" The master said, "The *Documents* says: 'Filial, only filial, friendly with elders and youngers, extending this into governing.' This, then, also is engaging in governing. Why must there be that active engagement with government?" (LY 2.21)

This attitude toward service is crucial because when power structures are corrupt, it is wrong to participate in them. In that case, one can only act by other means.

In the *Greatest Learning*, one step remains:

When the state is ordered then the world is at peace.

Our actions and concerns need to go to the broadest political context. Kongzi and Mengzi did not have a global perspective, but even they saw that one country could not be secure and prosperous without a stable international order. That is far more obvious now, when the most pressing local issues— inequality, racism, sexism, climate change, poverty—are embedded in global systems of power.

The basis for influencing the world differs little from what is required in the family or state: extend feelings, overcome self-bias, lead by example. The explanation begins:

What is meant in saying that bringing peace to the world lies in managing a state is this: If those above treat the elderly as elders, then the people will rise up in filialness. If those above treat seniors as senior, then the people will rise up in fraternal respect. If those above care for the vulnerable, then the people will not go against it. Using this, the noble have a way of marking and measuring. What one detests in those above, do not use in employing those below. What one detests in those below, do not use in serving those above. What one detests in those ahead do not use in leading those behind; what one detests in those behind, do not use in following those ahead. What one detests on the left, do not use to engage those on the right. What one detests in those on the right, do not use to engage those on the left. This is having a way of marking and measuring. (TX11)

This passage presents several forms of extension. One is seeing the elders of others as like my own, extending feelings of familial concern. Another is seeing others as like oneself, treating them as we would want to be treated, but this passage recognizes the complexity of that process. We are not all the same, nor do we play the same roles. We need to attend not just to what we would want but to what we would want if we were in the same position. So, in managing other people, we should not do the things that we dislike in our boss.

Another version of extension appears with a line from the *Songs*:

The *Songs* says: "Joyful indeed are the noble, the father and mother of the people." Love what the people love and detest what the people detest. This is called being the father and mother of the people. (TX11)

We can't just project our desires onto other people; we need to determine what they want and incorporate that into ourselves. That includes addressing their material needs but also considering that people want to be respected, to have caring relationships, and so on. This extension culminates in caring for those who are vulnerable beyond our own family, community, or state. Kong Yingda explains:

Those people who are vulnerable and weak are neglected and abandoned by other people. If rulers and leaders above can care for the vulnerable and weak without neglecting them, then the people below will learn from them and will not abandon or reject these people. (TX11, 1.2)

World peace

The explanation of bringing peace to the world is the longest in the text and is the only stage that introduces specific policies. The main concern is the distribution of wealth. The *Greatest Learning* says:

Virtue is the root and wealth is the branches. If one neglects the root and embraces the branches, the people will struggle and compete. For this reason, when wealth is concentrated, the people disperse; when wealth is dispersed, the people are concentrated. (TX12)

The Confucians are not opposed to wealth, but when those with power concentrate on accumulating wealth it leads to inequality, instability, strife, and poverty. A direct concern with wealth turns out to be counterproductive: "Do not take benefit as benefit but take rightness as benefit" (TX15). Benefit is good, but it is best attained through an ethical social order.

Early Chinese philosophers did not see poverty as necessary or natural. It results from harmful policies and the unequal distribution of goods. The *Greatest Learning* says that those who draw money from the people to support the elite are worse than robbers. Mengzi says that in good years, the powerful overconsume and waste resources. In bad years, people die (M 1A3). In another passage, he says simply that those with wealth are not benevolent (M 3A3). If those with power and wealth would cultivate simpler pleasures, there would be enough resources for everyone. The *Greatest Learning* explains:

> There is a great way for generating wealth. Let those who generate it be many and those who consume it be few; let those who make it be urgent and those who use it be restrained. In this way, wealth will always be sufficient. The benevolent use wealth to express themselves; the unbenevolent use themselves to express wealth. (TX14)

The *Greatest Learning* distinguishes two ways of relating to wealth. A benevolent person uses wealth to promote the things they most care about, based in the heart. We might think that the unbenevolent person is just selfish, but the text seems to say the opposite. They place their self in service of wealth. Such people are like King Hui of Liang, who sacrificed the people he loved to gain territory he didn't need (M 7B1).

Two passages juxtaposed in the *Lunyu* discuss the problem of distributing wealth. In the first, Zihua is sent on a mission to the state of Qi and requests grain for his mother. Kongzi suggests a month's supply. Zihua asks for more, and Kongzi agrees to a small increase, but in the end, his disciples give Zihua even more. When Kongzi finds out, he scolds them: '

> When Zihua went to Qi, he had fat horses for his carriage and wore light furs. I have heard this: the noble assist the distressed but do not make the rich get richer. (LY 6.4)

That does not mean that one must turn down a salary:

> When Yuan Si became governor, he was given nine hundred measures of grain, but he declined them. The master said, "Don't! May you not give them away to the households in your neighborhood and district?" (LY 6.5)

Given the criticism of Zihua's greed, Yuan Si thinks he is doing something noble in turning down a high salary, but he misses the point. Both passages illustrate the same imperative: the noble help the distressed but do not enrich the rich.

A second key policy related to world peace is meritocracy. The *Greatest Learning* begins with a quotation from the *Documents* that imagines two ministers. One has no exceptional abilities but when he encounters others with abilities he treasures and employs them, as if their skills were his own. The other minister has exceptional skills but is threatened by others, driving them away. The former will bring benefits and the latter will bring danger. A genuine willingness to promote those with talent is more important than any particular ability. Promoting the worthy requires correcting the heart and cultivating the embodied self so as to avoid biased judgments of other people. The text follows the above description with a line attributed to Kongzi in the *Lunyu* (4.3): "This means that only a benevolent person can love other people and detest other people" (TX13). Everyone feels attraction and aversion, love and hate. Only a benevolent person can do so without bias.

A concern with attracting and promoting good people was not particular to the Confucians. One of the central Mohist positions was elevating the worthy (*shàngxián* 尚賢). China had a long tradition of revered ministers like Yi Yin. The ultimate paradigm was Yao, who gave power not to his son but to Shun, the most capable person. Shun did the same in choosing Yu as successor. It was only with Yu that power was passed within the family, founding the Xia dynasty. By the time of Kongzi and Mengzi, much of the work of governing was done by officials and bureaucrats. A crucial part of effective governing was selecting and utilizing talent. The *Greatest Learning* explains:

> To see the worthy but be unable to raise them to office, or to raise them to office but not give them priority—this is negligence. To

see those who are unworthy but not send them away, or to send them away but not far—this is error. (TX13)

Kongzi and Mengzi both sought to take positions as officials and to influence rulers, but their primary role was training those with ability to take up influential positions.

For a meritocratic system to function, education must be open to anyone, regardless of background. Everyone has potential:

> The master said, "Those born later should be held in awe. How do we know that those who come will not be equal to the present? If they have still learned nothing by age forty or fifty, then they are not worthy of awe." (LY 9.23)

Kongzi would accept any student who made a small offering:

> The master said, "From the one bringing a little silk or some cured meat upward, I have never refused instruction to anyone." (LY 7.7)

In another passage, Kongzi's disciples are reluctant to allow in a boy whose village had a bad reputation. Kongzi scolds them, saying that if he purifies himself, he can be accepted regardless of his past (LY 7.29). Mengzi was criticized for a similar reason:

> Mengzi went to the state of Teng and resided in the upper guesthouse. There was a partially woven shoe by the window, and when another guest looked for it they could not find it. Someone asked Mengzi, "Is that what your followers are like—they pilfer?" Mengzi said, "Do you think they follow me in order to steal shoes?" The resident said, "I guess not. But in setting up your teachings, master, you do not chase those who go or refuse those who come. If they come with this heart, they are just accepted." (M 7B30)

Apparently, Mengzi had a reputation for accepting students with dubious backgrounds. He only cared about the sincerity of their intentions.

This final stage of leadership is specifically connected to bringing peace, *píng* 平, but the *Greatest Learning* itself says nothing directly about avoiding war. Peace follows naturally when the system distributes wealth and positions fairly and when people have what they need. War comes from scarcity and injustice. Mengzi explains this connection explicitly in many passages. If people are formed through their environments, then desperate conditions form desperate people. That follows from the embodied nature of our existence. As Mengzi says, hunger distorts the preferences of the heart in the same way that it distorts our taste in food (M 7A27). Bad conditions lead to bad actions, setting off a vicious cycle. Mengzi explains to Duke Wen of Teng, the ruler who asked Mengzi for advice about funerals:

> The people have a way: those who have a steady livelihood have steady hearts. Those who lack a steady livelihood lack steady hearts. If they lack a steady heart, in dissolution, corruption, deviance, and excess, there will be nothing that they will not do. To set a pitfall that drops them into crime, and then to follow that up by punishing them—this is to entrap the people. When there is a benevolent person in power, how can there be the entrapment of the people! Thus, a worthy sovereign must be respectful and frugal, treat subordinates with propriety, and take from the people with a regulated system. Yang Hu said, "Those for wealth are not benevolent; those for benevolence are not wealthy." (M 3A3)

In desperate situations, people will break laws, using almost any means to stay alive. Rather than ease their suffering, the usual response is something like a war on crime or a campaign for law and order. This adds injustice to injustice, as the people are made desperate and then punished for the actions that naturally follow.

The crackdown on lawbreaking only increases the desperation. In a more positive moment, Mengzi describes what happens when people have what they need:

> The people cannot live without water and fire, yet if you knock at a person's gate in the evening, seeking water or fire, no one will refuse to give it, because there is enough. Sagely people manage the world so that beans and grains are had like water and fire. When beans and grains are like water and fire, how could there be those among the people who are unbenevolent? (M 7A23)

As Mengzi says elsewhere, in years of plenty the people are mostly good and in years of scarcity they are mostly bad (M 6A7). Their natural dispositions are the same, but they react to different environments, just as barley grows differently in different settings.

Power and the limits of government

In the Confucian ideal, the best people should be the most powerful people. No one thinks that is actually the case. The Confucians responded to this reality with a two-pronged strategy: persuade those with power to become better people and persuade good people to seek more power. The progression of the *Greatest Learning* reads in either direction and the same message applies at all levels: "From the son of heaven all the way down to commoners, all must take cultivating the self as root." If you happen to be king, realize that success depends on treating your community well, which depends on correcting your biases, which depends on making your intentions authentic. If you are a regular person making progress in cultivating virtue, work to be a more effective leader, extending your influence in the community and beyond.

Many of the Confucians traveled and tried to persuade rulers to take up their principles, but they were most concerned and had the most success with the bottom-up approach. The real audience of these texts was not a handful of kings but the *shi* 士, people of some talent and education. The goal is to bring them into public service and action. That is where Confucianism remains most relevant politically. This contribution gets lost in the standard divisions between "moral philosophy" and "political philosophy," but that will be true of any philosophical way of life dedicated to social change. No fundamental difference exists between the way a good person relates to those around them and how a good person holds a "political" position. Kongzi and Mengzi rarely had official power.

The belief that good people gain more influence might seem like wishful thinking, a desperate attempt to maintain hope in bad times, but Mengzi's understanding of power is less top-down than the presence of kings and lords suggests. The foundation of power lies with the people. This belief goes back to early conceptions of *tiānmìng* 天命, the Mandate of Heaven. The success of sage kings like Yao or Tang was not attributed to their military prowess but rather their virtue and goodness. The term I have been translating as virtue is *dé* 德. In the earliest documents, *de* is a power that comes from heaven in response to virtuous conduct and reverence toward ancestors. If a leader has *de*, the people will follow along and the result will be harmony and prosperity.

In its explanation of bringing peace to the world, the *Greatest Learning* invokes this history as a warning:

The *Songs* says: "Before Yin [i.e., the Shang dynasty] had lost power, it was as if they matched with the High Lord (*Shàngdì* 上帝). Take the Yin as a mirror: maintaining the mandate is not easy." The way is to attain the masses and then you attain the state. If you lose the masses, then you lose the state. Therefore, the noble are most conscientious about virtue. If there is virtue then there are other people; if there are other people then there is land; if there is land then there is wealth; if there is wealth then there is effectiveness. (TX12)

For Confucians of the Warring States period, the power of virtue is not explained by heaven but by natural human dispositions. If those in charge love what the people love and detest what the people detest, then the people will support them. Care for the people requires ensuring that their basic needs are met, but people want more than material things. Everyone has what they love more than life and detest more than death. People want a system that incorporates caring relationships and lets them have certain things they would not do. They have a sense of dignity and don't want to be bullied or humiliated.

Abuse of power is destabilizing. Several passages in the *Mengzi* rationalize violence against the ruling classes (e.g., 1B12). Rebellion results from natural human reactions to being poor and exploited, just as crime is a natural expression of human beings put into desperate conditions. In both cases, the cause and the blame lie in the power structures and those who dominate them. In one passage, Mengzi goes so far as to justify a coup:

> King Xuan of Qi said, "Tang banished Jie and King Wu attacked Zhou—is it so?" Mengzi replied, "In what has been transmitted, it is so."
>
> The king said, "Can a minister kill his sovereign?"
>
> Mengzi said, "One who robs benevolence is called a robber; one who robs rightness is called cruel. A cruel robbing person is called a commoner. I have heard of the execution of that commoner Zhou. I have never heard of killing a sovereign." (M 1B8)

This passage plays on an idea that Kongzi describes as "correct naming" (*zhèngmíng* 正名): someone named a father should act like a father, a son should act like a son, and a king should act like a king (LY 12.11). That is easier to convey in classical Chinese, where the same character acts as the noun and the verb: a father fathers (*fù fù*

父父), a son sons (zǐ zǐ 子子). Mengzi turns this doctrine in a radical direction—if you are not acting like a king, you are not really a king, and if you act like a bandit, you are a bandit, regardless of your official title. One owes no loyalty to a "king" who acts like a bandit, because such a person is not really a king at all. The point, though, goes even deeper. Abusive kings like Jie and Zhou lose the power that goes along with the position of being king. It is not just that they no longer deserve the title of king. In some sense, they no longer have the power.

These stories explaining the changes in dynasties point toward two distinct sources of power. One is the overt power that comes from being a king or being very rich. The other is the power of virtue itself. That kind of power is open to anyone.

The distribution of power is further complicated by the fact that power does not just control what we do but also shapes what we are—our ideas, values, emotions, and desires take form through interaction with our social environment. A good system strengthens the feelings of the heart by using natural feelings of care, shame, and reverence. A bad system attempts to control people through the fear of punishment and lure of material rewards. That just makes them greedier and sneakier:

> The master said, "If the people are led [dao] by governmental power and kept in line through punishments, they will avoid them but have no shame. If they are led by virtue and kept in line through propriety, they will have a sense of shame and also will be correct." (LY 2.3)

This contrast in ways of leading others expresses the deeper contrast between the concern for benefit and the concern for virtue, which itself extends the distinction between the heart and the other senses. The sense of shame is the sprout of rightness. For Mengzi, all have this sprout. That makes it possible to have a peaceful and stable social order without the threat of violence.

This interplay of internal and external is fundamental to leadership at all levels. Everyone affects other people and is affected by them. Members of a community will tend toward sharing the same goals and methods. Those with leadership positions have more influence. A greedy and ruthless leader will make those around them greedy and ruthless. A caring and respectful leader will make those around them caring and respectful. The influence is the same either way, but the results differ. If Mengzi can be described as optimistic, his optimism lies here. A leader who makes those they depend on greedier and more ruthless will be undermined by those very people. Prioritizing benefit inevitably leads to conflict, since the limits of what can be attained are always narrower than the limits of greed. The people in such a community will be at cross-purposes. Leading by virtue has the opposite result. Having more people care more about each other makes that community stronger. The whole Confucian way of life described in this book can be seen as a project of greater and greater integration and harmonization. The individual extends the feelings of the heart and trains the desires of the other senses so that they rarely conflict. Such a person authentically desires what is good. That cultivation naturally integrates itself with the broader community. Ideally, this process of integration leads to world peace.

That full vision of integration must include Mengzi's belief that the heart expresses dispositions that derive from nature itself. It is not just that a greedy or ruthless leader will cultivate the kind of people who ultimately undermine him. If Mengzi is right, there is something inherently unsatisfying about a life driven by greed and competition. People want to have caring relationships, they want to avoid what they find shameful and disgusting, and they want to feel and demonstrate respect toward others. These sprouts are fragile. They can be weakened, perhaps destroyed, but that is not what most people want. Leading through virtue builds a constructive community by using feelings that come naturally to human beings.

Working with those feelings is like going with the flow of water or letting plants naturally grow.

Mengzi explicitly links heaven to authenticity:

> For this reason, authenticity is the way of heaven; to attend to becoming authentic is the way of humanity. To reach the utmost authenticity and not set others into motion—that never happens. In lacking authenticity, one can never move others. (M 4A12)

The "way of heaven" refers to cultivating virtues through our heaven-endowed dispositions. It is the way that integrates what we truly want with the rest of our desires and the world around us. Authenticity aligns us with the efficacy of the natural world. The *Zhongyong* describes the culmination of this power:

> Only those in the world with utmost authenticity can fully express their natural dispositions. Those who can fully express their natural dispositions can fully draw out the natural dispositions of other people. Those who can fully draw out the natural dispositions of other people then can fully draw out the natural dispositions of other things. Those who can fully draw out the natural dispositions of other things can thereby participate in the transformative nurturing of heaven and earth, and thus they can form a triad with heaven and earth. (ZY22)

The power of authenticity involves a creativity that channels and joins with the forces of nature. Forming a triad with heaven and earth involves creating a sustainable relationship with the natural world, but it also expresses a spiritual or religious vision. It culminates in something like the Daoist idea of *wuwei*, nonaction:

> The master said, "One who governs by virtue is like the north star—it dwells in its place and the masses of stars revolve around it." (LY 2.1)

The Confucians are not naïve in taking this goal as readily attainable. They hope for it, but no one knows if it will ever be achieved:

> Zilu passed the night at Stone Door and the gate keeper said, "Where do you come from?" Zilu said, "From the house of Kong." The gate keeper replied, "Isn't he the one who knows it cannot be yet does it anyway?" (LY 14.38)

This seemingly pessimistic account must be read alongside another description of Kongzi, one he gives of himself:

> The Duke of She asked Zilu about Kongzi. Zilu did not reply. The master said: "Why did you not say to him—he is the kind of person who in his eagerness forgets to eat, whose joy makes him forget worries, and who does not recognize that old age is approaching?" (LY 7.19)

Regardless of the prospects of success, Kongzi is happy, happy because he is doing what he really wants.

Notes

Introduction

1. Ch. 28; Sun Yirang 孫詒讓, *Mozi Xiangu* 墨子閒詁 (Beijing: Zhonghua Shuju, 2001), 214–216. For an alternate English translation, along with the Chinese text, see Ian Johnston, trans., *The Mozi: A Complete Translation* (New York: Columbia University Press, 2010), 273.

2. Yuri Pines, *Envisioning Eternal Empire: Chinese Political Thought of the Warring States Era* (Honolulu: University of Hawai'i Press, 2009), 117.

3. Kurtis Hagen and Steve Coutinho, ed. and trans., *Philosophers of the Warring States Period: A Sourcebook in Chinese Philosophy* (Peterborough: Broadview, 2018), 45–46.

4. For a critical study of philosophy as a contemporary academic discipline, see Robert Frodeman and Adam Briggle, *Socrates Tenured: The Institutions of 21st Century Philosophy* (New York: Rowman & Littlefield, 2016).

5. Speaking of the Hellenistic and Roman periods, Hadot explains: "philosophy was a mode of existing-in-the-world, which had to be practiced at each instant, and the goal of which was to transform the whole of the individual's life" (Pierre Hadot, *Philosophy as a Way of Life: Spiritual Exercises from Socrates to Foucault*, trans. Michael Chase [Malden: Blackwell Publishing, 1995], 265).

6. Once Buddhism came into China from India, this become a point of criticism between the two schools. For an example, see the debates in A. Charles Muller, *Korea's Great Buddhist-Confucian Debate: The Treatises of Chŏng Tojŏn (Sambong) and Hamhŏ Tŭkt'ong (Kihwa)* (Honolulu: University of Hawai'i Press, 2015).

7. Xu Fuguan, *Zhongguo renxinglun shi* 中國人性論史 (Taibei: Taiwan Shangwu Yinshuguan, 1969), 20–24.

8. "Records of Yueyang Tower" (*Yueyang Louji* 岳陽樓記) in Fan Zhongyan, *Fan Zhongyan quanji* 范仲淹全集 (Chengdu: Sichuan Daxue Chubanshe, 2002), 195.

9. For an interesting account of how Yang Zhu has been perceived across Chinese history, see Carine M. G. DeFoort, "Five Visions of Yang Zhu

before He Became a Philosopher," *Asian Studies* 8, no. 2 (2020): 235–256, https://doi.org/10.4312/as.2020.8.2.235-256.

10. For an excellent study of the philosophy of the *Mozi*, see Chris Fraser, *The Philosophy of the Mòzǐ: The First Consequentialists* (New York: Columbia University Press, 2016).

11. The best translation of the *Zhuangzi* is Brook Ziporyn, *Zhuangzi: The Complete Writings* (Indianapolis: Hackett Publishing, 2020). For a recent and interesting interpretation of the text, see Hans-Georg Moeller and Paul D'Ambrosio, *Genuine Pretending: On the Philosophy of the Zhuangzi* (New York: Columbia University Press, 2017).

12. Burton Watson, trans., *The Complete Works of Chuang Tzu* (New York: Columbia University Press, 1968); Ziporyn, *Zhuangzi*.

13. The most significant collection was unearthed in 1993 near Guodian 郭店, in what is now Hubei province. The texts were buried around 300 BCE in what was then the state of Chu. Another significant collection of philosophical materials was purchased by the Shanghai Museum in 1994. These texts were looted and their original location is unknown, but they are thought to come from roughly the same time and place as the Guodian bamboo texts. An even larger collection of Warring States bamboo strips were acquired by Tsinghu University in 2008, once again coming from an unknown source. The Guodian texts have been translated by Scott Cook and published, along with the Chinese texts and extensive notes, in *The Bamboo Texts of Guodian*, 2 vols. (Ithaca: Cornell University East Asia Program, 2012).

14. For a good range of interpretations of the *Mengzi*, I recommend James Behuniak Jr., *Mencius on Becoming Human* (Albany: SUNY, 2004), Kwong-loi Shun, *Mencius and Early Chinese Thought* (Stanford: Stanford University Press, 1997), and Bryan Van Norden, *Virtue Ethics and Consequentialism in Early Chinese Philosophy* (Cambridge: Cambridge University Press, 2007).

Chapter 1

1. Voltaire, *Toleration and Other Essays*, trans. Joseph McCabe (New York: G.P. Putnam's Sons, 1912; reprint in The Online Library of Liberty), 134, https://oll.libertyfund.org/title/mccabe-toleration-and-other-essays.

2. Voltaire, *Toleration*, 136.

3. Albert Camus, *The Myth of Sisyphus and Other Essays*, trans. Justin O'Brien (New York: Vintage Books, 1955), 21.

4. The text is known as the *Shangshu* 尚書 (*Shang Documents*) or *Shujing* 書 經 (*Classic of Documents*). I quote these lines from Mengzi, who attributes them to the "Great Declaration" (Taishi 太誓) chapter.

5. "Yu wu zheng" 雨無正, Mao number 194, based on the Chinese text in Zhou Zhenfu 周振甫, *Shijing yizhu* 詩經譯注 (Beijing: Zhonghua Shuju, 2002).

6. "Zhan yang" 瞻卬, Mao number 264, based on the Chinese text in Zhou, *Shijing yizhu*.

7. The *Laozi* is cited by chapter number in the traditional ordering. The Chinese text is based on the Mawangdui B manuscript as reconstructed in Gao Ming 高明, *Boshu Laozi jiaozhu* 帛書老子校註 (Beijing: Zhonghua shuju, 1996).

8. Attempts to explain the emergence of things in the world have been found among recently excavated bamboo texts, suggesting it was a common concern at the time. In addition to the *Laozi*, there are three other cosmogony texts: *The Great Oneness Generates Water* (Taiyi sheng shui 太一生水), *Constancy First* (Hengxian 恆先), and *All Things Flow into Form* (Fanwu liuxing 凡物流行). For an overview of the ideas in these texts, see Franklin Perkins, "The *Laozi* and the Cosmogonic Turn in Classical Chinese Philosophy," *Frontiers of Philosophy in China* 11, no. 2 (2016): 185–205.

9. *Taiyi sheng shui*, slips 1–8; Cook, *Bamboo Texts of Guodian*, 343–348. Cook includes a full English translation.

10. For a thorough study of yinyang thinking, see Robin R. Wang, *Yinyang: The Way of Heaven and Earth in Chinese Thought and Culture* (Cambridge: Cambridge University Press, 2012).

11. For an interesting and accessible discussion of the use of nature metaphors in early Chinese thought, see Sarah Allan, *The Way of Water and the Sprouts of Virtue* (Albany: SUNY, 1997). For a broader discussion of metaphor in Chinese philosophy, see Sarah A. Mattice, *Metaphor and Metaphilosophy: Philosophy as Combat, Play, and Aesthetic Experience* (Lanham, MD: Lexington Books, 2014), 1–19.

12. Ch. 20; Chen Qiyou 陳奇猷, ed., *Hanfeizi Xin Jiaozhu* 韓非子新校注 (Shanghai: Shanghai Guji Chubanshe, 2000), 421. For an English translation, see Sarah A. Queen, "Han Feizi and the Old Master: A Comparative Analysis and Translation of *Han Feizi* Chapter 20, 'Jie Lao', and Chapter 21, 'Yu Lao,'" in *Dao Companion to the Philosophy of Han Fei*, ed. Paul R. Goldin (Dordrecht: Springer, 2013), 197–256.

13. Ch. 18; Guo Qingfan 郭慶藩, *Zhuangzi jishi* 莊子集釋 (Beijing: Zhonghua Shuju, 1978), 614–615; cf. Ziporyn, *Zhuangzi*, 145–146.

14. *Yucong, yi* (語叢一), slip 98; Cook, *Bamboo Texts of Guodian*, 821.
15. Roger T. Ames, *Confucian Role Ethics: A Vocabulary* (Hong Kong: Chinese University Press, 2011), 154.
16. Ch. 2; Guo, *Zhuangzi jishi*, 93; cf, Ziporyn, *Zhuangzi*, 18–19.
17. Ch. 17; Guo, *Zhuangzi jishi*, 603–605; cf. Ziporyn, *Zhuangzi*, 141.

Chapter 2

1. *Apology* 92a–b, trans. G. M. A. Grube, in John Cooper and D. S. Hutchinson, eds., *Plato: Complete Works* (Indianapolis: Hackett Publishing, 1997).
2. For a sample of her work, see Anne Dufourmantelle, *In Praise of Risk*, trans. Steven Miller (New York: Fordham University Press, 2019).
3. Zhang Zai 張載, *Zhang Zai ji* 張載集 (Beijing: Zhonghua Shuju, 1978), 62.
4. *Liu de* (六德), slip 26; Cook, *Bamboo Texts of Guodian*, 786, 791.
5. *Yu cong, yi*, slips 18–21; Cook, *Bamboo Texts of Guodian*, 822–823.
6. See Book I, ch. 3 of John Locke, *An Essay Concerning Human Understanding*, ed. Peter H. Nidditch (Oxford: Oxford University Press, 1975).
7. The example occurs in a commentary to the *Five Conducts* (Wuxing 五行) text found at Mawangdui. I follow the Chinese text in Pang Pu 龐樸, *Zhubo* Wuxing *pian jiaozhu ji yanjiu*竹帛《五行》篇校注及研究 (Taibei: Wanjuanlou, 2000). For an English translation, see Mark Csikszentmihalyi, *Material Virtue: Ethics and the Body in Early China* (Leiden: Brill, 2004), 23.3.6–7.
8. Ch. 23; Wang Xianqian 王先謙, *Xunzi jijie* 荀子集解 (Beijing: Zhonghua Shuju, 1988), 437. For an English translation, see Eric L. Hutton, *Xunzi: The Complete Text* (Princeton: Princeton University Press, 2016), 249.
9. *Wu xing* (五行), slips 36–37; Cook, *Bamboo Texts of Guodian*, 510–511.
10. The phrase "like protecting a child" appears in the "Announcement of Kang" (Kang Gao 康誥) chapter of the *Documents*. Its use in the "Greatest Learning" (TX10) is discussed later, in chapter 8.
11. Ch. 5; Guo, *Zhuangzi jishi*, 190–191; cf. Ziporyn, *Zhuangzi*, 46.

Chapter 3

1. *The Bhagavad-Gita: Krishna's Counsel in Time of War*, trans. Barbara Stoller Miller (New York: Bantam Books, 1986), chapter 2, stanza 37.

2. "Adittapariyaya Sutta: The Fire Sermon" (SN IV, 19), trans. Ñanamoli Thera, *Access to Insight* (BCBS Edition), June 13, 2010, http://www.accesstoinsight.org/tipitaka/sn/sn35/sn35.028.nymo.html.

3. Marcus Aurelius, *Meditations with Selected Correspondence*, trans. Robin Hard (Oxford: Oxford World Classics, 2011), 8.48.

4. He Ning 何寧, *Huainanzi Jishi* 淮南子集釋 (Beijing: Zhonghua Shuju, 1988), 61–63. For an alternate English translation, see *The Huainanzi: A Guide to the Theory and Practice of Government in Early Han China*, trans. John S. Major, Sarah A. Queen, Andrew Seth-Meyer, and Harold D. Roth (New York: Columbia University Press, 2010), 1.14.

5. Epictetus, *The Handbook*, trans. Nicholas White (Indianapolis: Hackett Publishing, 1983), section 28.

6. Ch. 6; Guo, *Zhuangzi jishi*, 243; cf. Ziporyn, *Zhuangzi*, 56.

7. Ch. 6; Guo, *Zhuangzi jishi*, 228–229; cf. Ziporyn, *Zhuangzi*, 54.

8. Ch. 14; Guo, *Zhuangzi jishi*, 522; cf. Ziporyn, *Zhuangzi*, 124.

9. For an insightful discussion of this point and of Confucian views of mourning, see Amy Olberding, "Slowing Death Down: Mourning in the *Analects*," in *Confucius Now: Contemporary Encounters with the Analects*, ed. David Jones (LaSalle, IL: Open Court Press, 2008), 137–149.

10. Ch. 28; Guo, *Zhuangzi jishi*, 982; cf. Ziporyn, *Zhuangzi*, 235.

11. For an accessible overview of various early Chinese philosophers' views of *wuwei*, along with an analysis in terms of contemporary psychology, see Edward Slingerland, *Trying Not to Try: Ancient China, Modern Science, and the Power of Spontaneity* (New York: Broadway Books, 2015).

12. Ch. 21; Wang, *Xunzi jijie*, 403; cf. Hutton, *Xunzi*, 231–232.

Chapter 4

1. Immanuel Kant, *Foundations of the Metaphysics of Morals*, trans. Lewis Beck White (New York: Macmillan, 1990), 15.

2. Some of the ideas in this chapter are discussed further in Franklin Perkins, "Mengzi, Emotion, and Autonomy," *Journal of Chinese Philosophy* 29, no. 2 (June 2002): 207–227.

3. One might think the proper conclusion would be to stop eating meat. Mengzi either thinks that is impossible or is improper. He does not explain why. For a Buddhist criticism of Confucianism on this point, see sections 6–7 of Kihwa's *Exposition of Orthodoxy*, in Muller, *Korea's Great Buddhist-Confucian Debate*, 89–95.

4. Ch. 21; Wang, *Xunzi jijie*, 387; cf. Hutton, *Xunzi*, 224.

5. For a thorough and interesting account of early Chinese views of the senses and their operation, see Jane Geaney, *On the Epistemology of the Senses in Early Chinese Thought* (Honolulu: University of Hawai'i Press, 2002).

6. Translation modified from Philip J. Ivanhoe, trans., *Readings from the Lu-Wang School of Neo-Confucianism* (Indianapolis: Hackett, 2009), 160–161. The passage occurs in the first question of the "Questions on the *Greatest Learning*" (Daxue wen 大學問).

7. Amy Olberding, *Moral Exemplars in the* Analects: *The Good Person Is* That (New York: Routledge, 2012).

8. Augustine, *On Free Choice of the Will*, trans. Thomas Williams (Indianapolis: Hackett, 1993), particularly sections 12–16 of Book One.

9. Henry Rosemont Jr., *Against Individualism: A Confucian Rethinking of the Foundations of Morality, Politics, Family, and Religion* (Lanham: Lexington Books, 2016), 36.

10. *Xing zi ming chu*, slips 1–2; Cook, *Bamboo Texts of Guodian*, 697–700.

11. *Xing zi ming chu*, slip 9; Cook, *Bamboo Texts of Guodian*, 703, 705.

Chapter 5

1. Some of the ideas in this chapters are developed in different ways in Franklin Perkins, "Love of Learning in the *Lun Yu*," *Journal of Chinese Philosophy* 33, no. 4 (December 2006): 505–517, and "The Sprouts of Wisdom and the Love of Learning in *Mengzi*," in *Liebe—Ost und West/Love in Eastern and Western Philosophy*, eds. Hans-Georg Möller and Günter Wohlfart (Berlin: Parerga Verlag, 2007), 89–98.

2. See Plato's *Phaedrus* (particularly 249c–252c) and *Symposium* (204a–212c), trans. Alexander Nehamas and Paul Woodruff, in Cooper and Hutchinson, *Plato*.

3. *Apology* 38a, trans. Grube, in Cooper and Hutchinson, *Plato*.

4. John Cottingham, Robert Stoothoff, and Dugold Murdoch, eds. and trans., *The Philosophical Writings of Descartes*, Vol. 2 (Cambridge: Cambridge University Press, 1985), 12.

5. Locke, *Essay Concerning Human Understanding*, book I, chapter 5, section 25.

6. Philip J. Ivanhoe, *Confucian Reflections: Ancient Wisdom for Modern Times* (New York: Routledge, 2013), 8–9. Ivanhoe provides a general defense of tradition from a Confucian perspective (1–16).

7. Ch. 1; Wang, *Xunzi jijie*, 4; cf. Hutton, *Xunzi*, 2.

8. Ch. 1; Wang, *Xunzi jijie*, 2–3; cf. Hutton, *Xunzi*, 1.

9. Ch. 17; Wang, *Xunzi jijie*, 317; cf. Hutton, *Xunzi*, 179–180.

10. The bamboo strip is damaged here.

11. *Yucong, yi*, slips 42–43, 38–39, 44, 36–37, 40–41; Cook, *Bamboo Texts of Guodian*, 835–836.

12. See Ji Xusheng, 季旭昇ed., *Shanghai Bowuguan zang Zhanguo Chuzhujian I duben* 上海博物館藏戰國楚竹簡 (I) 讀本 (Taibei: Wanjuanlou Tushu Fufen, 2004).

13. See Ji Xusheng, 季旭昇ed., *Shanghai Bowuguan zang Zhanguo Chuzhujian III duben* 上海博物館藏戰國楚竹簡 (III) 讀本 (Taibei: Wanjuanlou Tushu Fufen, 2005).

14. The passing wise man is said to be Zigong, the disciple of Kongzi we have encountered several times. His suggestion of new technology, though, is not typical for a Confucian, and the whole story is probably fictional.

15. Ch. 12; Guo, *Zhuangzi jishi*, 433–434; cf. Ziporyn, *Zhuangzi*, 104.

16. Farai Chideya, "Philosophers Don't Get Much Respect, But Their Earnings Don't Suck," *Five Thirty Eight*, November 11, 2015 (https://fivethirtyeight.com/features/philosophers-dont-get-much-respect-but-their-earnings-dont-suck/#:~:text=And%20when%20it%20comes%20to,from%20entry%20to%20mid%2Dcareer).

17. See Frodegman and Briggle, *Socrates Tenured*, 13–45.

18. The line appears in the *Chuan xi lu* 傳習錄, section 116. For a translation, see Wing-tsit Chan, trans., *Instructions for Practical Living and Other Neo-Confucian Writings by Wang Yang-Ming* (New York: Columbia University Press, 1963), 73.

19. "Cula-Malunkyovada Sutta: The Shorter Instructions to Malunkya" (MN I, 426), trans. Thanissaro Bhikkhu, *Access to Insight* (BCBS Edition), November 30, 2013 (http://www.accesstoinsight.org/tipitaka/mn/mn.063.than.html).

20. Ch. 1; Wang, *Xunzi jijie*, 14; cf. Hutton, *Xunzi*, 5.

Chapter 6

1. For accessible interpretations and defenses of the contemporary relevance of Confucian propriety, see Ivanhoe, *Confucian Reflections*, 31–58; Michael Puett and Christina Gross-loh, *The Path: What Chinese Philosophers Can Teach Us about the Good Life* (New York: Simon & Schuster, 2016), 23–54; and Amy Olberding, *The Wrong of Rudeness: Learning Modern Civility from Ancient Chinese Philosophy* (Oxford: Oxford University Press, 2019).

2. For discussions of the philosophical significance of music in early China, see Erica Brindley, *Music, Cosmology, and the Politics of Harmony in Early China* (Albany: SUNY, 2013); So Jeong Park, "Sound, Tone, and Music in Early China: The Philosophical Foundation for Chinese Sound Culture," in *Inter-culturality and Philosophic Discourse*, edited by Yolaine Escande, Vincent Shen, and Chenyang Li (Cambridge: Cambridge Scholars Publishing, 2013), 271–290; and Meilin Chinn, "Representing the Great in Music," *Philosophy East and West* 71, no. 1 (2021).

3. *Yucong, er* (語叢二), slip 1; Cook, *Bamboo Texts of Guodian*, 849.

4. Ch. 20; Wang, *Xunzi jijie*, 379; cf. Hutton, *Xunzi*, 218.

5. Ch. 17; Wang, *Xunzi jijie*, 316; cf. Hutton, *Xunzi*, 179–180.

6. *Xing zi ming chu*, slips 18–19; Cook, *Bamboo Texts of Guodian*, 712–715.

7. *Xing zi ming chu*, slip 23; Cook, *Bamboo Texts of Guodian*, 715–719.

8. Ch. 19; Wang, *Xunzi jijie*, 372; cf. Hutton, *Xunzi*, 212.

9. Ch. 19; Wang, *Xunzi jijie*, 376; cf. Hutton, *Xunzi*, 215.

10. *Xing zi ming chu*, slips 24–27; Cook, *Bamboo Texts of Guodian*, 716–720. My reconstruction of the Chinese text here differs from that of Cook on several points. In reading this passage, I am grateful to help from Ding Sixin.

11. Micheal Puett, "Ritual and Ritual Obligations: Perspectives on Normativity from Classical China," *The Journal of Value Inquiry* 49, no. 4 (2015): 543–550. For a more accessible account, see chapter 3 of Puett and Gross-loh, *The Path*, 23–54.

12. *Xing zi ming chu*, slip 36; Cook, *Bamboo Texts of Guodian*, 726–728.

13. Ch. 19; Wang, *Xunzi jijie*, 355; cf. Hutton, *Xunzi*, 204.

14. For a thorough and subtle study of harmony in Confucianism, see Chenyang Li, *The Confucian Philosophy of Harmony* (New York: Routledge, 2014).

Chapter 7

1. Amy Olberding describes the *Analects* as a moral manual that "provides a guide for living, serving as a handbook of sorts that can assist anyone who wonders what to do, how to feel, or how to think about the circumstances, people, and events of her life" (Olberding, *Moral Exemplars*, 2). The same would apply to the *Mengzi*.

2. Stephan Bodian, "Simple in Means, Rich in Ends: An Interview with Arne Naess," in *Deep Ecology for the Twenty-First Century: Readings on the Philosophy and Practice of the New Environmentalism*, ed. George Sessions (Boulder: Shambhala Press, 1999), 36.

3. Ch. 18; Wang, *Xunzi jijie*, 324; cf. Hutton, *Xunzi*, 198.

4. *Crito* 44c–d, trans. Grube, in Cooper and Hutchinson, *Plato*.

5. The discussion is in the "Models of benevolence and rightness" chapter of the *Chunqiu fanlu* 春秋繁露. The authorship of the chapter is uncertain but usually attributed to Dong Zhongshu. For an English translation, see Sarah A. Queen and John S. Major, trans., *Luxuriant Gems of the Spring and Autumn* (New York: Columbia University Press, 2016), 29.1.

6. *Lu Mu Gong wen Zisi* (鲁穆公問子思), slips 1–2; Cook, *Bamboo Texts of Guodian*, 425–426.

7. A similar explanation appears in *Lunyu* 13.21.

Chapter 8

1. See Simon Kow, *China in Early Enlightenment Political Thought* (New York: Routledge, 2017), 38n6.

2. For a broader study of Leibniz's interests in China, see Franklin Perkins, *Leibniz and China: A Commerce of Light* (Cambridge: Cambridge University Press, 2004). For Bayle's views and a more critical take on Leibniz, see Kow, *China in Early Enlightenment Political Thought*.

3. Daniel Cook and Henry Rosemont Jr., eds. and trans., *Gottfried Wilhelm Leibniz: Writings on China* (Indianapolis: Open Court, 1994), 48. Louis XIV revoked the Edict of Nantes in 1685. Kang Xi issued the Edict of Toleration in 1692.

4. Haun Saussy, *Great Walls of Discourse and Other Adventures in Cultural China* (Cambridge, MA: Harvard University Asia Center, 2002), 17. The Chinese source is *A Treatise for Removing Doubts* (*Dài yí piān* 代疑篇). Saussy comments: "If this little dialogue had become the foundation for East–West cultural exchange, we might now be in the habit of contrasting Chinese free enterprise and liberty of information with European despotism" (Saussy, *Great Walls of Discourse*, 19).

5. An immense amount has been written on Confucian political philosophy in the past few decades. For an overview, see Sor-hoon Tan, "Democracy in Confucianism," *Philosophy Compass* 7 (2012): 293–303, and Stephen C. Angle, *Contemporary Confucian Political Philosophy* (Cambridge, UK: Polity, 2012). For a roundtable discussion among a number of prominent scholars involved with reviving Confucian political philosophy, see Stephen C. Angle, "The Future of Confucian Political Philosophy," *Comparative Philosophy* 9, no. 1 (2018): 47–87.

6. For an interesting explanation of this process of depoliticization with application to China, see Wang Hui, "Depoliticized Politics: From East to West," in *The End of Revolution: China and the Limits of Modernity* (New York: Verso, 2009), 3–18.

7. For an insightful criticism of the link between individualism and politics from the perspective of Confucian philosophy, see Rosemont, *Against Individualism*.

8. Thomas Hobbes, *Leviathan*, ed. C. B. Macpherson (New York: Penguin, 1985), part I, ch. 13, 185–186.

9. On this point, see Sin Yee Chan, "The Personal Is Political: Confucianism and Liberal Feminism," in *The Politics of Affective Relations: East Asia and Beyond*, eds. Hahm Chiahark and Daniel A. Bell (Lanham: Lexington, 2004), 97–118. See also Ivanhoe, *Confucian Reflections*, 63–67.

10. These layers are now accessible through the English translation of Johnston and Wang, who translate the original text along with multiple commentaries and interpretations. They also include the original Chinese. Ian Johnston and Wang Ping, trans., *Daxue & Zhongyong* (Hong Kong: Chinese University Press, 2012).

Bibliography

"Adittapariyaya Sutta: The Fire Sermon" (SN IV, 19). Translated by Ñanamoli Thera. *Access to Insight* (BCBS Edition), June 13, 2010. http://www.accesstoinsight.org/tipitaka/sn/sn35/sn35.028.nymo.html.

Allan, Sarah. *The Way of Water and the Sprouts of Virtue*. Albany: SUNY, 1997.

Ames, Roger T. *Confucian Role Ethics: A Vocabulary*. Hong Kong: Chinese University Press, 2011.

Ames, Roger T., and David L. Hall, trans. *Focusing the Familiar: A Translation and Philosophical Interpretation of the* Zhongyong. Honolulu: University of Hawai'i Press, 2001.

Ames, Roger T., and Henry Rosemont Jr., trans. *The Analects of Confucius: A Philosophical Translation*. New York: Ballantine Books, 1999.

Angle, Stephen C. *Contemporary Confucian Political Philosophy*. Cambridge, UK: Polity, 2012.

Angle, Stephen C. "The Future of Confucian Political Philosophy." *Comparative Philosophy* 9, no. 1 (2018): 47–87.

Augustine. *On Free Choice of the Will*. Translated by Thomas Williams. Indianapolis: Hackett, 1993.

Aurelius, Marcus. *Meditations with Selected Correspondence*. Translated by Robin Hard. Oxford: Oxford World Classics, 2011.

Behuniak, James, Jr. *Mencius on Becoming Human*. Albany: SUNY, 2004.

The Bhagavad-Gita: Krishna's Counsel in Time of War. Translated by Barbara Stoller Miller. New York: Bantam Books, 1986.

Bodian, Stephan. "Simple in Means, Rich in Ends: An Interview with Arne Naess." In *Deep Ecology for the Twenty-First Century: Readings on the Philosophy and Practice of the New Environmentalism*, edited by George Sessions, 26–36. Boulder: Shambhala Press, 1999.

Brindley, Erica. *Music, Cosmology, and the Politics of Harmony in Early China*. Albany: SUNY, 2013.

Camus, Albert. *The Myth of Sisyphus and Other Essays*. Translated by Justin O'Brien. New York: Vintage Books, 1955.

Chan, Sin Yee. "The Personal Is Political: Confucianism and Liberal Feminism." In *The Politics of Affective Relations: East Asia and Beyond*, edited by Hahm Chiahark and Daniel A. Bell, 97–118. Lanham: Lexington Books, 2004.

Chan, Wing-tsit, trans. *Instructions for Practical Living and Other Neo-Confucian Writings by Wang Yang-Ming*. New York: Columbia University Press, 1963.

Chen Qiyou 陳奇猷. *Hanfeizi xin jiaozhu* 韓非子新校注. Shanghai: Shanghai Guji Chubanshe, 2000.

Chideya, Farai. "Philosophers Don't Get Much Respect, But Their Earnings Don't Suck." *Five Thirty Eight*, November 11, 2015. https://fivethirtyeight.com/features/philosophers-dont-get-much-respect-but-their-earnings-dont-suck/#:~:text=And%20when%20it%20comes%20to,from%20entry%20to%20mid%2Dcareer.

Chinn, Meilin. "Representing the Great in Music." *Philosophy East and West* 71, no. 1 (2021): 173–192.

Cook, Daniel, and Henry Rosemont Jr., eds. and trans. *Gottfried Wilhelm Leibniz: Writings on China.* Indianapolis: Open Court, 1994.

Cook, Scott, ed. and trans. *The Bamboo Texts of Guodian.* 2 vols. Ithaca: Cornell University East Asia Program, 2012.

Cooper, John, and D. S. Hutchinson, eds. *Plato: Complete Works.* Indianapolis: Hackett Publishing, 1997.

Cottingham, John, Robert Stoothoff, and Dugold Murdoch, eds. and trans. *The Philosophical Writings of Descartes.* Vol 2. Cambridge: Cambridge University Press, 1985.

Csikszentmihalyi, Mark. *Material Virtue: Ethics and the Body in Early China.* Leiden: Brill, 2004.

"Cula-Malunkyovada Sutta: The Shorter Instructions to Malunkya" (MN I, 426). Translated by Thanissaro Bhikkhu. *Access to Insight* (BCBS Edition), November 30, 2013. http://www.accesstoinsight.org/tipitaka/mn/mn.063.than.html.

DeFoort, Carine M. G. "Five Visions of Yang Zhu before He Became a Philosopher." *Asian Studies* 8, no. 2 (2020): 235–256. https://doi.org/10.4312/as.2020.8.2.235-256.

Dufourmantelle, Anne. *In Praise of Risk.* Translated by Steven Miller. New York: Fordham University Press, 2019.

Epictetus. *The Handbook.* Translated by Nicholas White. Indianapolis: Hackett Publishing, 1983.

Fan Zhongyan 范仲淹. *Fan Zhongyan quanji* 范仲淹全集. Chengdu: Sichuan Daxue Chubanshe, 2002.

Fraser, Chris. *The Philosophy of the Mòzǐ: The First Consequentialists.* New York: Columbia University Press, 2016.

Frodeman, Robert, and Adam Briggle. *Socrates Tenured: The Institutions of 21st Century Philosophy.* New York: Rowman & Littlefield, 2016.

Gao Ming 高明. *Boshu Laozi jiaozhu* 帛書老子校註. Beijing: Zhonghua shuju, 1996.

Geaney, Jane. *On the Epistemology of the Senses in Early Chinese Thought.* Honolulu: University of Hawai'i Press, 2002.

Guo Qingfan 郭慶藩. *Zhuangzi jishi* 莊子集釋. Beijing: Zhonghua Shuju, 1978.

Hadot, Pierre. *Philosophy as a Way of Life: Spiritual Exercises from Socrates to Foucault*. Translated by Michael Chase. Malden: Blackwell, 1995.

Hagen, Kurtis, and Steve Coutinho, eds. and trans. *Philosophers of the Warring States Period: A Sourcebook in Chinese Philosophy*. Peterborough, Canada: Broadview, 2018.

He Ning何寧. *Huainanzi jishi* 淮南子集釋. Beijing: Zhonghua Shuju, 1998.

Hobbes, Thomas. *Leviathan*. Edited by C. B. Macpherson. New York: Penguin, 1985.

The Huainanzi: A Guide to the Theory and Practice of Government in Early Han China. Translated by John S. Major, Sarah A. Queen, Andrew Seth-Meyer, and Harold D. Roth. New York: Columbia University Press, 2010.

Hutton, Eric L., trans. *Xunzi: The Complete Text*. Princeton: Princeton University Press, 2016.

Ivanhoe, Philip J. *Confucian Reflections: Ancient Wisdom for Modern Times*. New York: Routledge, 2013.

Ivanhoe, Philip J., ed. and trans. *Readings from the Lu-Wang School of Neo-Confucianism*. Indianapolis: Hackett, 2009.

Ji Xusheng, 季旭昇, ed. *Shanghai Bowuguan zang Zhanguo Chuzhujian I duben*上海博物館藏戰國楚竹簡 (I) 讀本. Taibei: Wanjuanlou Tushu Fufen, 2004.

Ji Xusheng, 季旭昇, ed. *Shanghai Bowuguan zang Zhanguo Chuzhujian III duben*上海博物館藏戰國楚竹簡 (III) 讀本. Taibei: Wanjuanlou Tushu Fufen, 2005.

Jiao Xun焦循. *Mengzi zhengyi*孟子正義. Beijing: Zhonghua Shuju, 1987.

Johnston, Ian, trans. *The Mozi: A Complete Translation*. New York: Columbia University Press, 2010.

Johnston, Ian, and Wang Ping, trans. *Daxue & Zhongyong*. Hong Kong: Chinese University Press, 2012.

Kant, Immanuel. *Foundations of the Metaphysics of Morals*. Translated by Lewis Beck White. New York: Macmillan, 1990.

Kow, Simon. *China in Early Enlightenment Political Thought*. New York: Routledge, 2017.

Li, Chenyang. *The Confucian Philosophy of Harmony*. New York: Routledge, 2014.

Liu Baonan劉寶楠. *Lunyu zhengyi* 論語正義. Beijing: Zhonghua Shuju, 1990.

Locke, John. *An Essay Concerning Human Understanding*. Edited by Peter H. Nidditch. Oxford: Oxford University Press, 1975.

Mattice, Sarah A. *Metaphor and Metaphilosophy: Philosophy as Combat, Play, and Aesthetic Experience*. Lanham: Lexington Books, 2014.

Moeller, Hans-Georg, and Paul D'Ambrosio. *Genuine Pretending: On the Philosophy of the Zhuangzi*. New York: Columbia University Press, 2017.

Muller, A. Charles, ed. and trans. *Korea's Great Buddhist-Confucian Debate: The Treatises of Chŏng Tojŏn (Sambong) and Hamhŏ Tŭkt'ong (Kihwa)*. Honolulu: University of Hawai'i Press, 2015.

Olberding, Amy. *Moral Exemplars in the* Analects: *The Good Person is That*. New York: Routledge, 2012.

Olberding, Amy. *The Wrong of Rudeness: Learning Modern Civility from Ancient Chinese Philosophy*. Oxford: Oxford University Press, 2019.

Olberding, Amy. "Slowing Death Down: Mourning in the *Analects*." In *Confucius Now: Contemporary Encounters with the Analects*, edited by David Jones, 137–149. LaSalle, IL: Open Court Press, 2008.

Pang Pu 龐樸. *Zhubo* Wuxing *pian jiaozhu ji yanjiu* 竹帛《五行》篇校注及研究. Taibei: Wanjuanlou, 2000.

Park, So Jeong. "Sound, Tone, and Music in Early China: The Philosophical Foundation for Chinese Sound Culture." In *Inter-culturality and Philosophic Discourse*, edited by Yolaine Escande, Vincent Shen, and Chenyang Li, 271–290. Cambridge: Cambridge Scholars Publishing, 2013.

Perkins, Franklin. *Heaven and Earth Are Not Humane: The Problem of Evil in Classical Chinese Philosophy*. Bloomington: Indiana University Press, 2014.

Perkins, Franklin. "The Laozi and the Cosmogonic Turn in Classical Chinese Philosophy." *Frontiers of Philosophy in China* 11, no. 2 (2016): 185–205.

Perkins, Franklin. *Leibniz and China: A Commerce of Light*. Cambridge: Cambridge University Press, 2004.

Perkins, Franklin. "Love of Learning in the *Lun Yu*." *Journal of Chinese Philosophy* 33, no. 4 (December 2006): 505–517.

Perkins, Franklin. "Mengzi, Emotion, and Autonomy." *Journal of Chinese Philosophy* 29, no. 2 (June 2002): 207–227.

Perkins, Franklin. "The Sprouts of Wisdom and the Love of Learning in *Mengzi*." In *Liebe—Ost und West/Love in Eastern and Western Philosophy*, edited by Hans-Georg Möller and Günter Wohlfart, 89–98. Berlin: Parerga Verlag, 2007.

Pines, Yuri. *Envisioning Eternal Empire: Chinese Political Thought of the Warring States Era*. Honolulu: University of Hawai'i Press, 2009.

Puett, Micheal. "Ritual and Ritual Obligations: Perspectives on Normativity from Classical China." *Journal of Value Inquiry* 49, no. 4 (2015): 543–550.

Puett, Michael, and Christine Gross-loh. *The Path: What Chinese Philosophers Can Teach Us about the Good Life*. New York: Simon & Schuster, 2016.

Queen, Sarah A. "*Han Feizi* and the Old Master: A Comparative Analysis and Translation of *Han Feizi* Chapter 20, 'Jie Lao,' and Chapter 21, 'Yu Lao.'" In *Dao Companion to the Philosophy of Han Fei*, edited by Paul R. Goldin, 197–256. Dordrecht: Springer, 2013.

Queen, Sarah A., and John S. Major, trans. *Luxuriant Gems of the Spring and Autumn*. New York: Columbia University Press, 2016.

Rosemont, Henry, Jr. *Against Individualism: A Confucian Rethinking of the Foundations of Morality, Politics, Family, and Religion.* Lanham: Lexington Books, 2016.

Saussy, Haun. *Great Walls of Discourse and Other Adventures in Cultural China.* Cambridge, MA: Harvard University Asia Center, 2002.

Shun, Kwong-loi. *Mencius and Early Chinese Thought.* Stanford: Stanford University Press, 1997.

Slingerland, Edward, trans. *Confucius Analects, with Selections from Traditional Commentaries.* Indianapolis: Hackett, 2003.

Slingerland, Edward. *Trying Not to Try: Ancient China, Modern Science, and the Power of Spontaneity.* New York: Broadway Books, 2015.

Sun Yirang 孫詒讓. *Mozi Xiangu* 墨子閒詁. Beijing: Zhonghua Shuju, 2001.

Tan, Sor-hoon. "Democracy in Confucianism." *Philosophy Compass* 7 (2012): 293–303.

Van Norden, Bryan, trans. *Mengzi, with Selections from Traditional Commentaries.* Indianapolis: Hackett, 2008.

Van Norden, Bryan. *Virtue Ethics and Consequentialism in Early Chinese Philosophy.* Cambridge: Cambridge University Press, 2007.

Voltaire. *Toleration and Other Essays.* Translated by Joseph McCabe. New York: G.P. Putnam's Sons, 1912. Reprint in The Online Library of Liberty. https://oll.libertyfund.org/title/mccabe-toleration-and-other-essays.

Wang Hui. "Depoliticized Politics: From East to West." In *The End of Revolution: China and the Limits of Modernity,* 3–18. New York: Verso, 2009.

Wang, Robin R. *Yinyang: The Way of Heaven and Earth in Chinese Thought and Culture.* Cambridge: Cambridge University Press, 2012. Wang Xianqian 王先謙. *Xunzi jijie* 荀子集解. Beijing: Zhonghua Shuju, 1988.

Watson, Burton, trans. *The Complete Works of Chuang Tzu.* New York: Columbia University Press, 1968.

Xu Fuguan. *Zhongguo renxinglun shi* 中國人性論史. Taibei: Taiwan Shangwu Yinshuguan, 1969.

Zhang Zai 張載. *Zhang Zai ji* 張載集. Beijing: Zhonghua Shuju, 1978.

Zhou Zhenfu 周振甫. *Shijing yizhu* 詩經譯注. Beijing: Zhonghua Shuju, 2002.

Ziporyn, Brook, trans. *Zhuangzi: The Complete Writings.* Indianapolis: Hackett Publishing, 2020.

Index of Passages

For the benefit of digital users, indexed terms that span two pages (e.g., 52–53) may, on occasion, appear on only one of those pages.

Index

For the benefit of digital users, indexed terms that span two pages (e.g., 52–53) may, on occasion, appear on only one of those pages.